Purchase of this book
Made Possible by the
Post War Fund
of the
Walla Walla Chamber of Commerce
1944

THE ROAD TO
Foreign Policy

BOOKS BY

HUGH GIBSON

THE ROAD TO FOREIGN POLICY

BELGIUM

RIO

A JOURNAL FROM OUR LEGATION IN BELGIUM

With Herbert Hoover
THE PROBLEMS OF LASTING PEACE

THE ROAD TO
Foreign Policy

BY HUGH GIBSON

Withdrawn by
Whitman College Library

Doubleday, Doran and Company, Inc.

GARDEN CITY, NEW YORK

1944

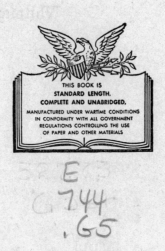

THIS BOOK IS
STANDARD LENGTH,
COMPLETE AND UNABRIDGED,
MANUFACTURED UNDER WARTIME CONDITIONS
IN CONFORMITY WITH ALL GOVERNMENT
REGULATIONS CONTROLLING THE USE
OF PAPER AND OTHER MATERIALS

E
G744
.G5

COPYRIGHT, 1944
BY HUGH GIBSON
ALL RIGHTS RESERVED

PRINTED IN THE UNITED STATES
AT
THE COUNTRY LIFE PRESS, GARDEN CITY, N. Y.

To
my friends and former associates,
the men and women of the Department of State
and the Foreign Service.

64343

Foreword

THERE IS NO DENYING that the problems we face today are alarmingly serious. For that very reason we need to focus public attention on them. There is altogether too much pontifical talk about world affairs as if they were on some plane above the heads of ordinary Americans. Much of this is based on the idea that we are called upon to deal with new and unprecedented problems. There is nothing to this. A reading of history brings us the reassurance that there is really nothing new under the sun—that men have repeatedly had to grapple with all the problems that trouble us today.

Athens and Sparta had the problem of democracy versus totalitarian militarism. Pericles had a New Deal with many of the modern fixings. Diocletian had his own version. Ancient Gaul was worried by Julius Caesar's fascist aggression. Charlemagne was, for his times, a big-scale totalitarian. And so on down the ages to Frederick the Great, Napoleon, Bismarck, and Hitler.

To deal with our problems we need to modernize our approach, but there is no need to bow our heads and admit the whole subject is beyond our ken.

There is no doubt that in the course of the last century the handling of our foreign affairs has got out of adjustment. It has come about more or less unnoticed, but the fact remains that we have drifted far from the intentions of the men who wrote the Constitution. We need to get back to the intent if not the letter of the Constitution in these matters, and it can be done.

Thus far in our history we have got along pretty well in spite of defects of policy and diplomacy, thanks largely to our favored geographical position, our wealth, and our resources. But this does not justify us in depending on luck as a system of government, for our favored position alone may not suffice to carry us indefinitely through the upheavals that lie ahead.

The problems that face us today, although not necessarily new, are bewildering in their nature and intricacy. Quite aside from protecting our interests we want our country to play a worthy part in the world, and this cannot be achieved by hoping for the best. We need a mature and considered approach to the problems we must solve. The sands are running out, and unless we get to work we shall be found unprepared.

I propose in this book, therefore, to examine the existing obstacles to our having an adequate foreign policy and then go on to make suggestions as to how we can overcome these obstacles and develop the sort of policy and diplomacy we need.

Contents

THE ROAD TO

Foreign Policy

CHAPTER I

Have We a Foreign Policy?

IF WE ARE to have a sound foreign policy it must be realistic. This statement often provokes the charge of cynicism, but it is not deserved. If we use the word to describe a policy that can be brought into operation to achieve desirable results, there is nothing in realism that excludes idealism. On the contrary, to be genuinely realistic a policy must be lighted by idealism. Here we need to do some clear thinking as to the nature of realism and idealism.

It is not always those who are most vociferous in their professions of idealism who have the best claim to it. In fact, the real idealist is likely to concentrate his efforts on the practical problem of getting things done and leave it to others to praise his motives.

We need to develop a wholesome contempt for bogus idealism and bogus idealists. A greater discrimination would enable us to get more effectively behind the genuine article. In some quarters, if you want to qualify as an idealist and humanitarian, it suffices to demand the More Abundant Life for the Hottentots. It does not matter if you don't know anything about the Hottentots. It does not matter if in close contact you would dislike them and their ways. It does not matter, because it is practically certain you can live through a long career of humanitarianism without laying eyes on a Hottentot. In fact, unseen and unknown, he better serves your purpose of displaying your idealism.

We also need discrimination about realism. The word itself has been abused by Hitler, Mussolini & Co. to justify their brutalities until it has become a term of reproach. They have merely used a respectable word to disguise stark cynicism. Talleyrand was franker when he said: "Base yourself always on principles. Lean upon them heavily. They will always give way. [*Appuyez-*

vous toujours sur des principes. Appuyez très fort; ils finiront toujours par ceder]." Using the word in its true sense, we need recognition of realities as never before. Only if our policy is responsive to realities can we hope to bring our ideals into operation.

I do not presume to specify the outlines of a foreign policy for our country, but rather to examine the means by which we can reach sound conclusions as to the sort of policy we need and to secure its adoption. This approach is based on the belief that we cannot formulate a policy without doing many other things first —that policy is not the first but the last step of a process. Thus the door is left open for the adoption of any one of the many plans now under discussion, perhaps a combination of several of them.

This approach should appeal to those who are willing to submit their plans to systematic scrutiny rather than to force them through by emotional appeal. As a practical matter, there is little prospect of any policy being adopted in this way. There are few people in this or any other country ready to adopt a policy unless it is really in the national interest. It would at least be one step forward if the advocates of all plans would unite their efforts in support of a concerted approach and depend on the merits of their ideas to win them support.

Nothing is more fatuous than belief in the miraculous power of political expedients. I hasten to add that no such powers are claimed for the expedients suggested in this book. They are brought forward with no pretense of creating a miracle machine, but in the conviction that there is virtue in improving our methods, in correcting mistakes and abuses, and in creating facilities for dealing with foreign relations on a realistic basis.

The prime purpose of this book is to stimulate discussion and criticism on a basis of reality.

The usual approach is to point out the defects of our present course in foreign affairs and advocate the adoption of something entirely different. We shall never reach our goal in this way. Policy is not a problem that can be isolated and dealt with alone. The best possible policy is lifeless without a competent diplomacy to make it work. Diplomacy, on the other hand, is aimless without a recognized policy to guide it. Both policy and diplomacy are ineffective except as they are approved and supported by public opinion. Hence, policy is only one part of a whole and can be discussed intelligently only in its setting of diplomacy and public opinion.

Perhaps our thinking would be clearer if we tried a somewhat more elementary approach. Justice Oliver Wendell Holmes put it wisely when he said: "We need education in the obvious more than investigation in the obscure."

We start with certain inescapable fundamentals.

We live with and among other nations.

To live, we must exchange goods with them.

If civilization is to advance, we must study their languages, their arts, their science, their literature.

Our citizens must live and travel abroad; theirs must live here.

We want peace preserved.

These fundamentals impose on us the need for clear-cut foreign policies and the implements to carry them out.

The implements are our Department of State and our Foreign Service. They must know their business, they must be adequately equipped, and they must be constantly in action.

As a matter of fact, there is nothing mysterious in diplomacy and no need for hocus-pocus. Foreign policy and the diplomacy which makes it work are an integral part of our daily life in time of peace as much as in time of war. They are part of the daily life of the farmer and the factory worker and the housewife—of anybody who buys and sells. They determine in some measure how much he gets for his produce or his labor, how much he pays for his shoes or his loaf of bread, perhaps whether his children will have a chance to better their lot. And, finally, they determine whether we live in peace or become involved in war.

We have, as a nation, certain principles and convictions which compose a sort of instinctive basis for foreign policy.

We desire to avoid wars and maintain peace.

We do not covet our neighbor's land.

We believe in the independence of all peoples who are capable of self-government.

We favor the expansion of representative government as promoting the maintenance of peace.

These principles and convictions give certain definite directions to our course in foreign affairs. They tend to simplify our problems because they are recognized as constant factors.

On the other hand, in foreign affairs we labor under many handicaps peculiar to this country.

The most workmanlike way to deal with these handicaps is to begin by taking account of stock and making an inventory of the state of our affairs.

We emerged almost overnight in the role of a Great Power, without long preparation and experience in world responsibilities.

Alone among the Great Powers we have important organized elements of citizens of foreign birth or descent whose affections and antipathies are constantly in play to influence our national thinking and action, with a view to serving the interests of foreign countries.

Alone among the Great Powers we have looked upon world affairs as a field for the indulgence of generous and reforming impulses.

Alone among the Great Powers we carry on our foreign affairs through a ministry with no consistent relation with the legislative branch of the government. Many other powers achieve this through the system of ministerial responsibility, but in our case there is an unfortunate amount of antagonism between the two branches of government.

When in possession of the facts, and given time, the American people have a way of reaching sound conclusions. However, they are not always afforded time nowadays to feel their way. And, as matters stand, they are not in possession of adequate facts about our foreign relations. This is not a reproach leveled against any particular administration. It is no more than a statement of deplorable fact. As a result of developments extending over a century and a half, we have reached a point where the American people have in practice little control over foreign affairs, either directly through force of public opinion or through their elected representatives. There is a vague awareness of this evil, and we hear much about the need for democratic control of foreign policy. This discloses an instinctive recognition of the undoubted fact that in our country there is in practice autocratic control of foreign affairs, brought about almost unnoticed because of the gradual relaxation of checks, controls, and provisions for collaboration.

The Senate and the House, separately and jointly, have been largely eliminated from the effective participation in the conduct of foreign relations prescribed by the Constitution. The people as a whole can register their approval or disapproval only at the ballot box. But these opportunities occur only at rare intervals instead of being continuous. Furthermore, in practice elections are rarely decided on international issues, which is due in some measure to a deeply ingrained feeling that "politics should stop at the water's edge."

Under our present setup there is no guarantee against the exercise of autocratic power by the Executive. Yet the Constitution sought to provide against this very danger by dividing authority between the President and the Senate, with a supposedly determining share reserved to the Senate. It was clearly intended that the Senate should exercise an effective control as is shown by the provision that the President should have the "advice" of the Senate in concluding agreements with other countries and that ratification of these agreements should be dependent on senatorial "consent." Beyond this, to Congress as a whole was reserved all authority in the declaration of war.

During the last century and a half we have moved steadily toward control of foreign affairs by the Executive. We have seen the growth of a system of appointments of personal representatives of the President clearly in violation of constitutional intent. We have seen the growth of a system of executive agreements which has been developed for the express purpose of sidestepping the Senate. And, finally, we have seen the growth of one-man control of negotiation with other countries which involves the power to lead us along the path to war regardless of the will of Congress. Our present machinery affords us no guarantee against the exercise of autocratic power by the Executive.

The situation has come on us without our realizing it. Although safeguards disappeared, affairs continued to be conducted by scrupulous methods, and the fact was not disclosed that the stage was set for autocratic control. But the control is autocratic, no matter how honorable the conduct of the Executive may be.

The great mass of the American people is inarticulate. Their silence, however, is made up for by the clamor of serried ranks of agitators, propagandists, pressure groups, and crackpots, all claiming to speak for America. The press and the radio are filled with their recommendations, arguments, and demands. They harass the government, always in the name of public opinion, and demand all sorts of things that the sober bulk of the people would never advocate.

All this confusion of tongues passes for public opinion, which it is not. But in the absence of a sound public opinion, all this chatter, much of it for selfish ends, much of it prejudiced, more of it irresponsible, does serve as the basis of discussion. As a result we present a strange spectacle, and it is a tribute to the inherent good sense of the American people that, given time, they end by discriminating between the true and the spurious. In the process we go through much travail of soul that could be better devoted to other things.

There is no need for us to look on this situation as the Will of God, something inherent in our system, something that cannot be remedied and must be endured.

One of our most vital problems is to find a way whereby the American people can come into their own, can run their own show directly through public opinion and indirectly through its elected representatives. We should have a totally different picture if we were doing this for ourselves rather than under the guidance of propaganda and organized emotion.

Most of those who have policies to propose for adoption are in agreement that our government's policy is deplorable. But there agreement ends. When we come to discussing what should be done about it, we enter the realm of utter confusion and name-calling. One reason for this is that so many people begin by reaching their conclusions and then set out to justify them. Our only real hope lies in reversing this procedure and reaching our conclusions as the last step.

Now and then we hear voices deploring the fact that we have no continuity of foreign policy. This is usually blamed on periodic changes of party in government. We might simplify the explanation even more by saying that we have no continuity of foreign policy because we have no comprehensive, recognized policy to continue.

We conduct our international relations by improvisation, sometimes well, sometimes badly. This method is costly to our national interests. We shall not correct the evil by adopting any one of the blueprints of foreign policy that have been made. We can correct it only by adopting measures which will lead step by step to the formulation of a real foreign policy responsive to our needs, and of an adequate diplomacy to implement it.

This is merely a statement of a chronic situation of long growth and development which calls for treatment. Without effective treatment much of the current discussion of foreign policy is unrealistic and inconclusive.

Readers will perhaps be critical of the suggestion that we are lacking in foreign policy. What about Mr. Hay's policy of the Open Door, Mr. Knox's policy of Dollar Diplomacy, Ballots instead of Bullets, Mr. Bryan's policy of Arbitration and Conciliation, Mr. Kellogg's Pacts, Mr. Hoover's policy of Non-recognition, Mr. Hull's policy of Bilateral Trade Agreements, and the like? There are perhaps dozens of them, if we care to go back far enough. That's just our trouble. There is nothing more confusing to the public mind than labels like these that are represented as a national policy.

The objection will at once be raised that we have the Monroe Doctrine. That is quite true. The Monroe Doctrine might be described as the essential basis of an incomplete American foreign policy, but no more than a basis.

It will be objected that we have a lot of other policies. Take the Good-Neighbor Policy, for instance. It is friendly and satisfying as a phrase, but in practice any enlightened foreign policy is a good-neighbor policy. The fundamental purpose of any considered policy is to get on with one's neighbors. Incidentally, what is popularly understood as the Good-Neighbor Policy with Latin America was a fact before the Roosevelt administration claimed it for its own.

It is, of course, possible to have a bad-neighbor policy. We are endeavoring at the present time to convince certain countries that such a policy cannot succeed or even continue beyond a limited time.

This is not to quarrel with these so-called policies in themselves, but with their description. They are not policies. They are, rather, scraps of policy—in some cases, no more than phrases indicating aims, purposes, or aspirations.

Many of us have a weakness for feeling that we have accomplished something when we have given three rousing cheers for some tinkling phrase. We need the sobering realization that even if they resound around the world such phrases begin to have value only when they are put to work.

We can find a useful analogy in the Declaration of Independence. The Declaration was an eloquent statement of our national aims. But alone it did not suffice to put those aims into effect. We have only to give our imagination free play to form an impression of what would have happened—the national chaos into which we should have fallen—if we had contented ourselves with the Declaration and had tried to govern the country according to each succeeding administration's interpretation of its meaning and the intentions of the Founding Fathers.

Instead of following this disastrous course, a group of our wisest men spent years of hard work devising means and machinery that would implement the aims and aspirations of the Declaration. If we had not been given a well-conceived Constitution, we should probably not have survived as a nation.

Any important enterprise needs a policy—the greater its importance and intricacy, the greater the need for policy. If a responsible man were to invest his savings in a large grocery, he would hardly be likely to open it with a dissertation on the virtues of private enterprise and the beauties of service to the public; at least he would not consider that an adequate plan for running his grocery. He would realize the need for a comprehensive plan, made up of a series of component plans, based on all available experience as to purchases, stocks, relations with employees, overhead expenses, advertising, collections, pleasing his customers, and a score of other matters. Without such plans the grocery would soon go out of business.

It is hardly fair to press too far the analogy between public and private enterprise. For one thing, the government is not required to make ends meet. But the fact remains that the government needs careful planning, just as does the grocery—only the need is greater. A government policy is nothing more mysterious than planning for the future.

To be more precise, a foreign policy is a well-rounded, comprehensive plan, based on knowledge and experience, for conducting the business of the government with the rest of the world. It is aimed at promoting and protecting the interests of the nation. This calls for a clear understanding of what those interests are and how far we can hope to go with the means at our disposal. Anything less than this falls short of being a national foreign policy.

We have referred to a number of fragments of foreign policy. They do not all merit that description. Some of them can be described not too unkindly as hobbies of successive secretaries of state, or even plans that the Secretary of State has been persuaded are good, or at least give off a goodly sound.

We should face the fact that under our system we rarely, if ever, have a Secretary of State of rounded experience in foreign affairs. Usually he is a complete amateur in diplomacy. This is not said in derogation, but rather in extenuation of many things that happen when a new Secretary of State comes into office. Not being able to survey the whole field for himself, and having no comprehensive recognized policy provided for him, the best he can do is to deal with questions as they arise and clamor for his attention.

On taking office, a new Secretary of State is expected to announce his policy before he settles down to work. He is expected to take it out of his hat, before familiarizing himself with his new job. Often he is only too anxious to oblige. A sound, workable policy does not suffice for the American people. It must, for political reasons, be something with a resounding slogan that will get over to the people the idea that at last we have the superior article.

Under present conditions, a Secretary of State can hardly be expected to do better. As soon as he comes into office, a multitude of questions come crowding upon him. Some, by their urgency, force themselves upon his attention. In some cases he singles out questions that interest him particularly. One Secretary may manifest special interest in Far-Eastern questions, or in our relations with Latin America. Although he realizes that other questions are important, there is an inevitable human tendency to let them fall into second place. An essential quality of foreign policy is its comprehensiveness, and so long as this vague, particularistic emphasis continues we shall have no real foreign policy.

Another essential quality of policy is permanence, continuity. The tendency toward personal hobbies seldom has the advantage of permanence. Only too often the opposition party, having denounced the policy of the party in power, feels it essential to scrap everything the old party stood for and produce something new of its own—the main concern being its newness. That is a body blow to our hopes of having a foreign policy. You can't have a four-year policy followed by another four-year policy. That is nothing but improvisation cut off in four-year stove lengths.

Many of these so-called policies are good in themselves, good for the limited field to which they apply. Many of them are imposed by circumstances and either party would take approximately the same line. Many of them would find a place in any well-rounded plan for handling our foreign affairs. But it has been a general and recurrent error to proclaim that each of these fragments in turn was all-inclusive and sufficed to avert war, win friends and influence people, and promote world-wide prosperity.

We stand alone as a Great Power without a policy. Almost any other grown-up country has one. It may be a bad policy, but it is one that can be recognized, and is recognized, throughout the world. And it is continuous.

It may help to examine the workings of other governments. Let us assume a change in the British Government. A new Foreign Secretary comes in. Whether he be Conservative, Liberal, or Labor, he goes to work to carry out the national policy. He finds a group of permanent officials who support him loyally and guide him as to the fundamentals of policy. Other countries know what to expect—that as regards fundamentals there will be no change.

A British Foreign Secretary feels no humiliation in carrying on the policy he finds. It is not the personal policy of his predecessor. It is national policy, the one his predecessor found when he came in and handed on when he went out. The last thing the new Foreign Secretary wants to do is to scrap a policy made of the precipitate of the experience of centuries. He knows that the country would grumble if he were to tinker with the policy. It would be outraged if he were to trumpet a brand-new policy of his own. It would be staggered at his presumption in thinking that he could improvise something better than the combined wisdom and experience of generations had been able to evolve. And the improvisor would be turned out of office.

We should not lose sight of the fact that in many ways the British system lends itself to continuity of policy better than our own. In our country, the Executive handles foreign affairs independently of the Legislature, which leads to clashes when there is need for ratification of executive commitments. The British cabinet not only consults with Parliament, it might accurately be described as the executive committee of Parliament. Thus the course of the government is subject to continuing readjustment to maintain unity of purpose. It may even be said that such disunity as we often suffer from is impossible under a system where, if disagreement is acute, the cabinet falls. Under this system there is an entirely different attitude in both legislature and administration.

This is not to advocate that we adopt the British system, for that would involve an impossible and in many ways an undesirable change in our own. But the success of Britain in dealing with problems of policy is obviously due in large measure to close and constant consultation between the executive and legislative branches, and we can, without imitating the British form of government, seek to achieve in our own way the benefits of consultation.

What it all boils down to is that with our unpredictable handling of foreign affairs we are not dependable associates for governments with continuity of policy. This is an obvious disadvantage at all times, and is bound to render particularly difficult the sort of postwar international co-operation we shall need. We cannot do our part in building a better world if we can never think more than four years ahead. This may seem to be a brutal statement. It is not made as a reflection upon our honesty or good will. But we may as well face the unpleasant fact that we are fundamentally undependable in foreign affairs as long as we are subject to abrupt and violent reversals in our course of action.

So it behooves us to consider what we can do about it.

It cannot be too strongly emphasized that long-range planning is the essence of policy. There can be no long-range planning except about fundamentals, for everything else is in a constant process of change. The interests of governments change, and with this, their attitudes toward each other. We all recall the radical change in the alignment of the powers since the last war. We must be prepared for similar shifts as inevitable in planning for the future. If we know how to profit from it, this limitation to fundamentals is a blessing, for it may save us from dissipating our efforts on immediate and non-essential questions. Any attempt to handle foreign affairs by short-range planning labors under a grave handicap. It is bound to be unrealistic in that it can deal only with the immediate. This leads instinctively to approaching everything from the standpoint of the *status quo*. Regardless of the questions at issue, this is a bad approach, for change is the essence of diplomacy, as it is of human life, and any attempt to prevent change is doomed to failure. If it cannot come about peacefully, it will come by violence. The only realistic foreign policy—the one we should seek to achieve for our own country—is one that concentrates on fundamentals and plans far enough ahead to foresee the need for change and prepare to bring it about by peaceful means.

History gives us a long list of cases where, in the light of available information, governments should have been able to anticipate events and solve problems before they became acute. Our country is by no means the only one in need of education in foresightedness. Indeed, we have to our credit several cases where we sought to give leadership, but where other governments were unable to take their gaze from some immediate advantage and events moved on to the inevitable crash. But our immediate task is to put our own house in order.

One defect in much of our thinking is that we persist in looking on policy as a program of action. It is advocated, for instance, that we should decide on a "policy" of ousting a government we dislike in Argentina or on a "policy" of supporting Tito. These are not policies. They are current decisions on action. Policy is the formulation of fundamental objectives. Once the objectives are clear, the decisions on action fall into their true perspective. Even with the foundation of true objectives diplomacy is hard put to it to keep up with events.

By way of illustration we may note briefly current adjustments of British policy. We start with the knowledge that it is a fundamental of that policy to throw Britain's weight into the balance against the most powerful country in Europe or against any power which threatens to dominate the Continent. It can be called more than a fundamental of policy; it is almost a national instinct.

Britain never deviates from this policy. Her basic policy has persisted through the centuries, but her specific aims have often been changed in order to maintain fundamentals.

It is often charged that British policy is one of opportunism. This is true only in the sense that there is opportunism in current diplomacy to attain fundamentals which remain constant.

Britain became involved in this war because she inevitably found herself aligned against the aggressive might of Germany which had again become a menace. But suddenly, in the midst of war, there are signs of change. Germany is pushed aside as the strongest power and Russia emerges in that role. Not in the sense of military victory over Germany, but rather as a power which arrogates to itself the right to decide the fate of other nations. Britain has never been able to view with indifference the disappearance of the countries that maintain the European balance of power. In 1939 she went to war against Germany on that ground; and now the same threat reappears, this time from another source.

We have many indications of the turmoil into which Britain has been thrown by this development. There are many signs of British recognition of shifting values.

On November 25, 1943, Marshal Smuts offered his testimony in favor of the balance-of-power system—strange testimony from this fierce advocate of collective security. The marshal faced the hard fact that Britain would probably emerge from the war as the weakest of the three great world powers. He foresaw that Russia would dominate the Continent unless Britain took early measures to correct the balance of power. He therefore proposed the building of a British sphere of influence on the Continent by bringing Belgium and Holland (with their colonies) into the British Empire.

Lord Halifax approached the subject from another angle and advocated greater centralization of the Empire as regards foreign policy, defense, and economic affairs. This did not evoke a favorable reception but at least the possibilities had been explored.

Mr. Eden on January 26, 1944, served notice on Russia that Britain was not prepared to scrap her policy by way of appeasement. This was achieved by a statement that Britain would not recognize any territorial changes in Poland unless "they take place with the free consent and good will of the parties concerned."

Although these developments have, for the most part, been played down in the American press, they clearly indicate a shift in the British attitude to meet a new situation. The fundamental aim is unchanged. The specific aim is adjusted to changing conditions. There will doubtless be further developments before these words appear in print and we can do no more than take this opening scene as an illustration of a basic and continuing policy maintained by change and adjustment in action to meet changing conditions.

Illustrations could be multiplied, but this will suffice to underline one idea we should master—that without a basic policy all such change as we have indicated becomes no more than improvisation.

Much of the present discussion assumes that once we have put a policy on paper the task is done. As a matter of fact, even when we have adopted a policy we shall have done no more than to get ready to begin. For, although policy should be definite and continuous, it can be kept that way only through skilled adaptability in operation. Any rigidity, any refusal to modify operations to meet changing conditions, means the end of continuity and of policy.

A policy is nothing without diplomacy. Policy is no more than the formulation of guiding principles. Diplomacy is the machinery to make them operate. We must face the fact that the effectiveness of our policy will be determined by the effectiveness of our diplomacy. That will involve a radical change in our attitude, for we have long had a national allergy to any sort of intelligent and expert diplomacy. Our thinking has been in terms of policy first and diplomacy nowhere.

When we come to the actual implementing of our diplomacy, we find that we have inadequate tools for the task. We shall get nowhere if we merely look on our present weakness as something incurable. There is a great deal that can be done about it, but only if we have a clear idea of what we want to do and how it can be done.

In most of our discussions diplomacy is taken as meaning the operation of our diplomatic service. It is much more than that. It is the process of making our policy effective by peaceful means. In any comprehensive discussion we should take diplomacy as including every official and unofficial activity that affects the conduct of our foreign relations. If Congress passes a tariff act, that is diplomacy; if it repeals an exclusion act, that is diplomacy; if the fleet is sent to stand by during an emergency to protect American lives, that is diplomacy; if Congress appropriates money for famine relief in Soviet Russia, that is diplomacy; if high officials of the government make speeches at home and abroad, giving their purely personal views of a Brave New World, that is diplomacy. Of all this greater diplomacy which determines policy, the diplomatic service performs only the function of professionally trying to carry out the expressed wishes of the government, which may be brilliant or stupid, fumbling or well conceived.

We hear many phrases about the influence of public opinion on foreign policy. Many of these are empty phrases, because those who utter them don't believe what they are saying, but are merely seeking to butter up their listeners. Nevertheless, no government in this country can ignore any determined trend of public opinion, whether it be wise or unwise, whether it tend toward the Santa Claus complex or withdrawal from world affairs. Public opinion, therefore, plays a determining role in our policy, and thus it becomes our foremost problem to have not only an active but an informed public opinion, for only thus can it react advantageously on our diplomacy.

As matters stand now, our public opinion is vocal but often uninformed. The reproach does not lie against those who are not informed; neither does it lie against those who fail to inform them, but rather against a situation in which there is so little coherent that can be communicated to the people. It is only when we have a clearly recognizable policy that the government will have something definite to communicate and the people will have some standard by which to measure the conduct of government and develop an informed and intelligent opinion.

With this achieved, we might set out to build a foreign policy with a definite aim—the use of the same forces and resources that make for war, to conquer poverty and do away with resentment and envy with a view to making peace secure.

In the last few years there has been a tremendous and wholesome growth of interest in foreign affairs. There is an increasing amount of discussion of foreign policy, of plans and proposals. In the course of this discussion many wise and practical ideas have been developed. There is no doubt that their adoption would strengthen the hands of our government.

Unfortunately, advocacy of a sound proposal does not accomplish much more than promote public discussion, for we are not now equipped for adopting a policy and putting it to work. One difficulty is that arguments for and against proposals are too often emotional and develop more heat than light. They tend to cancel each other out. Their presentation is largely controversial, although this is exactly the contrary of what we need, for in reaching conclusions as to our common interest it is obvious that what we need is co-operation rather than controversy. To achieve this co-operation we need more than anything to devise a workmanlike method for arriving at sound conclusions as to the form of foreign policy most responsive to our needs.

A large part of our present discussion is prompted by our national concern for building a better world order after this war and determining the part America shall play in that order. It deals chiefly with postwar problems. We should plan for more than this, for however important these problems, in the long range of history they are no more than immediate questions. We must pass through the postwar period, but a real foreign policy must plan not only for the crisis, but for the long vista of the future as well.

I am tempted to begin by outlining the measures we might take to achieve these purposes, but it is difficult to state these proposals convincingly without first indicating the difficulties that are to be overcome. For immediate purposes it suffices at this stage to say that in a later chapter I shall suggest measures calculated to eliminate existing frictions and conflicts and bring about continuing co-operation between all the agencies of government playing some role in foreign affairs, and further measures to build an informed public opinion capable of exercising an intelligent control of foreign policy.

CHAPTER II

Why We Need a Foreign Policy

WE SOMETIMES hear it said that we are fortunate in having a foreign policy that is not fixed—without continuity; that it is more democratic to have a policy responsive to the public will through change of administration. We are told that the continuity of policy of other countries is an evil thing, due to the working of power politics, secret diplomacy, and the system of balance of power. It seems we can thank our stars we are free to adapt ourselves to changing conditions.

We may wonder whether unfettered opportunism is an unqualified blessing. Possession of a definite policy does not preclude us from adapting ourselves to changing conditions. Any intelligent policy must be adaptable. But adaptability cannot be intelligent unless fundamentals are fixed and clear. It might be well to recall that the essential purpose of a policy is to enable us to take care of our own interests in relation with the rest of the world. If we are to play our part in the world we must know that we can plan ahead and that other countries can plan with us. Otherwise there is no hope of long-range international collaboration. A nation, like an individual that is notoriously capricious and unpredictable, is hardly at an advantage in dealing with others who know what they want and how they propose to get it, and who keep on year in and year out striving for the same objective.

We may as well make up our minds that until we have a well-considered and settled plan for the conduct of our foreign relations, based on a true conception of the purposes of government, we shall never deal with the rest of the world on equal terms.

To look after our own national interests is the first duty of government. It is the function of foreign policy and of our diplomacy to afford those interests maximum protection consistent with good international relations. This does not imply a cynical and selfish attitude, but it does call for a definition of American interests which can, for present purposes, be divided into two categories.

First, the direct function of defending our territory, protecting our citizens, and promoting our trade.

Then the less direct function of working with other nations to promote the general interest in the maintenance of peace, prosperity, and justice.

Both of these phases are essential parts of an intelligent and enlightened diplomacy. The first alone is cynical and shortsighted. The second is needed even from a selfish viewpoint, if only for the benefits which we share with others.

On the other hand, it is far from reality to assume that the second alone suffices and that the first is unworthy of a generous people.

Only through a carefully planned policy can we hope to maintain a true balance of the two phases.

The enlightened course is one of fairness, often of generosity. But generosity as distinct from justice is not in itself a function of government. Generosity alone is not calculated even to promote good international relations. If capricious or calculating it will actually disturb them. We are likely to go further in the right direction by keeping our own house in order and limiting our promises and commitments within the bounds of our ability to perform.

In the course of long experience, no diplomat has ever encountered any two international situations sufficiently alike to be codified. After all, diplomatic situations and problems are, in a larger and more intricate way, like the situations and problems of private life; and nobody has yet produced a ready reference book of rules to govern all our everyday actions.

As in private life, experience and mellowed wisdom are as sure a guide as any. And what experience is for the individual, tradition becomes for a continuing diplomatic service. Not tradition in the sense of empty forms and formalities, but tradition as the precipitate of long and varied experience. A government that has at its command a sound tradition, carried on by experienced men, is on the right track.

We, unfortunately, have neither. Constant political change keeps us from developing a tradition of our own and scraps experience as fast as it is acquired. One indication of this is our failure to utilize the experience of ex-presidents, to say nothing of our diplomats, military leaders, and colonial officials once they leave active service.

Some people will take issue with this statement and say that we have a governmental tradition of our own. We don't. The nearest we can come under our system is to build up a fund of precedent. Fundamentally, precedent is no more than the memory of how things have been done in the past. Precedent, tempered by experience and tradition, is a valuable guide; but precedent alone is Byzantine, deadening, and stupid, and no substitute for the living reality of tradition and experience.

To put it in another way, we need a foreign policy, a known and recognized foreign policy for a number of definite reasons. To begin with, the day we have a policy our diplomatic agencies at home and abroad will tend to operate toward a common goal, instead of wrestling independently with the day-to-day problems that confront them. There will be less waste effort and more of a chance to secure essentials. Instead of squandering our energy on something today, only to abandon it tomorrow, we should concentrate on recognized fundamentals and work with a definite purpose.

Such a policy is imperative if we are to build up our foreign trade. The root of such a policy is that we give diplomatic protection to our business with other countries. Exchange of goods is vital to our own welfare and to the welfare of other nations. Development of economic life and of raw materials by our citizens in other countries and by foreigners in our country is a necessity if we are to have exchange of commodities. Our citizens must, therefore, reside and do business abroad and foreigners must reside and do business in the United States. Our citizens must have confidence that so long as they comply with the laws of foreign countries they will not be harassed and discriminated against, just as foreigners must have these assurances within our borders. This must be our policy, and it follows that our diplomacy must support this policy by proper action—not to support dishonesty and exploitation, but to support honest effort.

Business recognizes, even if the government does not, that long-range planning is the essence of investment in the foreign field. Business cannot make important commitments if it can never see more than four years ahead. Our present system is the worst conceivable from this point of view. One administration supports business to the limit, perhaps indiscriminately. The next may pull all support from under it and leave American enterprise to shift for itself.

We sometimes hear the voice of the fundamentalist, who maintains that the place for an American is in the United States, and if he goes abroad to live and do business he deserves any misfortunes that befall him. Mr. Bryan went through a phase of this when he advocated that we should deny protection to American citizens and enterprises abroad and thereby avoid complications. Curiously enough, this idea has often been advanced by professed internationalists, who seem to have no notion that they are advocating rigid isolationism.

This is based on a fuzzy idea that controversies over trade are unworthy and that by withholding protection we shall avoid irritating foreigners. Curiously enough, it is never suggested that foreign enterprise be barred from this country lest foreigners irritate us.

We have never had an established national attitude toward American foreign trade in the sense of an attitude that is maintained unchanged from one administration to another. Our business is thus at a grave disadvantage in competition with the business elements in other countries, which are able to plan far ahead in agreement with government.

If we were to decide once and for all that we do not value foreign trade enough to afford it assurances of protection, business would at least know where it stood. Any firm that was bent on doing business abroad would know that it was operating entirely at its own risk and could weigh its conditions and take its decisions accordingly. American investors would also have a better idea of what they were investing in. From some points of view this would be a better and more satisfactory position than present uncertainty.

We need to straighten out our thinking about foreign trade. The same people who look upon a business in the United States with approval, and even admiration, often view it with suspicion as it extends its operations overseas. The same men may direct it, with the same standards of honesty, but there seems to be some sort of moral turpitude that comes into play abroad.

On the face of it this seems absurd, but it may be accounted for, in part at least, by the deplorable conditions under which our business is required to operate in the foreign field. Responsible and important business concerns are held down to those operations where they can plan ahead without need to consider possible political changes at home. This leaves a tempting field to gamblers, who are prepared to accept the risks in the hope of rich pickings. These people attract attention quite disproportionate to their importance and numbers. A respectable enterprise may operate abroad for years without attracting public attention. But let a wildcat company get into trouble, and it is sure to make the headlines and thus help keep alive the impression that there is something inherently evil about American business operating overseas. It must be said that this evil is no longer so pronounced as it was a generation ago. There is, perhaps, a certain historical justification for suspicion which has been slow in dying out.

Experience shows that in our time American businessmen in foreign countries are quite as honest and reliable as those at home. Most of them show a high sense of responsibility in conforming carefully to high business standards. The American business community in any foreign country is exacting as to the conduct of its members which, save for the adventurers referred to, is every bit as high as in any community at home.

There is widespread impression that we cannot hope to excel in foreign trade. This is based on realization that we labor under serious handicaps, but the real handicap usually is ignored. Sometimes our unfavorable position is attributed to lack of official support and we hear that British and German business have carried off all the prizes because their governments back them at every stage. There is a persistent old myth that American businessmen must go to a British consulate for support. In fact, there was long current in the Far East a pleasantry to the effect that an American had to go to a British consulate for protection, to a German consulate for information, and to an American consulate for a drink.

The reproach that our government never supports American enterprise abroad is by no means justified. The Departments of State and Commerce, the diplomatic and consular services, commercial attachés and others, are as able and zealous as any others in the world. But the support they can give is immediate. They cannot promise support in the indefinite future. This is the crux of the problem. What really keeps American business at a disadvantage is the fact that it is never in a position to plan far ahead. This leaves our business without the fundamental assurances that enable British business to plan and invest for a long-term future, knowing that British policy will be unchanging and that the support enjoyed today will be the same years hence.

An illustration of the need for long-range planning of American business is to be found in the problem of developing oil resources in different parts of the world. The American oil business has for years been at the mercy of the whims of the government, and it is high time this was remedied if oil development is to be carried out to the advantage of the country. There has been a tendency in the past to look on all American oil interests abroad as commercial imperialism for the enrichment of greedy corporations. As a result the corporations have had to battle for their lives, both at home and abroad, when they might have been better occupied developing resources in consultation with our government.

An excellent illustration of how not to determine policy is Secretary Ickes' recent announcement of long-range commitments which plunge the United States Government into large-scale oil operations in one of the most politically volcanic regions in the world.

Here we have no problem of American oil companies forcing their way into dangerous fields to the embarrassment of the government. On the contrary, we have a spectacle new in American diplomatic history, of reluctant private business being coerced into serving as the instrument of government in strange new enterprises. By a "release" from Mr. Ickes' office on February 5, 1944, we were informed of a startling innovation in these terms:

The United States Government will construct a pipe line for transportation of petroleum products from the Persian Gulf area to a point on the eastern shores of the Mediterranean, and will obtain in that area reserves of one billion barrels of oil, Secretary of the Interior Harold

L. Ickes announced on behalf of the Petroleum Reserves Corporation, of which he is president.

There is every indication that this far-reaching decision was taken without adequate consideration, although it plunges us into what the Truman Committee rightly calls "as delicate and complex a diplomatic and economic situation as can be found in the world."

As Dr. Felix Morley remarks in the excellent newsletter *Human Events* (February 23, 1944), determination of a national policy on petroleum "should include inquiry as to why the Secretary of the Interior, rather than the Secretary of State, is taking leadership in a diplomatic undertaking about as remote from the interior of this country as terrestrial geography permits."

This is far more serious than any mere business enterprise, however gigantic. To begin with we plan to have a trunk pipe line extending from the Persian Gulf across Arabia to some port on the Mediterranean. There will obviously be need for various feeder pipe lines stretching away to distant fields. There are to be great refineries in various places. There will be need for docks, roads and airfields, tank farms, compressor stations, gathering lines, terminal lines, and power stations. There will even be a city built at Râs Tanura in Saudi Arabia. This means we plan to move into the Near East in a big way—as a government. This huge installation is to be spread over a broad area seething with all the political complications arising from the Pan-Arab movement, the Arab-Jewish feud, the rivalries of Britain, Turkey, and Russia, and the commitments of British foreign policy in Egypt, the Suez Canal, the Gulf of Aden and the Persian Gulf, Palestine, and India. It is hardly to be expected that we will invest hundreds of millions in such an enterprise and depend on a pious hope that our property will be respected. We know the explosive forces in the region—at least the State Department knows them. Once our government has gone into business there we know that any attack on pipe lines of refineries or cities will be an attack on the United States. That puts squarely up to us the need to decide what we shall do in such a contingency. The question cannot be decided when the attack comes. Elementary prudence demands that we know the answer before we embark on the enterprise. How far will that lead us?

Before being swept into an enterprise so alien to our tradition it would seem reasonable for the American people to be given some information. Have all these problems been considered and solved? If they have not, we have a perfect example of a feverish diplomacy with complete disregard of elementary prudence. If they have been considered and settled, we have a perfect example of autocratic control of foreign affairs in complete disregard of Congress and the people.

There are a large number of problems involved in the decision of concern to different government agencies, many of them of interest to Congress. The oil questions do not dominate the picture nor is the Department of the Interior chiefly concerned. Let us take a few of the questions that should have been discussed and settled in agreement with the government agencies concerned.

Are we really in need of oil from abroad?

If so, could that need be met from countries in this hemisphere without new political entanglements?

In order to secure oil, is it necessary for the government to go into business as now proposed?

In view of our possession of a great fleet of tankers is it necessary to build a pipe line to move oil to the Mediterranean?

What military provision must be taken to protect the pipe line, feeder lines, refineries, docks, bases, other properties and investments? How far will that lead us? Are we to maintain troops and airfields? Shall we require naval bases? If so, where? In the Persian Gulf, the Red Sea, and the Mediterranean? And how can we secure them?

Incidentally, we might well consider how such an enterprise is to be reconciled with the statement by President Roosevelt and Prime Minister Churchill in the Atlantic Charter that "their countries seek no aggrandizement, territorial *or other*."

As will be seen, these questions are only a few of those that require consideration and decisions by a wide range of authorities. There are military, naval, and air problems. There are questions of merchant marine. There are, of course, oil problems affecting not only the handling of oil in a far-distant theater, but their effect on our domestic oil industry, and our economic and political relations with countries in this hemisphere. But far transcending these in importance are the political implications of any such plan, the commitments we should be obliged to take to protect our holdings. For one thing it is difficult to see how we could protect our new holdings in the Persian Gulf, Saudi Arabia, and the Mediterranean without close intertwining of our interests and forces with those of Great Britain. It is absurd to believe that we could move into this region and operate in a vacuum, pursuing a completely independent course regardless of other powers.

In some particulars our interests would run parallel with those of Great Britain and we could act jointly to defend our holdings. In others there might be conflict—but in all particulars anything affecting British interests would become of concern to the United States—over the vast range of the Mediterranean, India, and the Middle East. There would be new relationships with other nations as well, and we should consider the implications of all of them, how far they involve us in a new brand of imperialism, and whether we have the equipment and the popular support for the commitments we are accepting. These questions are of fundamental importance to the American people and cannot be settled out of hand by the Executive—even with more study than is indicated by such announcements as have been made to the public. They call for study by the Department of State and for close consultation with Congress.

Without such over-all study there is danger that we shall find we have embarked lightheartedly on an ill-considered enterprise which may at any time involve us in another war.

The best policy in the world is useless except as far as the power of the country is there to uphold and enforce it. Most of the discussion nowadays ignores this, and appears to be based on the assumption that it suffices for the Secretary of State to come to a conclusion and decide on a good policy. This reveals one of our weaknesses, in our readiness to believe we can adopt policies without bothering to consider how far we are prepared to go to enforce them. We fall easily for the dangerous assumption that if our hearts are pure we cannot be called on to back up our aim with force—that there is some sort of moral sanction involved in disregarding our behests.

We need a complete re-examination of our international position from the angle of "put up or shut up." Where we are not ready to back up our views on a given question with force, if need be, we should do well to drop them—not even to preach about them—and save our energy for things we care enough about to act.

As a rich and powerful nation there are three choices open to us:

Collaboration with other governments.

Power politics.

Isolation.

To take them in inverse order, the last is something nobody really believes in—something that is impossible in the modern world.

As a people, we disapprove of the game of power politics and scorn the idea of participating in it. This is fortunate, because we are not equipped for it.

That leaves us collaboration, which seems the wisest course for us, one for which we are equipped by our character; and it remains our obvious choice.

Unfortunately, we have dabbled in all three, and have consequently secured the disadvantages of all and the advantages of none. Until we remedy this we are going to be buffeted on the stormy seas of diplomacy, to drift on treacherous currents and to get shipwrecked in wars.

We have a weakness for escapist methods and feel that we can act on high moral grounds without being called upon to make good. "No entangling alliances," "Non-recognition," "Cash and carry," "Arsenal of Democracy," "Lend-lease"—in all of which we seek to achieve the results of positive action while avoiding responsibility.

In our discussions of international collaboration we are prone to assume that our readiness to collaborate is enough. As a matter of fact, we can do no more than contribute our part, and although our flagellants are always ready to explain that world failures are due to our shortcomings, American readiness to collaborate has often been frustrated by lack of similar readiness on the part of other powers.

Abandoning the idea of the miraculous solution, one of the strongest factors for the maintenance of good international relations is the growth of representative government. While any representative government may make mistakes and be led to war, it is obliged to harken to the public will, and more likely to exhaust peaceful remedies before resorting to arms. Where the declaration of war depends upon the decision of one man or group of men, there is greater danger of resort to war through exasperation, to increase territory and power, or to distract attention from domestic difficulties.

When we speak of the need for fostering representative government in foreign affairs, we can begin at home. We may well concentrate our efforts on developing the role of representative governments to replace autocratic control of our own foreign affairs.

We can use the term representative government instead of democracy, because we can at least agree as to what it means.

There is a clear distinction between representative government and democracy, the first being a method and the second an ideal. Democracy can perhaps best be achieved through the growth of representative government, but we must be on our guard against the assumption that democracy is synonymous with the republican form of government. There is plenty of experience—ancient and modern—to show the most hideous tyrannies under republican forms. We must also be on our guard against the assumption that democracy is a natural state, and that it will burst into flower as soon as the weight of tyranny is removed. This state of mind is illustrated by a recent peace plan which prescribes that any dictator should be required to "restore democracy" before being admitted to the super-alliance. Just how would Hitler go about restoring democracy?

It is a fallacy to believe that democracy can be achieved by revolt. It seems a rather prevalent idea that if only you can remove tyranny and dictatorship, democracy will spring up fully developed. Experience has shown that revolt and the disappearance of tyranny do nothing more than clear the air for exercise of the talent for democracy which may already be latent in the people. We have seen a good many instances of this, but it is doubtful whether the results can be called democracy. In some instances there has been a gallant effort at better government, perhaps the first steps in the experience that lead toward democracy, but democracy cannot be imposed on people as dictatorship can. It is a game that two must play at, the government and the governed. We should free ourselves from the eager and wishful belief that at the end of the last war democracy suddenly sprang up all over the world. True, peoples in many lands set up the machinery of representative government, but even where there was a distinct improvement it could seldom, if ever, be called the achievement of democracy.

What we are primarily concerned with now is the preservation of representative governments, so that when the war is over they may be prepared to exercise their liberty. A good many of us feel that there are other countries going through the evolution toward some form of democracy, and that their hopes for the future are to a large extent measured by the survival of those who have trodden the long road and achieved freedom for themselves. We must hope that these countries will come through with enough strength to struggle against the forces at large in the world which are perilous to democracy.

Life would be much simpler if there were no dictators and if all governments were conducted on the liberal representative basis of Sweden and Switzerland. This truth has led to the growth of a widespread assumption that peace can be achieved by the elimination of dictators—it being assumed that as they disappear they will automatically be replaced by democracy everywhere. We are told that we cannot live in the same world with dictators, that the world cannot be half slave and half free.

That statement will hardly bear scrutiny. There have always been dictators in the world, and however much tyrannies have complicated life, we free societies have always had to live in a world that was half slave and half free. We shall probably have to go on doing so for a long time to come, although it should always be our aim to foster and strengthen representative government and reduce the area of despotism.

Our real task is to work out some way to make the dictators keep within certain bounds, partly by disarming the aggressive ones, partly, perhaps, through depriving their peoples of grievances on which they thrive—not by way of appeasement but by intelligent recognition of situations calling for peaceful remedies. We have repeated examples of this sort of thing in the last few years. If there had been effective international co-operation for reasonable settlement of controversies, it is probable that Hitler would never have come to power in Germany.

No matter how insufferable a dictator is, he seldom comes to power except to supplant some more reasonable form of government which has failed to secure national needs. He has little chance of seizing power unless he has some measure of real grievance to exploit and to exaggerate.

Perhaps this is what Mr. Wilson had in mind in his much-derided phrase about "making the world safe for democracy." As a matter of fact, that comes pretty close to being our real problem today. We did not succeed in it last time, but we would do well to have it in mind for the future.

People do not even agree easily on the definition of democracy —the democracy we want to make the world safe for. You may approach the subject from another angle and draw up a list of countries that qualify as democracies. Again it is difficult to get people to agree as to which countries would qualify. We are all rather prone to include in our lists countries that we like and exclude countries we don't like.

There remains still another consideration—that democracy is a matter of age-long growth, development, and education. If we put our sympathies aside, the only democracies that really stand the acid test are those countries where over a long period the people have been insistent on personal freedom, and have wrested a considerable share of sovereignty from their rulers in a struggle that has sometimes lasted for centuries.

There are certain countries that have gone through this experience—the United States, Great Britain, France, the Scandinavian countries, Holland, Belgium, and Switzerland, at least.

But when we venture far beyond that restricted list we are not always on solid ground. It is questionable whether democracy can be achieved without this long struggle, without the sacrifices that it involves, without the inner knowledge of the value of the liberties the people have been fighting for.

Even with a carefully planned policy, the interplay of forces, the quick movement of events, make heavy enough demands upon our diplomacy and upon public opinion. But if the people know what our policy is they will have a yardstick by which to measure and judge the conduct of the government. With an informed public opinion the people would have an effective control of foreign policy.

CHAPTER III

Diplomacy, Trained and Untrained

HOWEVER GOOD the policy we build, it must be constantly nurtured and helped along its way. This work can be done only by diplomacy. Perhaps diplomacy working in new ways with new instruments, but still diplomacy. Nothing else can take its place.

To begin with a helpful definition, diplomacy is simply the conduct of business between governments.

We must examine diplomacy, both from the national and the international point of view—that is, the use of American diplomacy to defend our national interests and, on the other hand, systematized international co-operation to promote common aims.

First, as to the American aspect.

It is often said, tritely but truly, that diplomacy is our first line of national defense. It follows that if the first line is adequately held there is less chance of our having to fall back on the second line. Or, to put it in another way, war comes only with the failure of diplomacy. If we can strengthen both national and international diplomacy, we can get better results. If we don't, we must be prepared for more failures—and more disastrous failures. The most disastrous failures of all end in war.

We have urgent need of national understanding of what diplomacy is and isn't. It is no more than a method of conducting international relations that has grown up through centuries of experience. The mystery and hocus-pocus of diplomacy are largely existent only in the minds of a mystery-loving public. In reality, diplomacy is a laborious business, singularly free from glamor and mystery. We can deal with it as a serious business, like any other method of working for the government.

Practical ends cannot be achieved by anything but hard, patient work, preferably by people who know the game. Diplomacy is a grim business with the underlying objective of getting as much as you can for your own country. The unfailing courtesy which should characterize it is not based, as is so generally assumed, on a spineless desire to make yourself agreeable to foreigners and give everything away. It is a reciprocal recognition that the current negotiation is a mere incident in a continuing relationship: that both parties to any controversy will have an unending series of matters to be settled in the future and that agreement will be favored by maintenance of good temper and good feeling. Either negotiator is often in a position to take all he wants if prepared to disregard the feelings and rights of the other. So is the gangster who makes a smash-and-grab raid. But the latter does not plan to return the following day and resume relations.

One of the reproaches leveled at diplomats in general is that they bring on wars. This is always good for a few lines in the papers if you have nothing to say. I have before me a newspaper dispatch reporting the return from overseas of a foreign "star of stage and screen." She "expressed a fervent wish formulated from what she had seen on her travels entertaining American soldiers."

"I wish," she said, "that every diplomat in the world could spend a day or two at the fighting fronts—and this mess would soon be over."

From this it would appear we have never appreciated the power of our diplomats. By all means let's hurry them off to all the fighting fronts and let them stop the war.

The young lady in question and others of her kind overlook the fact that the chief function of diplomats is to avoid war and maintain peace. If war comes, it proves that the diplomat has failed. It seems rather absurd that a whole profession should devote its energies to proving itself a failure. In general, war is brought about by deficient statesmanship on the part of political leaders whom the diplomat serves. No amount of ability on the part of trained diplomats can suffice to avert war when the political leaders lead a country straight into it.

We pride ourselves on being a nation of specialists. Medicine has endless specialties. So has the law. Engineering has an even wider range. If need for a specialty arises, we are more than likely to develop it and produce the specialists.

But as regards what should be the most highly specialized profession in the world we do a rightabout-face. In fact, we deny that a specialized need exists. We as a people are convinced we should be better served if the career diplomats were turned out and their places taken by plain Americans from private life. They alone will stand no nonsense from foreigners and know how to talk to them.

The American people have long looked on diplomacy as a mysterious activity on another plane that does not really concern them. Diplomats are a strange breed sent abroad by the government for some unfathomable reason, apparently to go to parties. Foreign lands are full of foreigners whose ways are past finding out. Anyway, what can those diplomats do about it?

In reality there is nothing that is more the concern of the American people than diplomacy. Diplomats, too, are their concern—to get the best-qualified diplomats possible to defend and promote our interests. For the diplomats defend those interests just as definitely as the soldiers in the jungles of the South Pacific.

The methods of diplomacy have undoubtedly lagged behind changing conditions. Some efforts have been made at modernization, but for the most part they have been unfortunate in their conception and have not given the desired results. There is much to be done in this field, and it may be that we can hope for progress in our time.

For some years efforts to build an adequate diplomacy have been undermined by propaganda from many sources, to convince the American people that the whole character of diplomacy has changed and that what we need in the Department of State and the foreign field are businessmen and not diplomats. We are told that diplomacy has become entirely a matter of business, and that we no longer have use for the traditional diplomat.

Diplomacy has not become a matter of business but, under the exacting conditions of modern organized life, business has become so international in character that it has more and more need for the expert assistance and support of diplomacy.

One might as well say that the legal profession has become entirely a matter of business, whereas we all know that under modern conditions business concerns need more and more the advice and active assistance of legal counsel, and the lawyer is assuming a larger and larger role. It would never enter anybody's mind, however, to suggest that the law has become so entirely a matter of business that we should disbar all practicing lawyers and put in their places men who have had experience in running banks, factories, and railroads. Instead of that, we try to broaden the training of our lawyers in order that they may render better service to business. In the same way, we should seek to train more efficient diplomats in order that they may afford effective assistance and support to our business at home and abroad.

There are doubtless special occasions when it may be desirable to choose an individual businessman because of special qualifications for a given post at a given time. It can hardly be said, however, that businessmen are better fitted than anybody else to act as chiefs of mission, because they have only one phase of the training that is necessary, whereas the trained diplomat should have a complete and well-rounded training to handle all phases of his work.

There is another fallacy in this idea that a businessman is the best material for diplomacy. We assume that it suffices to have business experience in almost any form. It might at least be assumed that the businessman should be chosen from among those having some knowledge and firsthand experience in the field of international business. But this limitation has never been applied. What we need is not less training in and understanding of diplomacy, but more.

One test is the case of the representative of an American enterprise who goes overseas to examine the possibilities of foreign trade, or to deal with difficulties encountered by an established enterprise. He sometimes goes to an embassy for help. In this case, he does not go for advice on business methods. He is qualified to deal with those himself or he would not be sent overseas. When he turns to the embassy, it is to get advice and guidance in matters beyond his ken. He may need expert knowledge of the political situation in the country which will enable him to judge as to the safety of investment, of the dangers to foreign enterprise, of trends which warn him that although investment is safe today it may be unsafe in the years to come. This kind of information can be furnished only by men trained in understanding political trends and interpreting events. Aside from the advice given by our representatives, the visiting businessman must depend upon them to put him in touch with sources of information which will permit him to arrive at sound conclusions. This indicates our need for diplomatic representatives who, over the years, have built up an acquaintanceship which enables them to sort out the valuable sources of information and discard the less reliable, although perhaps more obvious.

Any diplomat of long experience knows that when an American businessman brings in his troubles it is not to ask advice on strictly business matters, but to seek guidance through the unfamiliar waters of diplomacy, politics, and foreign customs. The expedient of appointing a wholesale grocer or lawyer from home to the post of ambassador deprives the visiting businessman of the very sort of guidance he needs most.

It is often said that the work of the diplomat has lost most of its importance in modern times, as he is able to receive his instructions from home by telegraph and merely has to repeat what he is told; that he has become a mere glorified messenger boy. As a matter of fact, there never was a time when it was so important to have highly trained diplomatic representatives. It is true that modern facilities of communication have, during the past hundred years, completely transformed the conditions under which diplomats work. But that is no ground for assuming it has rendered them superfluous. This very development has made the world a much smaller place, much more highly geared and, therefore, more sensitive to developments, and has made the career diplomat's duties more important than ever before. It is more than ever important that he keep himself and his government informed as to developments which, in former times, could have had no effect on international relations.

In the earlier days of diplomacy the Ambassador dealt with the foreign sovereign and reported only to his own. He had no public opinion or parliamentary majorities to think about. The reaction of the press had not been developed, and things were relatively simple—aside from certain occupational hazards such as the dagger and the poisoned cup.

Nowadays the diplomat is beset at every turn by perils for the unwary. Whereas in the old days couriers took weeks upon their journeys, nowadays events are known half round the world sometimes before they reach the local population. The diplomat's first and most essential task is to keep his government informed as to diplomatic trends in order that it may not be taken by surprise. And this task of keeping informed is something that must be handled by a man on the spot versed in the methods of diplomacy, who knows what sort of information to look for, where to find it, and how to appraise its value when he gets it. This is not the sort of information that can be secured by telephoning to a Foreign Minister from halfway round the world.

Moreover, as intelligent public opinion grows, there is an increasing desire to exhaust every possible means of peaceable negotiation and to have recourse to conciliation and arbitration, rather than accept the rupture of diplomatic relations and war. This has done, and will do, much more to elevate the duties of the diplomat to a still higher plane. It is, therefore, of the greatest importance that he should be so assisted and equipped as to make him an efficient instrument for obtaining information and conducting negotiations with foreign governments.

If, through the improvement of communications, the diplomat has become superfluous and diplomacy can be conducted by telephone, is it not curious that others with analogous duties have not been similarly affected? You would think the foreign representatives of Standard Oil could also be recalled and business conducted by telephone. Yet nobody suggests recalling the foreign representatives of American business. On the contrary, as communications have improved there has been a steady increase in the number of American business representatives abroad—and increasing demand for a higher standard of qualifications. Somehow this new conception seems to apply only to diplomacy, which is more important and has more responsibility than all our businesses put together.

We need a trained service as a political weather bureau for the country. Nobody questions the statement that an untrained man is useless in a meteorological station, where he is expected to read physical phenomena. It is not only unwise but sometimes dangerous to send an inexperienced and unqualified man to a diplomatic post, where he is called upon to read in a strange language the political, economic, and psychological phenomena of a strange people. Such a man must either plunge into the situation and try to muddle through, regardless of the help or guidance of those about him or, as the only alternative, he must depend upon others until he has learned his lesson. This means that he acquires his elementary education in a responsible position at the expense of American interests. If he is an appointee from private life, the chances are that by the time he has learned to do his work well he will be replaced by someone else, and the process of education will begin afresh. We take a gambler's chance every time we send an inexperienced man to a responsible post.

To revert to the phrase that diplomacy is our first line of national defense—in reality it is just that. Our diplomats are observers in the field to keep our government informed as to trends and developments that may affect our national security. We have an example fresh in our memories of the distinguished service rendered by Mr. Grew in keeping our government advised as to Japanese preparations for war and Japanese intentions toward the United States. None of this was directly concerned with the promotion of American trade. It was, rather, a matter of national security. And it was work that could be done only by a trained and experienced diplomat.

It must be remembered that diplomacy concerns itself with the whole range of intercourse between nations. These relations depend on many factors—economic, political, and psychological. To lay stress on the economic side to the exclusion of all the others is to take a one-sided and distorted view. A businessman, appointed to a diplomatic post, is rarely equipped to estimate accurately the value of these different factors—it would be surprising if he could. His natural intelligence may conceivably compensate for the deficiencies of his training, and he may achieve remarkable success, but it would be unfair and unreasonable to expect this of him merely because he had been a successful businessman.

It is quite true that we have had some exceptionally brilliant men who were successful in taking over an embassy or legation without previous training, but it must be remembered that this success was due largely to the fact that they were themselves extremely adaptable. We must also remember that a far larger number of the people appointed from private life have been complete failures. In the main, appointments from outside the service have given us men who have had to be largely guided by their subordinates, and who were not qualified by their training to do a great part of the directive work of the mission.

Walter Hines Page, who was himself a natural diplomat of remarkable ability, expressed himself briefly and forcibly on this subject. Among other things he said in one of his published letters:

"But the realness and the bigness of the job here in London is simply oppressive. We don't even know what it is in the United States, and, of course, we don't go about doing it right. If we did, we shouldn't pick up a green fellow in the plain of Long Island and send him here. We'd train the most capable male babies we have from the cradle."

The same idea was expressed in other terms by James Kearney, editor of the Trenton *State,* who was sent to Paris in the last war on an important mission and got into difficulties because of his lack of knowledge of French ways. At a particularly embarrassing moment he remarked:

"There's one thing I've discovered over here. There's a hell of a lot of difference between Paris and Trenton—and you notice it more in Paris than you do in Trenton."

There is a world of wisdom in that statement, and the American people would do well to give weight to the shrewd words of Jim Kearney in choosing their representatives.

The American career system, not the service itself but the system which determines how it shall be recruited, is probably the worst that could be devised, for we are prone to keep the conduct of the most important and intricate matters in the hands of inexperienced men and give all the training to their subordinates. In this way we effectively deprive ourselves of the opportunity of attracting large numbers of capable men, ready to devote long years to learning the profession of diplomacy in the knowledge that they are in a service like the Army or Navy, where they can rise as high as their abilities take them.

Other countries train their diplomats, and we shall continue to be at a disadvantage in dealing with them until we train ours. We have got along so far without enough trained diplomats, but this has been in spite of our lack of training and not because of it. We should certainly not come to depend on lack of training as a system for the conduct of government any more than a lawyer would prefer untrained men to assist him.

During the last twenty-five years the political leaders in most countries have made a mess of diplomacy. They could not be expected to succeed because they ignored the forces in operation; because they sought to settle everything by the methods of domestic politics; because they were ignorant of the methods of diplomacy and resolutely refused advice from the diplomats who could have helped them. They cannot, of course, be blamed for their ignorance, but we can blame them for their arrogance in assuming that they alone could settle everything and that they could succeed by pure improvisation.

We should not be justified in advocating that we bar the use of men from private life, but we might well follow the common-sense course followed by most other governments of using trained men where they can serve us best, and in exceptional cases utilize the services of men from private life who have special qualifications for dealing with a special situation. It is the duty of the government to secure the best possible service for the country in each case, whether that be through the use of a career diplomat or a man from private life. If this is done, we shall witness a great improvement in the handling of our foreign affairs.

While we need a trained diplomatic service, it is to be hoped that we shall never go to the extreme of having complete security of tenure. Those countries that have gone farthest in this direction have produced conspicuously incompetent diplomats. There is nothing more deadly than the knowledge that if you only live long enough you will be an ambassador. This encourages men to avoid all initiative in the belief that the end and aim of life is to sidestep responsibility and run no risks.

This state of mind was well illustrated by the old diplomat who said that he never answered a letter but filed all his correspondence in three drawers labeled as follows:

1. Letters that need no answers.
2. Letters that time will answer.
3. Letters that God Himself couldn't answer.

There is as much humbug about the diplomat as there is about the African witch doctor—with the difference that the witch doctor makes up his own mumbo jumbo as the necessary trappings of his trade. That of the diplomat is made up for him by people who know nothing about his business.

The ordinary detective is so little like the glittering figure in detective stories that he enjoys his Sherlock Holmes along with the rest of us. Ordinary diplomats are utterly unlike the heroes of E. Phillips Oppenheim, and most of them are thriller fans.

You will never find a diplomat in real life who has wrapped the Stars and Stripes around the lovely heroine to save her from the fury of the mob. He would probably be rather vague as to how much good that courtly gesture would do—outside the covers of a book.

You will have just as much trouble finding one who has whispered state secrets in the shell-like ear of a duchess—if he did, she would probably yawn.

None of them have had their lives brightened by dazzling adventuresses with stolen treaties to be recovered after breathless adventures—in fact, they have never done any of the things that seem to be the daily routine of the diplomat of fiction.

As regards the death-defying, daredevil diplomat of the thrillers, we may as well face the fact that there is no such animal. Life would be much more colorful if there were. But it is to be hoped that their authors will continue to send them on their palpitating journeys of three hundred pages. It is such a help in the prosaic life of the real diplomat.

Glamor is about as rare in diplomacy as it is in a grocery. Few of our representatives ever glimpse the sort of high society we read about. We seem to assume in this country that any society outside the limits of the United States is glamorous. This is not the case—in most places it is just as dull and provincial as it is in Squeedunk.

Let's look into this high-society aspect of diplomacy. Just what happens to a beginner in the Foreign Service?

He passes his examinations, is given some basic training in the Department of State, and is usually sent to some distant and forsaken post as a Vice-Consul. Here, instead of moving in a daze among the exalted, he settles down to deal with visa applicants, trade inquiries, distressed seamen, and the like. Humility and help-fulness and his own insignificance are dinned into him. He learns that in the official order of precedence he ranks "with, but after, a worm."

Through the years he works his way up, but must find his rewards in other things than high society. It is rare that he will have a post where the so-called "social advantages" are equal to what he would have had if he had stayed at home. Our diplomats are kept at it all their lives, not from social ambition as is widely believed, but by sheer spunk and devotion, coupled with pride in their work.

It may be that during the present upheaval the American people will be ready to do something about this problem. Common sense dictates that we equip this first line of defense as adequately as possible. We are ready to spend billions for military defense and we should be shocked if the high posts of command were entrusted to even the most competent lawyers, bankers, and politicians—to say nothing of diplomats. However, there is in normal course no public outcry—indeed very little public interest—in the equipment given to the Foreign Service; no protest if the most responsible positions are entrusted to utterly unqualified people.

Even under existing discouragements we have been able to build up a career service which, so far as it goes, is second to none. It is surprising that we have been able to attract and keep men of outstanding ability. It can be explained only by a high sense of public service.

Nevertheless, it is always open season on career diplomats. The man who comes to an embassy innocent of training or experience can get away with murder, and only in exceptional cases would the press take a fling at him. But there is some sort of turpitude in learning this profession, and it has become the mark of the liberal publicist to roast career diplomats as such.

When no other offense can be charged to them, they are denounced for drinking tea.

Perhaps some of them do drink tea, but what of it? Does tea sap their virility and their patriotism, and make them as clay in the hands of foreigners?

For the moment, some of our representatives are being freely denounced as reactionaries—or worse. A case in point is Mr. Murphy, who has done an outstandingly able job in North Africa. He was stingingly criticized for dealing with Darlan, and in some quarters there were shrill demands that our government recall him for his misdeeds. This sort of appeal to the government seems to be based on the assumption that Mr. Murphy made up his mind as to what he wanted to do, and that an ignored and henpecked government meekly followed along.

Much of this criticism arises from a fundamental misconception of the diplomat's duties. We do not hire him to be amiable to those he likes and rude to those he disapproves. So long as we maintain diplomatic relations with a country, it is the duty of our diplomat to get along with those in office. He may thoroughly disapprove the same men that people at home are denouncing—he may yearn to explode in righteous anger. But he is not there to indulge himself in that way. The day he adopts an attitude of public hostility his usefulness is ended and he is under the additional reproach of having made things harder for his successor.

What the impatient critic does not always realize is that the diplomat, while maintaining a public attitude of friendliness, is often speaking with plain and brutal frankness in private. This need not impair his usefulness if he confines his frankness to those with whom he has to deal officially, and if he does not allow any personal animosity to creep into his behavior.

Only on occasion is he justified in blowing off steam publicly, and then not to relieve his personal feelings but to serve some clear public interest and with full realization of the possible consequences. An illustration of this is Admiral Standley's carefully considered outburst over the failure of the Soviet Government to let the Russian people know about the importance of our Lend-Lease aid. He knew exactly what he was after and he got it.

A diplomat can always be sure of applause if he indulges in rough talk. That is supposed to be proof of his sterling Americanism. It is proof of nothing of the sort—only of his unfitness for his job.

Many people fail to realize that our greatest need for skill and restraint arises when an international situation becomes acute. Then our people demand service. They expect our representatives to work wonders. If they lose their heads or their tempers at a time like this, our interests suffer.

We hire our diplomats to get what we want. They cannot always get what we want from congenial people. Sometimes, indeed, we want things from people they dislike intensely. But the diplomat has to swallow his feelings, go to his post, and do his best to get on with the government to which he is assigned. In doing this, he has to bow his head to the storm and make up his mind to carry out the wishes of the President and the Secretary of State, instead of winning the approval of the bleachers.

This modern practice of pillorying individual diplomats for their conduct in current negotiations is mischievous in the extreme. The diplomat is our agent. Anything that impairs his prestige or creates an impression that he lacks respect at home lessens his standing in representing us. His best chance of achieving what we want is to work in freedom from publicity. When sniped at by critics at home, his freedom of action is impaired and his prestige undermined with the government to which he is accredited.

This is a peculiarly American practice. In other countries, the press criticizes the policy of the government, but it usually refrains from efforts to discredit the Ambassador who is seeking to defend the interests of the country.

These attacks are often amusing to people who do not realize their vicious effects. When the people of this country do realize how hurtful this sort of thing is to our own interests, they will show their disapproval and the practice will not long survive.

We have another curious complex about our diplomats. We criticize them if they appear to like the country where they serve. There is no more deadly charge against an American Ambassador in London than that he is pro-British. Curiously enough, we never hear such misgivings about foreign representatives in Washington. If a British Ambassador is reported as being pro-American, we do not consider his recall is indicated. On the contrary, we are gratified, and feel this proves him the right man in the right place.

Just what is the reason for this?

Is it some inferiority complex that questions the sturdiness of our own patriotism? Is it to be assumed that our representatives are such weak sisters that unless they keep a chip on their shoulder they cannot be trusted to defend our interests? In that case, foreigners must be made of stouter fiber, for there have been plenty of them in Washington who managed to serve their countries ably in spite of liking America and Americans.

There is one permissible exception. Our representatives are permitted to like any country with which we, as a nation, are infatuated at the moment. In such a case, all restrictions are off. Our representatives are free not only to like that country but to love it with a fierce and consuming passion—to do propaganda for it, regardless even of the interests of their own country.

Sometimes we go in for a new and wonderful sort of diplomacy to appease public clamor. This is occasionally justified as recognition of democratic control of foreign policy. Here is how it works.

Ninety-nine per cent of the American people keep their views to themselves. The remaining one per cent wants action of one sort or another—usually quick and direct action. They demand that the Administration declare a boycott or impose economic sanctions. If they cannot have war they want to break diplomatic relations. Of all the foolish steps perhaps the most foolish is the breaking of diplomatic relations for the purpose of persuading the other fellow to come around to your view. When conditions are difficult and exasperating is precisely the time when we most need to keep our heads and work for a sane solution. By breaking relations we deprive ourselves of the means of getting our own way peacefully. It is on a par with the man who loses his temper in a discussion and storms out, slamming the door. He has, in a sense, put himself in the wrong by losing his temper, and even if he does return he does so with a certain loss of dignity.

In recent years we have developed a totally new technique. Some vociferous minority clamors for severance of diplomatic relations—as a protest against this or that development which, incidentally, may be only one phase of our relations. The government wants to satisfy the minority and at the same time keep the door open for continued negotiations. So we have developed a new method which has all the disadvantages and none of the advantages of a clean break.

We withdraw the Ambassador and leave the rest of the staff.

If that does not suffice, we withdraw the next ranking official, leaving only inexperienced junior officials to represent us.

We don't exhaust the possibilities of negotiation first. If we did, we should withdraw the whole establishment. In a moment of impatience—or rather in an effort to appease the impatience of some influential element at home—we withdraw our highest representative. We are the chief sufferers from this procedure. The Ambassador alone has the right to demand interviews with the chief of state. In some cases the withdrawal of our Ambassador is a distinct relief to the other government. Once he is gone our junior representative can be referred to subordinate members of the Foreign Office, and if they give him scant consideration there is little he can do about it.

This is the most stupid of all systems, because it deprives us of our most effective representation. It is at times when nerves are taut that we need to keep our ambassadors at their posts.

There is one further refinement in this childish procedure. Strictly speaking, we do not withdraw our Ambassador. We recall him "for consultation." This is a perfectly normal thing in itself, but we do it with a difference. We allow it to be known that this is really an expression of our displeasure, and that the return of the Ambassador to his post will be considered later in the light of developments. Thus we convey to the other government and to the wide, wide world the fact that we are annoyed. The other country cannot take this lying down and makes the next move by recalling its Ambassador "for consultation." Thus we achieve the result worthy of Alice in Wonderland, that both countries are deprived of their fullest representation at a time of high public feeling. Both governments are frozen upon their positions in an embarrassing attitude, like bad-mannered little boys, and it is seldom they have the dignity and good sense to return their ambassadors to their posts.

By way of illustration we may recall that when in November 1938 barbarous and systematic anti-Jewish outrages broke out all over Germany there was a general demand that our government do everything in its power to put a stop to the persecution. It was obvious that the campaign was being directed by Goering and other leading Nazis. The only conceivable way of exercising a moderating influence was through the Ambassador, our highest ranking representative, who at least had the right of direct access to all the leaders. It is precisely in such times of crisis that an Ambassador should be at his post. We were fortunate in having an able man on the ground. However, according to the methods of our new diplomacy, Hugh Wilson, our Ambassador, was ordered back to Washington "for consultation," with a clear intimation to the press that this was a mark of official displeasure. The inevitable result was that the Nazi Government, unwilling to accept a publicly administered slap of this sort, promptly recalled Herr Hans Dieckhoff, the German Ambassador in Washington, also "for consultation."

There might have been justification for recalling Mr. Wilson for consultation, that is to consider what measures we could take that would lead to alleviation of the desperate condition of the Jews in Germany. But there was no justification for failing to send him back to his post where he might have been able to accomplish much. For when Mr. Wilson was recalled we forfeited our only direct access to the Nazi leaders. A chargé d'affaires cannot demand such access as a matter of right. In this instance the Nazi leaders were relieved of embarrassment by Mr. Wilson's departure, for they stood on their rights and referred the chargé d'affaires to the Foreign Office where he was received by subordinate officials and shown the futility of such protests or comments as he delivered. From the time Mr. Wilson was recalled "for consultation" in November 1938 we were without effective representation in Germany. The war was approaching with giant strides, and more than ever we needed an Ambassador in Berlin to keep us informed. Instead we deprived ourselves of this needed information on no ground that has ever been discernible except the desire to maintain our expression of displeasure—futile displeasure so long as we took it out in making faces at Germany.

Then in September 1939 the war came in Europe. For ten months we had been without full representation in Berlin, and with the withdrawal of so many other ambassadors it became more than ever urgent that we should have our own at Berlin. But we were faced by some embarrassment about declaring the period of consultation at an end. So under the new diplomacy of the bite-off-your-nose-to-spite-your-face variety, we resigned ourselves to doing without our best representation, and Mr.

Wilson was kept in Washington twiddling his thumbs from November 1938 until the end of 1940, when he resigned as Ambassador to Germany.

It might be assumed that even if for some mysterious reason we preferred to remain at a disadvantage in dealing with Germany, we should have clung to the services of every qualified man available. But while keeping in office some of the strangest people who have ever represented us abroad, Hugh Wilson, like a number of other experienced and qualified men, remained unemployed in any responsible capacity and eventually retired from the service after Pearl Harbor.

We find another illustration in our dealings with Finland. An unsatisfactory situation arose. It was obvious that Mr. Schoenfeld, the Minister, should remain at his post where he could look after our interests. But we recalled Mr. Schoenfeld, leaving the legation in charge of the first secretary. The situation got no better with some rapidity, and we recalled the first secretary, who handed over the legation to the second secretary, who in the course of events withdrew in obedience to a summons home and left our interests in charge of a third secretary. At the time of writing our relations with Finland call for wise and experienced handling, but unless we have a fourth and fifth secretary of legation in Helsinki we shall probably either exhaust our stock of representatives or begin on the janitor and domestic staff.

Another illustration came in February 1944 when a revolution broke out in Bolivia. In such a time of crisis we need our most influential representative on the ground. But in what has become an almost routine development Pierre de L. Boal, our Ambassador, was hustled into a plane and flown to Washington. Again we were told by the press that the trip was for purposes of consultation and as a mark of our dissatisfaction with the faction that has made the revolution. Yet it does not require expert knowledge to know that Mr. Boal would have a better chance of influencing events by remaining at his post in La Paz.

These instances will suffice to show some of the disadvantages of scrapping the long experience of diplomacy and embarking on a new technique of bad temper and bad manners.

CHAPTER IV

Diplomacy, Trained and Untrained
(continued)

ONE OBSTACLE in the way to our having the sort of diplomatic service we need is the inadequate pay for the higher ranks.

The present rate of pay for our ambassadors was set in 1855—not much short of a century ago. In those days it was a generous allowance for the representative of a small power playing no great role in the world. Since that time the importance of our role in world affairs and the demands upon our representatives have increased by leaps and bounds even as the value of the dollar has declined.

Perhaps the obvious course would be to increase the pay of our representatives. This would call for drastic revision upward. For instance, to put our Ambassador in London on a financial level with the British Ambassador in Washington we should have to give him more than five times what he now receives.

Until we do something to make it possible for a suitable American of modest means, or no private means at all, to accept any post in the diplomatic service, we shall be maintaining an undemocratic service in which rich men are favored merely because they are rich. But there is no need to meet the situation with increased salary. Salary is presumably the remuneration a man receives for his work. It is his to do with as he likes. A diplomat's salary, even if greatly increased, does not answer that description. He must use it to pay the expenses of his post. This is almost as absurd as paying an admiral a handsome salary and then requiring him to use it to pay the expenses of his fleet.

Another drawback about granting much higher salaries is that it would bring about still greater pressure from unqualified office seekers and would delay still further the building of a trained service. An ambassadorship paying an amount adequate for the upkeep of the embassy would become the goal of hundreds of men intent on feathering their nests. And with this sort of incumbent our purpose would not be achieved, for we would have no guarantee that the money was spent in the public interest.

An alternative would be to leave salaries as they were fixed in 1855 and consider them the pay of the Ambassador. In addition to this there should be post allowances for the necessary expenses of the embassy, lighting and heating, servants, necessary entertaining, transportation, et cetera. Other countries have followed this course for many years. It has made it possible to choose good men for posts, regardless of their private means, and it has made certain that the money was spent for official purposes and not tucked away in a private bank account.

The cost of our diplomatic service is an infinitesimal fraction of our national expenditure. Even in a time of economy and retrenchment we would do well to double or triple our expenditures on the diplomatic service—provided we did some reforming of our diplomacy at the same time.

Our diplomatic service has suffered from the belief—systematically spread for various reasons—that diplomacy is essentially snobbish and undemocratic. This is based chiefly on the idea that diplomats associate with the rulers of foreign countries and move in glamorous social surroundings. There is a great deal of nonsense in this. As a matter of fact, a great part of the so-called social activity is far more of a chore to the diplomat than is his office work. It is, however, an essential part of his business, for it is in these social contacts that he builds up relationships which enable him to know what is going on and to secure what his government wants. However, anybody who looks on this as the end and aim of the diplomat's life has never lived through it.

This social activity is a deeply rooted grievance against the diplomatic service. It overlooks the fact that we send the diplomat for the express purpose of associating with the people of influence in the country to which he is accredited, and it is rather unreasonable to feel he should be punished for what he is sent abroad to do. Foreign diplomats are sent to Washington to establish good relations with the government and with influential Americans, and we see nothing reprehensible in their doing so.

There is a belief that our career diplomats are readily beguiled by the diplomats of other countries and that they never stand up for our interests. They are supposed to succumb to flattery and social attentions, and we are often told that plain Americans from private life would not fall for that sort of thing.

As a matter of fact the political appointee falls for just that sort of thing far more readily than a man with a career background. The career diplomat realizes that the courtesy and consideration shown him are addressed to the representative of the United States. He understands that they represent a normal attitude toward a foreign representative, calculated to lubricate the wheels of diplomacy. Very often the political appointee is surprised and gratified by these courtesies and accepts them as addressed to him personally. He has had the good fortune to land in a country where he is recognized at his true worth. There is something exhilarating about this and he feels called upon to tell the world how truly wonderful everything is—whether it be in France, Russia, Albania, or Spain. This often leads to his becoming an active propagandist for the country to which he is accredited. In some cases it goes so far that he ends by serving not as American Ambassador to Graustark but as second Graustarkian Ambassador to the United States. One striking example of this sort of thing was Alec Moore, husband of Lillian Russell and pal of Diamond Jim Brady, who served for a time as Ambassador to Spain. He was not particularly active in defending American interests but he was vociferous in promoting Spanish interests in the United States. It has been said that he was a mediocre American Ambassador but an active and zealous Spanish Ambassador to the United States.

Many of these temporary diplomats, not realizing that theirs is a fleeting importance, become considerably puffed up, and are bewildered and hurt at the change when they retire. As a wholesome *memento mori* certain pertinent Biblical selections might well be emblazoned on the walls of every Ambassador's office. Among them should be a quotation from the twentieth chapter of the Book of Job, which begins:

Though his excellency mount up to the heavens, and his head reach unto the clouds;

Yet he shall perish for ever like his own dung: they which have seen him shall say, Where is he?

He shall fly away as a dream, and shall not be found: yea, he shall be chased away as a vision of the night.

The eye also which saw him shall see him no more; neither shall his place any more behold him.

The theme is developed in further detail in such a way as to leave no doubt as to the transitory character of His Excellency's importance. A diplomat who has worked his way up from the ranks has no illusions as to the importance of the individual. On the other hand, he has probably developed a greater and more responsible understanding of the importance and power of the representative capacity, of what it really means to represent and speak for a great nation.

We need to free ourselves from self-important ambassadors and develop a service of men of personal modesty who realize that their standing is due to their office as representatives of the United States.

During the last fifteen years or so there has been a moderate amount of controversy over the admission of women to the diplomatic service.

When the question first arose there was one valid argument that women had to have preferred treatment in order to succeed in the diplomatic service. The equal rights demanded for them were not enough. They could not be sent to unhealthy posts, or to posts where they would be exposed to normal hazards of diplomatic life—for, although it is not generally known, there is more danger in diplomatic life than there is social glamor. Women in diplomacy would doubtless be prepared to face their share of the danger and to take the rough with the smooth, along with other members of the service. However, they would not be the ones to decide. The benighted males, who are responsible for assignments, still labor under certain old-fashioned prejudices about sending women out where machine guns are popping while they sit safely in their offices; and that women would have to have first claim on the most agreeable and comfortable posts and the men take more than their share of the unpleasant assignments.

In recent years, however, there has been a drastic change in the work of the diplomatic service. For one thing, the personnel has been greatly increased, and even after the war emergency there is no doubt that there will be a new technique calling for far larger numbers of trained officials. This involves a radical change from the old days, where a legation might have one lone secretary, and in the new setup there ought to be plenty of room for women diplomats without putting the men in a position where they would have to organize a campaign for equal rights.

In discussing the suitability of women for diplomatic work the fundamental test is very much what it is for men. There are women whom it would be disastrous to have in the diplomatic service. However, we have a large number of case histories where the same is to be said about men. Even with the small number of women admitted to the diplomatic service, we are fortunate in having some who have effectively disposed of most of the arguments against a coeducational service. There is no man in the service who could do us greater credit in the foreign field than Frances Willis, now Secretary of Embassy in Madrid, who has had a really distinguished career in diplomacy—of greater distinction in performance than in recognition. Any man who had such a consistent record of achievement would by this time have been recognized by appointment as chief of mission.

This suggests one drawback to the entry of women into diplomacy. It is the curious reluctance to recognize demonstrated ability by entrusting a woman with a highly responsible position. This again may be due to the reluctance we have mentioned—to expose a woman to the occupational hazards of diplomacy—but we cannot expect to get the best talent if women of proven ability are allowed to do the work without recognition.

When we talk about women in diplomacy, we usually have in mind service in the foreign field. We tend to overlook the fact that the Department of State directs the whole operation of our diplomacy and that there is much more of it in Washington than there is in Tokyo or Buenos Aires. Most arguments against women in the Foreign Service fall to the ground in Washington. The occupational hazards are less and, although it is not generally recognized, we have a long tradition of women in responsible positions in the Department of State.

Miss Margaret Hanna was for many years a recognized power in the department. Mrs. Ruth Shipley, Chief of the Passport Division, has had a long and distinguished career. Her efficient handling of the far-reaching and intricate problems of her division, at the most difficult period of our history, is rendered possible only by a lifetime of experience and responsible service. It seems that there is a greater field of opportunity and greater chance of recognition for women in the Department of State than in the foreign field.

There is another phase to this subject. It is not generally recognized that we have always had almost as many women as men in the diplomatic service, for the wife of a diplomat is just as much in the service of the government as her husband. In many branches of the government service, both military and civilian, it is of little moment whether an official is married or unmarried. His wife is not called upon to help him in his work. He does his daily grind and when it is done he is through. The diplomat's wife plays an integral part in representing the government for good or ill. She has clearly recognized duties and obligations and if she fails to perform them the Department of State is likely to hear about it from indignant citizens. Although our diplomats are notoriously underpaid, it is worse than appears on the surface, for in the diplomatic service alone the government gets the full-time services of two people for the pay of one.

The government would do well while examining the fitness of an appointee to look into the fitness of his wife to share in the work of her husband. A well-qualified wife is of immense value to her husband, and although we have had many disasters when wives were not up to what was expected of them, we have many cases of wives who greatly enhanced the value of their husbands to the government.

Any reference to the work done by the wife of a diplomat is almost certain to elicit an inquiry as to what on earth she does. There is a widespread impression that she is the pampered darling of fortune and that she has a rollicking life made up of an unending round of amusing parties. It is quite true that in many posts she does have what seems like more than her share of giving and attending dinners, lunches, receptions, and the like. But to describe all this as amusing is to reveal a lack of familiarity with the facts. No one without firsthand experience can realize how large a part of this social activity is pure boredom; nor can he realize how much of it, boring as it is, has a practical value for Uncle Sam.

The diplomat's value at any given post is largely determined by the sort of people he knows and the nature of his acquaintance. No one has yet evolved a substitute for social intercourse as a means of building up these relationships which are of value in the conduct of official business. The better your relations with an official outside his office, the better they will be when you go to his office, and the better your chance of getting what you go for. Of course in strict logic he ought to handle each transaction on its merits, but even officials are human enough to be well disposed toward their friends and anxious to do anything reasonable to please them. We can see the obverse of this in the case of a diplomat who keeps to himself and does not bother to see Foreign Office officials until he wants something. He will probably get courteous treatment, but there will usually be lacking that little extra desire to be helpful that calls resourcefulness into play to find a way.

Here the wife is expected to pull her weight in the boat. She is expected to make her home a center where government officials and colleagues of the diplomatic corps like to come on easy and friendly terms. Her skill and the amount of intelligence she puts into this may have an important part in building up a useful position for her husband in official quarters. In an active post this comes close to being a full-time job.

In addition to this there is the heavy burden laid upon the diplomat's wife by visits from Americans, both official and unofficial. The visitors usually look upon their own sojourn as an incident apart, a pleasant interlude for the diplomats and a breath from home for the exiles. To the diplomat the visitors are no more than part of a steady stream that he must take care of without regard to his own pleasure and convenience.

Many of these visits are useful, and it is important that they be turned to good account, and here is where the diplomat's wife is put to work. Let us assume that a group of four or five American senators arrive in town for a visit of three days. They rarely send ahead to inquire when it would be convenient to have them appear. They telegraph that they are arriving on Monday at noon and that during the short time at their disposal they want to see as many national leaders as possible. That means that the diplomat's own plans go out the window and that he and his wife settle down to make complicated arrangements that will ensure the best possible use of the visitors' time. On such short notice the national leaders are not always available and there is need for fitting them in when they can be had. It usually ends by the wife having to arrange a series of dinners and luncheons and perhaps a reception thrown in.

Visits of this sort can be of great value. It is important that the senators take home the fullest possible picture of the situation and of the state of our relations. On the other hand, it is important that the leaders of the other country get to know leading Americans and their point of view. Any effort involved is well worth while, but if a hurried visit of this sort is a success, there is seldom any appreciation of the fact that it went smoothly because of much hard work on the part of the diplomat's wife and to the established position that enabled her to get results.

In normal times official visits of this sort are frequent, and without firsthand experience it is difficult to realize the amount of time and effort the diplomat's wife devotes to making them go smoothly. In most posts there is in addition to this an unceasing flow of unofficial Americans who need help that only the embassy can give them. An American businessman or his lawyer comes to close an important deal approved by Washington, or to seek solution of difficulties. It is important that he establish contact with the officials who have the decision. Of course he could be given the names and addresses of these officials and left to fend for himself. Or he could be taken around and introduced to them in their offices. But there are many occasions when it is important they get off to a good start without loss of time. No better way usually suggests itself than to have him make the acquaintance of the men he is to deal with in the embassy. This may seem like a frivolous way of getting started but it is not so in the least. On the contrary, there is no more prompt and effective way of conveying to foreign officials that a visiting American is looked on by his own embassy as a man sufficiently substantial and trustworthy to be vouched for. By meeting thus under American auspices both parties get off to a friendly start, and the visiting American acquires a standing it might take him months to acquire by visits to a government office.

Or suppose the visiting American is a journalist or writer. He may be well known in his own country but unknown in the country he is visiting. Nothing gets him started under proper auspices better than meeting the right people—and by right people I mean those who can help him—and getting on easy, friendly terms with them at the embassy or in the home of a member of the staff. For in many posts the demands which it is desirable to meet are beyond the scope of a single establishment and have to be shared by all the official family even though this activity is not supposed to be a primary responsibility of any one of them.

If an American of distinction comes along there is a double purpose in having him meet the people of interest to him. It not only helps him, but it also helps to keep American standing high to have foreigners get to know our people who are distinguished in science, art, or literature. There is no more effective form of legitimate national propaganda.

The sum total of these visits and the cultivation of friendly relations with people of the country represent a continuing demand on the energy and hospitality of our official representatives— and, incidentally, a considerable demand on their private resources. Firsthand experience gives a picture of hard and devoted work and sacrifice of personal inclination quite at variance with the popular conception of a cast of frivolous men and women bent on social amusement.

The diplomat's wife is expected to take an active part in all sorts of local enterprises, American and foreign. If there is an American hospital, she is expected to take a working job of some sort and manifest a continuing interest. If there is an American school, there is much for her to do. If there is a local chapter of the American Red Cross and the Y.W.C.A., there is need for the diplomat's wife. The same is true for the American church. Each of these enterprises has its meetings and bazaars and sales and money-raising campaigns.

Then there is a whole range of charitable, educational, and other enterprises of the country in which the diplomat resides. It is essential that he and his wife demonstrate their friendly attitude by active participation in many of these activities. This involves another category of committee meetings, visits, and attendance at charitable, cultural, and sporting events. It is rarely fun, but it has to be done as part of the process of building a position of influence in the community.

In a busy post the wife has to be as businesslike as her husband with her own office, secretaries, and helpers, the only difference being that she pays for them out of her own pocket. We shall probably never get around to providing salaries as we should for the diplomat's wife, but we might well make provision for giving her secretarial assistance and paying her expenses.

We might even more properly get rid of the idea that she leads a life of undiluted amusement.

There is a good deal of talk nowadays of establishing a government school of diplomacy on the model of West Point or Annapolis. On the surface this may appear desirable, but there are a good many catches that we should do well to ponder before we go any further.

There is no identity of purpose in training for all services. West Point and Annapolis deal almost entirely with tangibles, with men and ships and guns and supplies and with training in exact sciences. This education is aimed at teaching men to think according to a pattern so that in great emergencies, where large numbers of men are involved, they can be counted on to think and act uniformly. That is essential if the armed forces are to maintain any orderly procedure in the midst of the confusion of battle.

The last thing we want in a diplomat is to force him into a mold—to teach him to fit a pattern of thought. He, unlike the military, has to deal with a minimum of tangible factors. He has to deal largely with imponderables and there is no rigid form of precise training that will suffice. Students can, of course, be given any amount of useful information—without which they would be handicapped in diplomatic work. But the essence of diplomacy cannot be taught. You cannot give classroom lessons in resourcefulness, tact, and the knack of getting one's own way. Your diplomat needs these qualities. They cannot be created in a school, but where they are latent they can be encouraged.

Diplomacy is not a thing that can be fully mastered by any system of training, and proficiency can be secured only after long experience. In a lesser degree this is true of the more exact science of law and medicine. A graduate of law school passes his bar examination and is authorized to hang out his shingle. Theoretically he is just as much a lawyer as any legal light in the country. But the big cases will come to him only after he has built up a fund of experience and a reputation for judgment. In the same way a young man may have passed his medical examinations and have about as much book learning as he can get and be certified as a competent physician. In fact, in the eyes of the law he is a competent physician. Nevertheless, we should hesitate to put him in charge of a serious medical case because we think he needs years of experience and practice in dealing with everyday cases before he can be expected to develop the qualities of judgment and resourcefulness which we consider essential.

It is exactly the same with diplomacy. A man coming from private life and taking charge of a great embassy has not the training which by law we prescribe as a preliminary for secretaries and consuls. He also lacks the constant application day by day of his own powers of discrimination and judgment to problems which he increasingly understands on the basis of his training and experience. We require that a young secretary coming into the service have a working knowledge of international law, diplomatic usage, languages, and a number of other subjects. We do not contend that this equipment makes him a trained diplomat—it doesn't—it only gives him some of the elementary knowledge which is necessary before he can be entrusted with the ordinary, everyday tasks of a legation. He becomes a trained diplomat only after he has worked for years with this equipment and has developed his powers of judgment, discrimination, resourcefulness, energy, and tact.

Having contested the desirability of a government school for diplomats it should be added that a number of our universities have excellent schools of political science which provide grounding in a wide range of subjects.

During the past twenty years there has been a great advance in the teaching of political science for men planning to enter the public service. Among a number we may cite the Fletcher School of Law and Diplomacy, administered by Tufts College with the co-operation of Harvard University; the Georgetown University School of Foreign Service; and the Graduate School of Princeton

University. Some idea of what the young diplomat ought to know may be gathered from the fact that among the subjects taught in such schools are International Law, International Organization and Government, Maritime Law, Consular and Diplomatic Law and Practice, International Commercial Law, Problems and Conflicts in the Law Merchant, Diplomatic and Consular Practice, Law of the Air, Public Administration. Then in the field of diplomacy and international politics we find such subjects as Political Theory, the Foreign Relations of the United States, the History of European Diplomacy Since 1815, Contemporary Thought on International Politics, Public Opinion and Diplomacy, Latin-American Problems and Inter-American Relations, Diplomatic Issues in the Far East, Problems of Central and Eastern Europe, Diplomatic Relations of the British Commonwealth of Nations, Japanese Institutions, Diplomatic History of Europe Since 1918, the Evolution of Diplomacy, Military Power in International Relations, the Conflict of Policies in the Far East, European Imperialism in Africa, the Nature and Problems of War, Military Science, Public Administration, Municipal Government, Pressure Groups and Propaganda, Geography and Geopolitics, Democracy and World Revolution, Revolutionary Technique.

Another field is that of economics and finance, and we find such courses as International Economic Relations: Theory and Policy, International Finance, International Financial Co-operation, Methods of Analysis in International Economic Relations, Money and Banking, International Finance and Exchange.

This does not cover such fundamental subjects as history, English and modern languages—the importance of which for the diplomat cannot be exaggerated.

Even this list of subjects is rather overwhelming, but to get a more adequate idea of the range of training considered essential for a young diplomat nowadays it is suggested that the reader turn to Appendix, 246, which gives as an illustration the courses offered by the Fletcher School, with a brief indication of the nature of each course. However impressive this list may be, it should be repeated that even the best courses can provide no more than preliminary training. Real training begins only when the student is put to work in a government office, whether it be the Department of State or an embassy, legation, or consulate. It is here that he comes in touch for the first time with living people and live issues. Among the intelligent students there is a feeling that the courses given in our universities are not sufficient in themselves, and I have had many inquiries as to what other subjects should be studied. It is difficult to be specific in answer to such queries. Almost any form of interest and study is of value to the diplomat. Among the most precious gifts for a diplomat are an insatiable curiosity and an interest in people.

Jules Jusserand was a great Ambassador largely because all his life long he was driven by a consuming desire to learn what was going on and why. His interests went far beyond his official dealings with the American Government. He had to know what the American people were doing, how they worked and how they played, what they liked and disliked, and what were their processes of thought. The result was that he developed an almost uncanny power of foreseeing how they could be expected to react in any given circumstances. His dispatches to his own government, based on deep understanding, were of far greater value than if he had confined his interests to purely official matters; they bear reading today in the light of subsequent developments. Jusserand, of course, was an exceptionally able man, but his value to his government can be attributed in large measure to a broad general education, a liking for people, and a burning curiosity which would not be denied.

James Bryce was another Ambassador who will long be remembered in this country. His fame and his usefulness to his own country were both due in large measure to this same sort of curiosity. He was not content to take things as they were. He wanted to understand the real nature of our republic, what lay behind the adoption of our constitutional forms, the development of local government, and the role of the citizen. In satisfying his own curiosity he became a foremost authority on American government.

Walter Hines Page was another example of the value of a genuine liking for people and a desire to learn. He had a talent for eliciting information and understanding from the most unpromising people. His interest in a wide range of subjects gave him access to information and influence beyond the reach of his less gifted colleagues.

Then there is the matter of languages. It is difficult to exaggerate the importance of a thorough knowledge of languages for a diplomat. It is perhaps easier to realize how much this means if we imagine a diplomatic official arriving in Washington speaking no English and only some language like Russian or Persian, which practically no Americans speak. He would be just about as useful as if he were deaf, dumb, and blind, for he would be unable to communicate directly with our people, to state the wishes of his own government, to read our newspapers, or form acquaintances. He might almost as well stay at home. One of our diplomats abroad increases in value to the government with every fresh language he learns.

In the matter of languages a little knowledge is a particularly dangerous thing. Sometimes an amateur diplomat acquires a smattering of a foreign language and sets out to make use of it. When this happens it is time to take cover, for although many of his mistakes are merely amusing, some of them lead to trouble and misunderstandings not easily dispelled. A venerable congressman who headed one of our delegations at Geneva, reveling in an extremely slender and inaccurate command of French, devoted much effort to thinking up phrases for conversational purposes, and as he had complete confidence in his own knowledge he would tolerate no suggestions or restraint. By dint of literal translation into French he evolved a form of kindly greeting and inquiry which he addressed benevolently to the ladies he met which threw the whole of Geneva into turmoil. As worded, it constituted an inquiry into most intimate matters, and in some quarters he had a greater measure of success than he knew. But it got serious when he persisted in carrying on official conversations from which he excluded members of his own delegation and after which he angrily denied the promises the other party claimed he had made.

Fortunately few of our amateur diplomats persist in negotiating alone after burning their fingers once or twice. They usually content themselves with tossing a few foreign words into their conversation now and then to show how cosmopolitan they have become. Sometimes this sort of thing finds its way into official dispatches, as when Governor Francis, Ambassador to Russia at the outbreak of the revolution in 1917, reported that he had been stopped in the street by Red Guards and allowed to proceed when he said:

"I am the American Ambassador," the *first two words* being spoken in the Russian language.

This does not mean that languages alone are a qualification for a diplomat. The mere fact that a man can speak languages does not prove that he is of value. It is only when these qualifications are added to the equipment needed by a diplomat that they become of first-rate importance.

No one is so quick to realize the value of languages as an Ambassador or a Minister appointed from private life who himself speaks nothing but English. He is entirely dependent upon the staff of his mission to keep him informed, to make his communications for him, interpret all his conversations, and carry on pretty well every step of his official life. If the Department of State sends him a secretary who does not speak the language of the country or a language which is of real value there, he is indignant—and rightly so. A thorough working knowledge of several languages is an absolute essential for a secretary, and should be considered practically an essential for an Ambassador or Minister. Our country is practically the only one which sends out ambassadors who do not speak any language but their own, and we pay for it dearly.

We periodically have an agitation in this country for the establishment of a federal department of peace with a cabinet member at its head, the idea being that we could thus work effectively for peace. The White House is sometimes inundated with resolutions and petitions in this sense.

This overlooks the fact that we already have a department of peace. What else is the Department of State? Its fundamental purpose is to conduct our relations with other countries in such a way as to keep the peace. No other department could take over that function because, in order to work effectively for peace, it would require the machinery of the Department of State, the constant flow of information that comes in from our representatives in the field, and contact with the representatives of other governments. But it is difficult to see in what way a department could be created for that particular purpose.

It may well be that the Department of State is not used to the best possible advantage. But if the people who advocate a department of peace seek ample scope for their energies, they can profitably exert themselves to see that the Department of State is adequately equipped with funds and personnel and they can support its efforts to keep the peace.

We have got along without trained men in diplomacy for so long that we have come to accept it as normal. But our present system has only to be translated into terms of everyday life to appear fantastic.

Why not make the daring experiment of trying diplomats in diplomacy? They are not supermen, it is true, but they are of far better caliber than we have any right to expect. If they were given a chance, it is probable that they would at least avoid a good many of the errors of the politician because they know the mechanics of negotiation as the politician rarely does; they know, from long experience, numberless expedients for working toward agreement; how to adjust proposals so as to make them acceptable, without sacrificing important objectives. On the negative side they have learned from experience many things not to do. The politician usually tries them all and sometimes does not give them up until after repeated barking of the shins. They work quietly, without self-advertisement, thereby increasing the prospects of success.

Finally, there is a great deal of talk about the failure of diplomacy. As a matter of fact, diplomacy has not failed. It hasn't even been given a chance to fail. What we have come to call diplomacy in the course of the past twenty years has failed to achieve results and has led us into all sorts of disasters. But it wasn't really diplomacy. It was the usurpation of diplomatic functions by politicians and inept amateurs; it was the new method of having the negotiation of infinitely complicated world problems handled by politicians, amateurs, and adventurers; the forcing on the world in critical times of new and untried methods; publicity stunts and hurried personal discussions between the political leaders, who should stay at home and be the heavy artillery in reserve rather than trying to direct operations on hurried visits to the front-line trenches. The result has been a contribution to a worldwide mess of unprecedented proportions.

CHAPTER V

The Sanctity of Treaties

LEGALISM is the negation of diplomacy, yet in many ways the conduct of our foreign affairs is hampered by legalistic outlook and by legalistic handling.

It is symptomatic that our Department of State has a larger proportion of lawyers than any other foreign office in the world, and their activity extends far beyond strictly legal matters.

I recall hearing a British colleague complaining some years ago of the difficulty of negotiation with the Foreign Office lawyers constantly interfering. He went on to say that the Foreign Office was lawyer-ridden, and to drive home his point he added that there were four legal officers stifling the work of the diplomats. Consultation of the State Department Register revealed that, excluding the Secretary and Undersecretary, both of them eminent lawyers, there were thirty-two of the profession in the Department of State at that time—eight times as many as in the Foreign Office.

More often than not the Secretary of State is himself a lawyer and instinctively seeks to direct our affairs as he would run a law office.

Yet the Department of State is the last place to apply such methods—it is the only branch of our government that is not and should not be governed by a book of rules. The others all have laws, rules, and regulations to govern practically any situation that may arise. In the State Department this is true only in regard to certain routine matters. In the many questions that come before the State Department there are seldom any two that are exactly alike, or that can be settled by thumbing a book of regulations. They call, instead, for adjustment, conciliation, and agreement with those who have conflicting interests.

We often hear it said that all international differences should be settled by law. It is not altogether that simple. What law? In many cases the international difference arises precisely because of differences between our law and that of the other party. So far as law exists there is deadlock. It is here that diplomacy steps in to seek a solution. This solution must be sought through mutual adjustment and accommodation, leading to a form of justice and satisfaction which cannot be found through the conflicting systems of law.

In spite of the fact that diplomacy usually steps in only when it is accepted that law, by itself, does not afford a solution, the lawyer often tends to cling to legal methods which are not applicable, to see controversies in terms of black and white, right or wrong, and is instinctively impatient with the diplomat who tries to find a middle way.

When you have in Washington a lawyer Secretary of State, intent on winning a case for his client, Uncle Sam, and out in the field, disguised as diplomats, businessmen who understand little of either law or diplomacy but are intent on putting over a deal for their firm, the U.S.A., Inc., there are sometimes fearful and wonderful developments. But the results can hardly be called diplomacy.

At the end of the last war the lawyers took over and diplomats went through heavy weather. There was a general assumption —gleefully adopted in America—that they had brought on the world war, either to justify their existence or, more charitably, through sheer incompetence. The poor diplomats had not been given a fair try and the failure was not theirs, but none the less they have remained low in public esteem for many years. There is some prospect that they will continue in disrepute as a result of the antics of some of our wild men who are not diplomats at all, for the public does not always distinguish between professional diplomats and amateurs. The fact remains that we have reached a stage where the public assumes that all professional diplomats are incompetent. Not only that, they are also habitually wrong. We have gone to such extremes that it is sometimes enough to say the diplomats favor this or oppose that for people to assume that the opposite course must be right.

In deference to those who disapprove having diplomacy handled by trained diplomats we may point out that there are certain safeguards against excessive expert influence. Under our system the final decision will always be in the hands of non-diplomats. The President is an amateur in the sense that he cannot be accused of having been brought up in the diplomatic service. The Secretary of State is an amateur in the same sense. This is as it should be, but it therefore becomes all the more vital that they should be supported and advised by men of specialized knowledge and experience. We have seldom had enough of this.

In the meetings at Casablanca and Quebec, Cairo and Teheran, for instance, great events were discussed and important decisions reached. On each occasion Mr. Churchill was accompanied by highly trained members of the Foreign Office. We may be sure they scrutinized all texts and that nothing was adopted until they had gone over it and made sure of its meaning. At none of these meetings did we have anybody with the same training, to make sure the documents expressed exactly what we had agreed to. If the day comes when there is a disagreement as to what was settled we shall have nobody but ourselves to blame.

During the Teheran conference, for instance, the press reported that each of the leaders was supported by his diplomatic advisers and gave their names—perhaps with tongue in cheek. Mr. Churchill was accompanied by Mr. Anthony Eden, the Secretary of State for Foreign Affairs, Sir Alexander Cadogan, Permanent Undersecretary of State, and others of long diplomatic training. Mr. Roosevelt was supported by Mr. Winant, Mr. Harriman, and Mr. Harry Hopkins. With all due deference to the last three gentlemen they can hardly be considered experts in the drafting of diplomatic documents—they certainly would make no such claim for themselves. Where we need some legal scrutiny it is conspicuous by its absence.

On the other hand, when Mr. Hull went to Moscow, he was accompanied by a number of trained men who could read a document with an eye to making sure it meant what we had agreed. This method is less likely to lead to unpleasant surprises.

These days we are given to vague and general declarations as to common purposes in war and peace. So far as these are no more than noble aspirations, we should be prudent enough to label them as such. However cautiously phrased, such declarations are more likely than not to be interpreted as undertakings with the resultant obligation to see them through by force, if necessary. Before issuing such declarations we should do well to scrutinize them with a view to determining how far they may commit us.

In the Atlantic Charter, signed on August 14, 1941, we said something about restoring the sovereignty and independence of those forcibly deprived of these assets. However this statement was worded, it created the impression at home and abroad that we had undertaken to remedy this sort of injustice—in fact, the declaration was obviously made to create just that impression—otherwise, why was it issued?

And there was no reservation to the effect that the promise applied only to aggression from a single quarter. The American position on this question had been admirably summarized by Mr. Sumner Welles, Acting Secretary of State, in a statement to the press on July 23, 1940, in the following terms:

During these past few days the devious processes whereunder the political independence and territorial integrity of the three small Baltic republics—Estonia, Latvia, and Lithuania—were to be deliberately annihilated by one of their more powerful neighbors, have been rapidly drawing to their conclusion. From the day when the peoples of these republics first gained their independent and democratic form of government the people of the United States have watched their admirable progress in self-government with deep and sympathetic interest. The policy of this government is universally known. The people of the United States are opposed to predatory activities no matter whether they are carried on by the use of force or by the threat of force. They are likewise opposed to any form of intervention on the part of one state, however powerful, in the domestic concerns of any other sovereign state, however weak. These principles constitute the very foundations upon which the existing relationship between the twenty-one sovereign republics of the New World rests. The United States will continue to stand by these principles, because of the conviction of the American people that unless the doctrine in which these principles are inherent once again governs the relations between nations, the rule of reason, of justice, and of law—in other words, the bases of modern civilization itself—cannot be preserved.

In time some misgivings arose as to Russia's intentions toward some of her western neighbors—misgivings created, it should be observed, from Russian statements. However, in the Moscow Declaration, signed on October 30, 1943, we were assured of recognition of "the principle of the sovereign equality of all peace-loving States." We were also assured that the signatory powers "will consult with one another and as occasion requires with other members of the United Nations with a view to joint action on behalf of the community of nations." This sounds like a clear undertaking that there shall be no unilateral action in matters of concern to the signatories and their associates. It sounds like an assurance that the ground for our misgivings had been removed.

Further assurances were expressed in the Teheran Declaration, signed on December 1, 1943. "We express our determination that our nations shall work together in the war and in the peace that will follow. . . . We recognize fully the supreme responsibility resting upon us and all the nations to make a peace which will command good will from the overwhelming masses of the peoples of the world and banish the scourge and terror of war for many generations. . . ."

If this means anything it is a promise of co-operation and abstention from unilateral action. It is also a restatement in other terms of the third provision of the Atlantic Charter:

They respect the right of all peoples to choose the form of government under which they will live; and they wish to see sovereign rights and self-government restored to those who have been forcibly deprived of them.

And also:

After the final destruction of the Nazi tyranny, they hope to see established a peace which will afford to all nations the means of dwelling in safety within their own boundaries, and which will afford assurance that all the men in all the lands may live out their lives in freedom from fear and want.

Here we have a number of unqualified statements providing collaboration among the signatories in all matters. Taken together they give the Baltic States and Poland our promise that they can "live out their lives in freedom from fear and want." At least that is what the texts say.

The Teheran Declaration says: "With our diplomatic advisers

we have surveyed the problems of the future." The future covers quite a long time, and only a few months of it have now elapsed, but enough has happened even in this brief period to justify us in checking the texts against events with a view to determining how far these documents represent a guarantee for "the future."

On December 12, 1943, before the ink on the Teheran Declaration could have been very dry, Russia and the Czechoslovak Government-in-Exile signed a twenty-year "Treaty of Mutual Assistance and Postwar Collaboration." Just where does an agreement of this sort fit into the Teheran conception of a "world family of democratic nations"? If the texts of our various declarations mean anything, they mean we are committed to a system of general security and to abandonment of special alliances of this character.

On January 4, 1944, Russian troops swept into Poland. The Polish Government-in-Exile, which we recognize, requested that the Soviet Government issue some declaration that their armies came as liberators and not as conquerors. This request was ignored, but the Soviet Government had already made clear its intention of annexing a great part of Poland.

Just how is this attitude to be reconciled with the assurances in the various declarations we have quoted? And if they cannot be reconciled, which one is abolished, the generous texts or the Russian actions?

On January 2, 1944, Mr. Wendell Willkie, in his enthusiasm for Russia and Stalin, published in the New York *Times* an article entitled "Don't Stir Distrust of Russia." In the course of this friendly plea for understanding of Russia and her difficulties, Mr. Willkie did remark almost apologetically that "the political integrity" of the states bordering Russia on the west was "one of the most pressing questions" in the minds of Americans—after all, no more than a statement of fact. But as if bent on reviving earlier misgivings, *Pravda* sent Mr. Willkie about his business with the statement that Russia would settle all these questions for herself and with no need of help from Mr. Willkie.

Again this raises a question as to whether the official organ of the Communist party had read what the Teheran Declaration had to say about "our determination" to "work together in the war and in the peace that is to follow."

On January 14 the Polish Government-in-Exile suggested that the United States and Great Britain proffer their good offices to bring about a discussion of all outstanding questions with Russia. Mr. Hull, acting in the spirit of the Teheran Declaration, tendered the good offices of the United States in the hope of promoting agreement. The Soviet Government lost little time in rejecting this friendly offer. It is a reasonable assumption that the rejection was not worded in terms calculated to improve the situation, for the text has not yet been published.

Just how is this attitude to be reconciled with the undertakings of the series of declarations, ending with that signed at Teheran, with its cheerful conclusion:

"We leave here friends in fact, in spirit, and in purpose."

On January 17 *Pravda* came along with the now-famous dispatch about British conversations looking to a separate peace with Germany—a back-page item containing a mere wisp of gossipy rumor—no more. That was one in the eye for Mr. Churchill. But is it friendship "in fact, in spirit, and in purpose"?

Rather reminiscent of the lines:

> It is all very well to dissemble your love,
> But why did you kick me downstairs?

On February 1, lest others feel neglected, *Izvestia*, official government organ, came out with an article attacking Pope Pius XII as pro-Fascist, and including in the denunciation all who acknowledged his spiritual leadership. What was the purpose of this unless to build up a case for dealing with Catholic priests in occupied Poland?

"Friends in fact, in *spirit*, and in purpose!"

And finally on this same day, February 1, the Supreme Soviet reorganized the country into sixteen Soviet republics. To make sure there was no nonsense about previous assurances that everything would be done by consultation and collaboration, it was pointed out that three of these republics were to be Lithuania, Latvia, and Estonia. The fact that these three countries are recognized by the United States as independent nations did not delay matters. It was also pointed out that Moldavia and Karelia are being taken in, and there would be little difficulty in expanding them into a Soviet Romania and a Soviet Finland. The formula seems excellent for the gradual absorption of other lands—China, Iran, Poland, the Balkans, and other parts of Europe.

In spite of these spirited developments in two brief months, many of our papers and writers continue to explain everything that has happened as the smooth and loyal application of the principles of the various declarations. It is maintained by many people who ought to know better that the splitting up of Russia into sixteen republics is the best possible proof she could give that she has no thought of aggression. That is not wishful but willful thinking, for it blandly overlooks the fact that in proving her benevolent, non-aggressive attitude, Russia has also gobbled up three independent republics recognized by us.

All this shows it is high time we came to an understanding on what we have agreed to and also being sure we agree to nothing we are not prepared to see through.

The only possible conclusion is that our resounding international declarations mean precisely nothing. The last declarations say we are in agreement with Russia on all "basic principles" governing the peace.

If the sovereignty and integrity of an allied power are not covered by a "basic principle" it would be interesting to know what a basic principle is. Perhaps it would be better if we had more conviction about principles and less loose talk about them.

It may well be said that when the Atlantic Charter was drafted it was not foreseen how far the statement about restored independence and sovereignty would lead us. Then it should not have been issued. Foresight was the task of diplomacy—the diplomacy where the writers of the Charter were so obviously at sea. It is the job of diplomats to see the implications of any statement. And here the implications led far afield. It did not require a fortune-teller to foresee the possibility that Russia might eventually be in the war on our side. That contingency was freely discussed at the time of the Hitler-Stalin pact, and again at the time Russia was invaded. If Russia came in there was always the possibility she would want some territorial compensation—for we had no justification for believing that in this respect Russia, under Stalin, would be radically different from Russia under the czars. And, to carry our thinking a step beyond the present—a primary duty of diplomacy—we should have considered how far these ideas of territorial compensation would be confined to Europe—how far they might extend to Asia and give rise to conflicts with our other ally, China, or to Iran and even Arabia with complications for our plans for oil.

Considering this should not have been an end in itself. It was merely a prelude to reaching conclusions as to what we were prepared to do about it all, and after that what we could say with a reasonable measure of prudence. If, in the light of full information and an understanding of our own interests, we felt in a position to go on record that we would restore the sovereignty of those nations that had been forcibly deprived of them, well and good. But if, on the other hand, we did not see our way to enforce our views as to what was right, it was elementary diplomacy to refrain from reckless declarations.

We are now in a fine mess.

If we had had a policy we should have had a clear picture of where our interests lay, what our resources were, what we could hope to accomplish, and what we must forego. We should not have loosed off broadsides of beautiful generalizations without the foggiest idea of the commitments involved.

We should also be on our guard against domestic documents that raise high hopes not justified by the measure of agreement behind them. We have had a series of texts introduced in Congress, not so much to register agreement on postwar settlements as to create an illusion of agreement where none exists. In order to achieve this language was skillfully devised to be acceptable or at least unobjectionable to people of widely divergent convictions. The Fulbright Resolution, to single out an example, was widely hailed as a triumph of agreement, putting an end to the dangers of isolationism and guaranteeing our membership in a world organization because it committed Congress to some form of "appropriate international machinery." We are told that the resolution has obviated the danger of our "standing aside" after the war. The resolution has done nothing of the sort. It merely revealed that there was nobody on the premises at the time it was passed who wanted to build a Chinese wall around the United States and avoid all dealings with the rest of the world. It left intact all existing differences as to the form of international machinery we should adopt. In the course of the discussion, Representative Karl Mundt of South Dakota declared pointedly: "I have heard 'appropriate international machinery' defined by individuals varying all the way from a superstate of some kind to a league of nations, to Union Now, clear over to the other extreme of a world tribunal or a Hague court or just a series of treaties."

We should do far better to face our differences of opinion honestly than to blind ourselves to them through adopting forms of words that create an illusion of agreement but bind nobody to anything.

These illustrations suffice to indicate one form of legalism from which we suffer as a nation. We should be on our guard against the legalist's almost superstitious belief in the value of signed documents. That is legalism at its worst; but this faith is widespread nowadays despite many disillusionments. Each time a new treaty or pact or charter is signed—particularly if it is done with pomp and circumstance—it is hailed as the advent of a new and better era. The text is analyzed and interpreted and explained as if there were some potent magic in each word. However often we are disappointed, we are always ready to welcome the next document with enthusiasm.

We shall avoid much trouble in the future if we realize that the contents of a treaty are far less important than the spirit and interests of the signatories. The agreement is good only so far as the signatories are ready to live up to their bargain and feel that there is advantage in doing so.

Our thought on this whole subject has been considerably obscured in the course of the last generation. We have had it simplified for us by the contention that treaties are nothing more than international contracts, and therefore, like contracts, sacred. Obviously, if they are sacred there must be some magic quality about them.

We should do well to scrutinize this idea that all treaties are like contracts and therefore equally sacred and binding. There are many analogies between treaties and private contracts, but the way of stating the question is misleading. To begin at the end, it is not accurate to say that all contracts are sacred or even binding in the eyes of the law. It is true that they are, as a rule, binding in law and must be observed under certain clearly prescribed penalties. But the law does not go so far as to say, as we might infer from much of the current discussion, that any contract signed under any circumstances is binding.

Contracts are voidable if they are obtained by force or fraud, or on the assumption of a condition which no longer exists. Clearly unfair and usurious contracts are voidable. The law goes even further and in many cases holds as invalid contracts of indefinite or even unduly long duration, and there are other grounds upon which contracts may not be enforced. Under the law, contracts entered into willingly by both sides on a basis responsive to existing conditions are legally enforcible. There would seem to be no reason on the ground of analogy to consider treaties binding under conditions that do not apply to contracts.

It would clarify thinking if we would adopt the guiding principle that treaties negotiated by both parties and signed voluntarily are to have the full force of contracts and may not be changed by unilateral action. We must be able to count on this if we are to return to the reign of law. We should also recognize the fact that treaties signed under duress are binding so long as the duress can be maintained, and no longer. In such cases we must recognize that the conflict is only momentarily stopped by forced signature, and we must not be surprised if it breaks out again.

There is one whole category of treaties that can be discarded at the start—treaties imposed on defeated nations by those strong enough to dictate their terms. The treaty is not entered into freely and willingly. In private life any contract signed under duress is readily voidable in the courts. A nation under similar duress has no resort to a tribunal, and its only recourse is avoidance of contract or resort to war. A nation coerced into signing what it considers an unjust peace will see nothing wrong in freeing itself by any means. And we must bear in mind that any people can readily convince itself of the injustice of a treaty signed under duress.

Then there are treaties that become onerous to one of the parties. In private life recourse can be had to the courts. In international life the sufferer can often get relief only by taking the law into his own hands. Here the analogies of legalistic diplomacy break down.

Any attempts to free a nation from such treaties are met with protests about the "sanctity of treaties." Treaties are sacred to the same extent that private contracts are sacred—if entered into freely and willingly, and to mutual advantage, and so long as they continue to apply in this way. Otherwise the question becomes one rather of the sanctity of the *status quo*.

There has been a great deal of talk in the last twenty years about the sanctity of treaties. It has become a slogan, and with it has come much moralizing and high feeling. Much of this talk has come from people who are concerned, as we all are, at the collapse of the regime of law in international dealings. But the disregard of treaties is no more than an incident in the behavior of those governments which have thrown overboard all the restraints that have grown up in the conduct of international affairs.

Before we begin to generalize we should look into the contents of the treaties that have been broken. We will obviously find many that were binding both legally and morally, but, in other cases, we must recognize that their very character made their violation inevitable. In fact, it was certain onerous, if not unfair, treaty provisions which served men such as Hitler as stepping-stones to power. It was violation of these treaty provisions which gained them enthusiastic support at home and opened the way for them to disregard all law, national and international.

We would do well also to scrutinize this entire subject and to bear in mind where most of this agitation about the sanctity of treaties has come from. It arose in the period between World War I and World War II to counteract agitation in favor of treaty revision. While the Covenant of the League recognized the principle of treaty revision by agreement, the victorious powers had a perhaps-understandable distaste for reopening subjects they considered settled. To their minds, the most effective way was to oppose the whole idea; to prevent the subject being opened, even in regard to unimportant matters; to oppose revision on high moral grounds of principle. This was found by proclaiming the sanctity of treaties and urging that any attempts at revision would merely open the door to destruction of the whole treaty structure. This line of argument was successful in confusing public thought on the subject. The campaign was successful in preventing any examination of real grievances and of treaty provisions that should have been revised, but in the long run it was disastrously unsuccessful. The people of the defeated powers were left to the conclusion that they had no hope of securing redress by agreement and that their only hope lay in unilateral action or, to put it more bluntly, through treaty violations.

When this war ends we shall impose treaties on the vanquished powers. If we want these treaties to remain in vigor, we must show discrimination as to what we put into them. We should scrutinize all the provisions we consider desirable and satisfy ourselves as to our ability to enforce compliance. Anything we embody in the treaties without assurance of enforcement will shorten their life. Much better forego something we should like than adopt it and then find it cannot be enforced. There will be many temptations of this sort, but we should never lose sight of the fact that a defeated nation will lose no time in freeing itself from any provisions it considers unfair or onerous. A recurrent error is that treaties are dafted on the assumption that the victor will always be able to enforce them. The real test for a treaty is not how much can be put into it, but how effectively and how long it can be enforced.

This indicates a problem that has been sadly neglected—the need for some method of peaceful change for treaty provisions when common sense shows the need for modification. Under existing circumstances there are no such facilities, and history reveals a large number of cases where treaties were ended by violence because there was no accepted method for adjusting them to changed conditions. Here there is need for modernization of diplomacy and a real opportunity for an international organization.

CHAPTER VI

Secret and Open Diplomacy

AT THE END of the last war, we were told that one of the safe-guards of the new order was to be open diplomacy. Secret diplomacy was to be done away with, and international affairs were to be regulated by open covenants openly arrived at.

Probably no group of phrases has led to more muddled thinking on fundamental methods.

People are not always clear in their own minds as to what secret diplomacy is, but it sounds reprehensible and they are against it.

The general assumption has grown up that the negotiations of diplomacy on international affairs ought to be conducted in the glare of pitiless publicity. There are, of course, certain reticences which are permissible for the priest, the lawyer, the doctor, or the father of a family, but governments and their negotiators should, it is held, operate under an entirely different regime.

If the Secretary of State is not forthcoming with public statements as to what he is discussing with this government or what he has said to that Ambassador, or what he has heard from one of our missions abroad, you instantly hear the cry of secret diplomacy. Secret diplomacy is one of those hobgoblins that hover around the idea of democratic control of diplomacy.

As a matter of fact, there is such a thing as secret diplomacy, and it is reprehensible. This might be defined as intergovernmental intrigue for wrongful ends, resulting in obligations for future action of which the people are kept in ignorance until they are called on to pay with their lives and fortunes. There are also secret negotiations between governments to infringe the rights of another.

There is no doubt that every effort should be made to do away with this sort of thing. But we should bear in mind that this brand of diplomacy has the same relation to the real article that smash-and-grab raids have to legitimate business. We must remember that there is a broad margin between hole-and-corner intrigue and diplomatic negotiations in the glare of the floodlights. Perhaps we shall find the best results are to be had by avoiding both extremes.

If the people know the aims of their government and are kept apprised of undertakings and commitments before effective approval is given there is nothing reprehensible in carrying on the day-to-day negotiations in private—in fact, that is the only way negotiations can be carried on, not only governmental negotiations, but private business negotiations or family discussions. The less publicity there is to negotiation the greater the chance of success, but very often the advocates of open diplomacy or democratic control want to sit at the elbow of our negotiator telling him what to say, what not to say, and usually pushing him on to do stunts which have the beauty of being dramatic but don't get him any "forrader." This is nothing more or less than back-seat driving, and is just about as valuable. The sound course is to choose your negotiators for their ability, tell them what they are to seek to obtain, and let them use their own discretion as to their procedure.

Perhaps the greatest proponent of open diplomacy and democratic control was President Wilson, but when he came to grips with the grim realities of international negotiation he forgot all about "pitiless publicity" and "open covenants openly arrived at," and resorted, not only to secrecy in negotiation, but in many cases to secrecy as to his objectives as well. Nobody could say that the Treaty of Versailles was openly arrived at, indeed few professional diplomats have proceeded by means that were so secret. Perhaps if we had had greater public knowledge of policy we should have had a better treaty.

Which brings us back to the point that we are wasting a great deal of energy talking about democratic control of American foreign policy. We can all advocate it subject to one condition, and that is that we have a foreign policy. Once we have formulated a plan and know what we seek to achieve, democratic control will have its chance, but while awaiting that time we should

do well to spread understanding of the important difference between policy and negotiation. If the people take an interest in
policy, they will insist on being informed as to the whys and
wherefors, with the wholesome result that the government will
be obliged to explain its policies and justify them.

Most people believe in the democratic control of foreign policy,
but very few of them have a clear idea of what it is. Most discussion on this subject ignores the fact that the Founding Fathers
sought to establish democratic control of foreign policy by allot-
ting to the people's elected representatives in Congress an important share in the control of foreign affairs. Many of those now
deploring the lack of democratic control propose that the remedy
should be found by depriving Congress of its present powers,
although it is not at all clear just what form of democratic control they propose to substitute for the people's elected representatives.

Then there are those who, while believing that delegation of
power to elected representatives is unsatisfactory, also believe
that decisions must be taken by the whole mass of the population. For instance, in an emergency we should hold a referendum
and count noses on the question of a declaration of war—this on
the ground that the mass of the people will be more sober and
self-controlled than Congress. How far is this belief justified by
history?

This may have a satisfying sound, but we should not think of
applying it even on a far smaller scale. A factory could hardly be
run successfully by publishing all the details of its prices, contracts, and opportunities, so that its operations could be directed
by mass meetings of the stockholders and workmen. Anybody
who suggested such a course would be denounced as a crackpot.
How, we would be asked, could a firm publish its confidential
information for the benefit of its competitors? How could anybody be simple enough to believe that a business enterprise could
be conducted by having hundreds, and perhaps thousands, of
stockholders leaning over the shoulders of the general manager
and the shop steward and directing them at every step?

Of course it sounds grotesque as applied to a factory, but it
would be far more grotesque and dangerous if applied to the conduct of our foreign affairs. In practice this would not result in

democratic control but in control by organized groups with all their attachments, antipathies, and yearnings to serve this country or to have revenge on that.

Open diplomacy comes pretty close to being a contradiction in terms.

This idea was first broached at the time, during and after the last war, when the political leaders in all countries took over the actual handling of international negotiations. Naturally, they brought their own methods to the new task. They have been at it for nearly a generation, and we have had a fairly good opportunity to see how far they have improved on the old methods.

Secret diplomacy, if we use the words in their real meaning, is nothing more than the established method of unpublicized negotiation. This method was evolved through centuries of human experience. It is predicated on systematic exploration of a subject in private by trained negotiators. Such exploration involves the exercise of resourcefulness, patience, and good will in order to arrive, perhaps after many failures, at a meeting of minds where conflicting interests are reconciled, at least in principle, under a form of agreement involving the common denominator of understanding.

The problems of diplomacy are often difficult and intricate. If they were not, they would tend to settle themselves and would not call for study by governmental representatives. It is the daily lot of the diplomat to tackle one of these problems and seek, through long and patient negotiation, to reach solutions. It is rare that he succeeds the first time of trying. More often than not he finds that the plan first envisaged cannot be accepted by the other side for reasons which emerge from the discussions. There is no clash about this, and both sides set to work to re-examine the problem in the light of what they have learned. It is the method of trial and error, and the chances are that if all concerned continue the discussions with a desire to meet each other's reasonable difficulties they will one day find an acceptable solution. It is neither showy nor speedy, yet it has a way of succeeding more often than not.

In striking contrast to this we have the method of public conferences as all too generally practiced. Here the negotiators meet in the presence of the public and numerous representatives of the press, to say nothing of microphones and newsreel cameras. At the start, each side states its case. It would not be politic at this stage to divulge how little you could be content with. You are obliged to state your maximum requirements, in order to allow a reasonable margin for future bargaining. But, unfortunately, the other man is obliged to state his case in the same way, and thus at the outset you are entrenched upon your positions—and extreme positions at that. There is an inevitable deadlock. You are obliged to call in the press representatives and make sure that they understand that you are right and the other side wrong. You must make a speech to strengthen your position at home, and incidentally make it harder to reach agreement. The representatives of your national press, being patriotic, rally round to support you. Their dispatches tend to show how sound and reasonable you are in your demands and how exorbitant are the demands of the other side. Editorial comment makes conciliation still more difficult. The press of the other party adopts a similar attitude from their own angle, and you soon find that you have to deal not only with your opposite number in the negotiation but also with a public opinion at home that has been aroused by your speeches and by the well-intentioned efforts of the press. It is often far easier to negotiate with the representative of the other nation than it is to convince the public opinion of your own country of the necessity for making some contribution to agreement. Indeed, the pressure upon any negotiator in a public duel of this sort is almost overwhelming to stand pat and fight vociferously for his original platform. Thus he becomes a hero in his own country, whereas if he makes any concession, however reasonable he may consider it and however he may have anticipated it in his own mind, he suddenly finds himself charged by the press with being spineless or having been bamboozled by the other side.

Almost anyone who has followed international conferences since the last war has seen for himself that they have almost uniformly failed to live up to our hopes and expectations. A careful study of them reveals that their failure is largely due to the fact that Pitiless Publicity and the consequent frozen position have made successful negotiations impossible.

Another thing that emerges from a careful study of international conferences is that their success is usually in direct proportion to the amount of confidential and expert spadework which has been done in advance, and to the measure of agreement that was already reached before they were convened. The most successful of all were those convened merely to adjust and ratify agreement in principle already reached.

This does not mean that we should leap to the conclusion that the conference method should be scrapped. That would be jumping from one extreme to the other. But it seems important to draw some lessons from our experience, correct our mistakes, and see if we cannot improve our existing technique.

Common sense is attracted by the apparent advantage of having negotiations conducted by a group of men gathered round a table, rather than by complicated exchange by cable. And it should be possible to get better results.

When we re-examine our earlier work, conferences seem to have suffered from two handicaps. They were conducted under a blaze of publicity. They were given impossible tasks.

If we are capable of learning from our mistakes, it should be possible to reduce and even eliminate the first.

The second calls for common-sense recognition of what conferences can do. They cannot be charged with solving fundamental problems. That is the task of governments, and these solutions must be reached by man-to-man negotiation before calling conferences. Once the general lines of agreement and the will to agree have become clear, the negotiators can be brought together to formulate the actual terms of agreement.

When two corporations seek solution to a conflict on business matters, they do not turn the problem over to their lawyers. The executives find a basis for agreement and then entrust to the lawyers the task of putting the agreement into proper form. Delegates at a conference should have somewhat the same function as the lawyers.

People at home are often impatient with our delegates at international conferences for failing to make other people go as far as we should like. They overlook one thing—that in a conference you cannot make anybody do anything. No one can make us do anything, and we labor under the same limitations in imposing our views. Many people assume that the decisions should represent the position of the most enlightened delegation, and that if only we are sufficiently advanced we should have our way. Unfortunately, things do not work out that way. The conference has to content itself with what is accepted by the most backward delegation. You can secure the adoption of only those things agreed to by everybody. The rule of unanimity is the dead hand of this sort of negotiation.

If we can give conferences a fair chance they may prove valuable instruments, but only after we have done away with the very attributes that most appealed to many loose thinkers on the subject.

One drawback to the conference method is that it imposes upon any delegates sincerely desirous of agreement the necessity for resorting to the despised methods of secret diplomacy. They are obliged to spend a good part of their time in back-stairs negotiation in hotel rooms and to urge upon this or that delegate that he withhold any statement of his real position in order to gain time for seeking a common ground. When a roomful of delegates get up in public session and express agreement on an important matter, it is usually because these same delegates have spent some time in dark corners ironing out their difficulties. The proceedings have been carefully rehearsed; the more spontaneous they appear, the more carefully they have been rehearsed. Two delegates will state divergent views; a third will intervene with a conciliatory suggestion to which the other two express perhaps seemingly reluctant, perhaps enthusiastic, agreement. Thus everybody's face is saved. But it is slow and difficult work, and amounts to achieving good by hole-and-corner methods.

The foregoing applies primarily to public conferences conducted by trained negotiators who are giving their whole time to the problem. It does not apply to the same extent to the political figures who so often come upon the scene for the announced purpose of pulling the rabbit out of the hat.

One great drawback about having intricate problems handled by political leaders is that they are busy men and cannot settle down long enough to do a thorough job. How often at Geneva, or elsewhere, have we seen a meeting called to order with the statement that we must press forward to reach a solution of this or that question because the French Foreign Minister is obliged to leave on Thursday morning. You may well ask what relation there is between these two statements. The solution need not be reached before the Minister leaves Geneva. It could be reported to him in due course by telegraph or telephone. But that is just the catch. The politician simply cannot go home with the press trumpeting the fact that he did nothing more important than sit in at the beginning of the discussion. He must have his little triumph.

And this has led to two of the worst products of open diplomacy—improvisation and the formula.

Improvisation is undoubtedly the worst possible method for settling problems in diplomacy—just as it would be in business. The mere fact that problems have been put on the agenda for treatment by the political leaders is evidence that they are difficult and call for careful, prudent handling. Such handling can be based only on study, preparation, and consultation with the people who know most about them. No amount of improvisation, however brilliant, can take the place of hard work in diplomacy any more than in the conduct of an intricate lawsuit.

So the politician puts forward some short cut to agreement, something that looks good on the surface but would not bear scrutiny and careful examination. While this shocks the professional diplomat, it is not at all shocking to the politician. He is merely applying his ordinary, everyday methods of dealing with questions as they arise. He will have his little moment of triumph, and if the solution does not work, the people will be thinking of something else by that time anyway, so why worry?

If improvisation will provide something that can be represented as a great achievement, so much the better. But, in any event, there must be something to convey the impression of progress, something to which the leader can point with pride. This has led to a whole technique of humbug—the technique of framing resolutions and reports which will hold together for the moment and can, during that period, be represented as successes. This is a delicate technique, and calls for great skill, for it is not enough to create the illusion of achievement for one country. There are various leaders present at the conference, and each one —each Prime Minister, Foreign Minister, and whatnot, must have his little triumph, must be able to point with pride, and all the rest. From this has grown up the gentle art of agreeing upon a formula. Whenever there is an obvious deadlock, some sympathetic statesman will arise and suggest a formula. If the formula can be accepted by all, there is a sigh of relief, followed by an exodus, and the conference is over.

But don't make any mistake about the nature of a formula. It is not necessarily a form of compromise on which all agree. It has, in fact, come to mean a form of words which has the outward appearance of agreement and settlement when read by the man in the street but which, either by tacit agreement among the delegates or from differences of wording in different languages, means different things to the parties.

The formula is a dangerous remedy. It does permit the delegates to get away and the conference to capture momentarily glowing headlines. Although all concerned have agreed upon a form of words for the purpose of creating an illusion of agreement, they have a tendency to forget that the words mean exactly nothing. More often than not, after reading and rereading the formula, one side comes to the conclusion that it has been promised something definite and substantial. The other side probably feels that it has got out of a tight corner and promised nothing at all. The inevitable result is acrimonious disagreement and very possibly intimations of bad faith.

The trouble with all this is that it is contrary to one of the most elementary requirements of diplomacy. A diplomatic settlement to be of value must be definite and precise, must mean exactly the same thing in the different languages in which it is drafted, and be incapable of any other interpretation.

The conference method is undoubtedly here to stay, although it is to be hoped that it will be used more discriminatingly, but there are several modifications in present procedures which would tend to secure a larger volume of agreement.

First, it is desirable that the maximum amount of preparatory work be completed by direct and private negotiation before the conference is convened, in order that its work may be narrowed down to the adjustment of minor difficulties and the drafting of the actual terms of the agreement.

Second, the conference itself should be put on a normal, workaday basis and cease to be treated as an emergency with a time limit. There is no real reason for a conference to be carried on differently from any other human activity. What we need most is the application of the laboratory method. If you are seeking a chemical formula, you do not call a meeting, choose sides, and announce to an incredulous press that everything will be tidied up before the end of the week, as Professor Snooks must return to his regular work by that time. Above all, you do not, in agreement with your scientific colleagues, and in order to meet the immediate demands of the situation, dish up a phony formula which you know any scientist with half an eye can see through. On the contrary, you assemble the members of your research staff and send them off to work in their laboratories until they notify you that they have found the answer. It may be days, or weeks, or months, or even years, but the time element is of secondary importance.

There is every reason why conferences should be conducted in the same way. The problems they have to tackle are no less intricate than those entrusted to the scientific research worker. Disarmament, for instance, is so deeply bogged in the soils of human nature that it is folly to expect a quick and simple solution. The only hope is to let men of training and resource and good will disappear into some retreat and work quietly and unhurriedly for as long as may be necessary, many years perhaps, in the hope that they will find ways and means of advancing along the road. Furthermore, conferences should, except for the purpose of stimulating public interest and announcing agreement, be held as private conversations with a minimum of speeches and publicity in order to lessen the temptation for the negotiators to cavort for the benefit of the press and public opinion. In other words, to make their first concern the solution of the problem and not ephemeral public approval for themselves.

The conference method can hardly be expected to give better results until the conference itself ceases to be regarded as a gladiatorial combat. We must get out of our heads the idea that a conference is like a football game: that we choose sides and that they continue to score until there is victory for one side or the other. That is the mentality that is expressed by the remark attributed to Will Rogers, that the United States never lost a war or won a conference. Will Rogers denied to me on several occasions with some heat that he had ever made this statement, but that is another story.

The fundamental purpose of a conference, or any other form of negotiation, is to secure agreement, not victory. In fact, victory and defeat are the negation of diplomacy. The diplomat should never forget that the problem he is working on is of only relative importance in that it is one of an unending series that must be discussed with the other party through the years, and therefore, while he must get as much as is expedient for his own country, it must be within such limits and under such terms as will obviate resentment and a sense of injustice in future negotiations. It is important to have everybody satisfied, so that they bring to the next meeting a desire for further agreement and not a yearning for revenge—the inevitable result of defeat.

This calls for a radical change in our mental attitude, for there is no doubt that the public in all countries consider international relations in terms of victory and defeat. But we may as well make up our minds that it is only when we have adopted the opposite attitude that we can hope for a larger measure of success.

If the day ever comes when a conference is conducted by these methods, while we cannot of course be sure of success, we can be sure that better machinery has been installed in order to bring that success about.

It is, of course, imperative that all international agreements, once they have been concluded, should be made of public record. For our own security and for guidance in formulating our foreign policy, it is important that we be acquainted with agreements existing among other countries. But, from a practical point of view, and disregarding the tyranny of slogans, it does not make a particle of difference whether these covenants are arrived at openly or otherwise. The method is of little importance and of no real interest to the public. The essential thing is that the covenants should amount to something when they are arrived at.

Some of the advocates of open diplomacy go so far as to maintain that the archives of the Department of State should be open to the public and that the press be at liberty to publish any documents they consider of sufficient interest. If this were done, they would probably be sorely disappointed in what they found. There would be precious little of what they would be led to expect from the thrillers of E. Phillips Oppenheim.

Just the same, it is a method that is not to be advocated. There are certain matters regarding which any decent government must maintain reticence. There is nothing abstruse about it. It is simply a matter of common sense.

We are often told that the same standards should be applied to publicity in national affairs as in private business. There is little to disagree with in this. Even in private business there is a distinct difference between secrecy to conceal swindling and dishonest activities and reticence such as that observed by a bank in regard to the affairs of its depositors and clients.

The sort of reticence that is observed by a bank or a lawyer or a doctor is not entirely confined to business affairs, but extends to everyday life. No man is considered dishonest and secretive because he does not discuss his family affairs in the presence of strangers. A prudent man may legitimately go even further than that and not audibly proclaim such a harmless fact as his intention to purchase a farm. If he does, he perfectly well knows that his waking hours will be consumed by the importunities of salesmen, and he usually goes about this business with a certain amount of caution and reserve—in other words, secret diplomacy.

In the same way the efforts of the government to secure fair treatment for its citizens, to promote trade, to protect its interests against discrimination or injustice, need not be advertised in order to be honest.

Another important phase of this question is that a government cannot, any more than an individual, repeat information that is given under the seal of confidence. Not only is such secrecy considered legitimate, but the government would be severely condemned if it were to publish this information on the ground that there was no such thing as legitimate secrecy. The raw material upon which our Department of State operates is chiefly in the form of information gathered in all corners of the world. Much of this information is given us by other governments and by individuals, and given because they are convinced that we can be depended on to respect their confidence. A steady stream of such information pours into the Department of State, and a great deal of it is clearly labeled as having been given under an injunction not to let it become public or even to impart it to anyone outside of the government. It is given us because the people who give it realize that it will be of value to us, and that we can be depended upon not to use it in any way that will harm their interests. They are encouraged to give us this information because of a regime of reciprocity which exists between most governments under which they hope to secure equally helpful and legitimate information from us. Respect for confidence is just as important in international dealings as in private life, and if it is not observed the government suffers just as directly as the individual.

Information—sound, reliable information—is more precious than rubies. If it is good, you want more of it from the same source. So even if you lack a high sense of honor, you keep it confidential. You are kept on the straight and narrow path by the knowledge that if you betray your informant once he will lay no more eggs of golden information. And from that time on you will have to be content with the sort of information the other government is willing and ready to give to the press.

To put it in other words, the effective conduct of our foreign relations is largely dependent upon the completeness of the information upon which that conduct is based. The greater the amount of confidential information we receive, the better for the conduct of our affairs; that amount is in direct relation to the confidence felt in our discretion in the handling of such information. The minute that confidence is undermined, the flow of information stops.

The experience of the last generation should demonstrate that we should be on our guard against two dangers—secret diplomacy and open diplomacy.

No government in this country can indulge in secret diplomacy without paying the penalty when the facts become known. If it makes secret commitments, they will not necessarily be considered binding when they do become known. Any other government that accepts such commitments at face value may find that it has been swindled.

On the other hand, we should recognize the dangers of diplomacy in the market place. We should have had time to recognize the futility of trying to negotiate publicly in international conferences. We shall get farther faster by returning to the tested methods of real diplomacy, negotiating in private and making the results public.

CHAPTER VII

American Leadership in World Affairs

UNDER THE SPELL of some of our global planners you may picture all the peoples of the world sitting by their firesides, or under their banana trees, or in the air-raid shelters, discussing the beauties of world organization, world courts, and world armies, all on the American model, with the democracies sitting at the head of the table and the others waiting respectfully outside until they have made good in our eyes and can be admitted. This is all very inspiring, but you can travel the world over without finding anything to justify this picture. True, in Britain there is interest in postwar problems, for the most part more realistic than our own. The cheers that hailed Mr. Churchill's remarks about not liquidating the Empire belied the idea that all and sundry are just waiting for us to tell them what to do. General Smuts, in his speech of November 25, 1943, dealt with the need for international co-operation, but in clear terms of balance of power. The approval that greeted this pronouncement hardly strengthens the belief that Britain is putting all her chips on immediate realization of Utopia on the American Plan.

The British attitude toward world problems is nearest to our own, but it is less marked with crystal-gazing and bubble-blowing. The British are more experienced politically than we are and their approach is, as a rule, more realistic. There is a general readiness to collaborate in solutions, but always with an eye to British interests. This is not a reproach. That is what government is hired for, and British opinion is sufficiently mature politically to realize that concern for the national interest is a sane and respectable approach to international affairs. There is no reproach against the citizen who does not consider it necessary to neglect his family as a preliminary to good citizenship. Instead of criticizing the British for defending their own interests, we should take a leaf out of their book and try to do as good a job of looking after our own.

In the continental countries we find the mentality a step further removed from the belief in miraculous solutions. There is a general skepticism toward high-sounding plans. Governments sometimes pay lip service to them for purposes of their own, but prefer to rely on old-fashioned ways rather than trust to untried methods. Often this skepticism amounts to cynicism, and we are obliged to cover our ears in order not to be offended by comments on our generous ideas from the statesmen who decide how far their countries are to go along the lines we indicate. We can travel far and wide without finding any powerful country yearning to embark on new and untried methods.

Even when there is no demand for American leadership, there is often an assumption among Americans that all other peoples want what we want; that all of them yearn for democracy as we conceive it; that all we have to do is to make up our own minds as to what is best, and the job is done. Hence, so many plans for reorganizing the world on the model of the American Republic.

Most of this is based on a tendency to judge other countries by our own standards. As a matter of fact, they are vastly different from us and from each other. They have started from different points and have developed in different ways. As a result, they have different standards and different points of view.

Our attitude is reminiscent of the old English lady who was taken to see *Antony and Cleopatra*. When the play was over, her only comment was that it was very interesting "but *so* unlike the home life of our own dear Queen."

Many of the people, foreign and domestic, who are instructing the American people as to their duty have developed a new type of simplification. In ringing phrases they tell us we *must* do this or that. Their whole technique is nothing more than just that— "The fangs of the aggressor nations *must* be drawn." "America *must* maintain peace and justice." "Isolationism *must* be abolished." "We *must* make provision for racial equality." "America *must* police the world for a hundred years." "We *must* do away with nationalism, militarism, and imperialism." And so on, indefinitely. The crowd cheers and says the orator is a great leader. But just what has he said that could not be said by any high-school boy? There is no leadership in saying things *must* be done! And, unless the assertion that something *must* be done is no more than a prelude to showing *how* it *can* be done, the orator does not qualify as a leader. He does no more than confuse the public mind.

It is not agreeable to act as a wet blanket on generous enthusiasms, for we need enthusiasm, but we may question whether these things can be accomplished by mere fiat. This is too much like a demand that there shall be no more rain. It will not suffice to proclaim "Peace, it's wonderful!" to have peace by incantation. If we really want a peaceful world we must face up to the fact that lasting peace must come the hard way. And here we come to the fundamental hope of peace—that we should abandon the idea of abolishing conflict by changing human nature and devote ourselves to finding how we can control and direct and allay the evil forces, how we can strengthen the forces that make for peace.

Conditions are not going to be more favorable to peace after this war. They will be less favorable. The earth will be swept by waves of nationalism like none we have known before. There will be grievances and hatreds clamoring for revenge. There will be conflicting ambitions. There will be active underground movements. There will be waves of revolution. There will be among the strong powers an inevitable reaction toward isolation from other peoples' troubles. And if we are to have peace we must not ignore these difficulties but rather seek to find out how they can be overcome.

In our own minds we might as well put peace in second place and strive to create conditions from which peace would follow. If we can attain conditions of justice and liberty and confidence we shall achieve peace by indirection—a peace that will endure while we maintain those conditions.

The "musters" tend to leap over the obstacles of reality and start from the assumption that once firing ceases we shall come automatically into a new and better world; that mankind will instantly shed selfishness and greed and hate and revenge; that a new type of human being will come into existence, a sort of international man who will be ready to act generously and intelligently; and that all we need to attain the millennium is to set up some simple machinery.

Outside our own country there is little belief in the miraculous power of plans, little identity of thought, and—despite the exhortations of some propagandists—no demand for American leadership as we understand the term. American help, yes, and the assurance of American collaboration in world affairs, but the desire for this is normal and not to be confused with a desire for American guardianship. When a foreigner holds forth on the need for American world leadership it is usually enlightening to weigh his pleas against the remainder of his remarks. He usually has some plan of his own to promote, and his idea of American leadership is support for his own scheme. This, incidentally, is not leadership. Experience has shown that if we venture to express opinions of our own, we are likely to hear admonitions about minding our own business and refraining from meddling in matters we do not understand, rather than encouragement to go ahead and decide what is best for the rest of the world.

We should do well to put aside the belief that we must press for the adoption of sweeping solutions on the ground that we are now lagging behind the rest of the world and holding up the forward march of humanity. This has been dinned into our people for years, largely by foreigners trying to educate us as to our duty to the rest of the world. Their voices have rarely represented anything beyond their own ideas. In most cases their own governments are in no way disposed to adopt the responsibilities and the measures urged upon the United States. In spite of this, they have succeeded in implanting in the minds of many Americans a misgiving that we are failing in our duty. And some Americans have taken up the cry and seem bent on stampeding us into saving our souls, according to some of these prescriptions.

There is a great deal we can learn from foreigners in this country. They can help us, those who are qualified by wisdom and experience, to get ready to face the tasks that lie ahead. They can enlighten us as to their national problems and their difficulties. They can tell us what they have learned from experience. There is a broad field for them in this sort of helpfulness, and we should seek to learn from them.

There is, however, another aspect to this—the foreigners, few in numbers but objectionable beyond their numbers, who make it their business to instruct us not in their problems but in our own. This has led to a development peculiar to our country, the freedom with which some foreigners rise up to criticize and instruct us in our shortcomings and our national and international duties. There is something very humble and touching in the way we sit at the feet of these people and take their admonitions to heart. There are a number of them who, picking up courage from the way they have got away with it, are increasingly free and easy, not only in admonishing us as a nation but also in mixing into our internal affairs and taking to task individual Americans they do not like.

It is interesting to conjecture what would be the fate of an American who settled in Norway or in France and undertook a campaign of systematic publicity against Norwegian or French parties and public figures. We have very little to go on, possibly because we do not go in for this form of activity, more probably because no American has ever been allowed to get off to a good start in such activities. But we do seem to recall a few cases where Americans have done something displeasing to the authorities and have been given short shrift. Mr. Hearst, for instance, was run out of France on a few hours' notice, not because he campaigned against anyone, but because his papers published a document the authorities would have preferred not to have had published.

While welcoming all the enlightenment that foreigners can give us on their own problems, it is about time it was made clear that meddling in our problems is not calculated to promote good international understanding.

Under the impact of this sort of propaganda there has grown up in many quarters an assumption that the rest of the world is rarin' to travel the road to Utopia and that we alone are holding back—that, paradoxical as it may seem, although we are lagging behind, we are for some reason undisclosed expected to give leadership, and that all the age-old problems of the world can be settled promptly if only we make up our minds to adopt this plan or that. It would be lovely if it were that easy, but it isn't.

It is this belief that America has some high mission to lead the world that accounts in some measures for those breast-beaters who proclaim that we are entirely to blame for the failure of the

League of Nations. Curiously enough this idea originated in the United States. True, after our people had shouted "Unclean, unclean!" long enough some other countries took up the idea and put it to work for their own ends. Hardly a foreign lecturer fails to rub in our responsibility for this war. "If only America had joined the League!" We are given to understand that everything would have gone smoothly and with our membership this war would have been avoided. Of course it is easy to understand why our foreign critics harp on this theme. They hope to shame us into doing more next time by way of atonement for our past sins. But why we should assume the blame is something of a mystery to anyone familiar with the workings of the League and the real reasons for its failure. I represented our country at League conferences for ten years and was a convinced advocate of the closest possible collaboration; but I confess I do not see how we could have had a whit more influence as a member state than we had as a collaborating non-member. If the League failed, or, to put it more fairly, if the member states failed to make it work, the reasons are there for all to see. There were fundamental defects in the whole conception of the League machinery and its operation—the lack of harmony in the provisions for settlement of disputes by peaceful means or force; the failure to meet the need for some method for peaceful revision of treaty terms which might constitute a threat to peace; the failure to formulate a peace policy for Europe, the greatest danger spot. And we must not forget that the League was born of liberalism—and it did not survive the death of liberalism in Europe.

It is a large assumption that by merely joining the League we could have prevented another world war. In order to do this we should have had to be prepared and have the power to resist all the Great Powers, by arms if necessary, to make our views of peace prevail. And we should have had to possess some miraculous power to control and direct all the destructive forces let loose by the last war and the treaties, to say nothing of the need to dominate and direct the nations operating outside the League. No power on earth could do any of these things.

And while there was disappointment at our failure to join the League, Europe did not throw up its hands in despair, certainly not until our own head-hangers rushed abroad to trumpet our shame.

Without being unduly cynical or even unhelpful, we should adjust our ideas of American leadership to other peoples' ideas on the same subject. We all use the same expression but with wide differences of meaning. Most of the talk of American leadership outside our borders is a quite honest use of words to convey the description of our readiness to help financially and to support the political views of other governments. The expression is frequently used in the foreign press, but wide reading fails to reveal its use in any other sense. There is a striking absence of demand for our leadership in reorganizing the world. Unless we keep this in mind we may be saddened and disillusioned if, before the war is much older, it is pointed out to us in all kindliness that we do not really understand European problems and that it would be better for all concerned if we were to leave the Europeans to straighten out things in their own way. By way of consolation we may be reminded that we have had a vast sphere of influence in the Western Hemisphere. There have recently been some pointed intimations to that general effect. This would be a courteous way of telling us to get out, like asking somebody to close the door—from the other side.

This is not said by way of complaint, but merely to take note of an existing state of affairs. We shall be dealing with realities only when we recognize that there is no disposition anywhere in the world to invest us with *ex officio* leadership, to acclaim the "American Century." We may then begin to recognize that we shall have our work cut out for us in a less ambitious but more practical enterprise, contributing effective collaboration in world affairs.

A reasonable amount of travel suffices to relieve us of the guilty feeling that we are holding up the forward march of civilization. Indeed, we may well come home convinced that, on the contrary, we are far out in front leading a charge alone, while the other nations sit quietly in their trenches and don't even encourage us by shouting "Bravo!"

It is to be hoped we shall not become cynical in our approach to world affairs—that would be a disaster. But, shocking as it may sound to the generous mind, it is to be hoped we shall become moderately skeptical. Skepticism is a word that has fallen into disrepute, but in its true sense means no more than refusal to accept ideas without first making sure they are reasonable. It does not mean refusal to examine any new idea. But a wholesome skepticism would lead us to scrutinize new ideas instead of adopting them with religious fervor; it would lead us to retain the good and workable elements and to recognize their true scope instead of looking on them as cure-alls. There is nothing incompatible between skepticism and generous idealism.

One reason for our weakness in foreign affairs lies in this lack of true skepticism.

Politically, we sometimes have the mentality of the man who hangs his coat in an overcrowded cupboard and quickly slams the door so as not to see it fall off the hook. There is often a readiness to proceed on the basis of assumption of what we should like to believe. If we are going to have solutions that work, they must be on the basis of fact. A good surgeon does not base his diagnosis on enthusiastic impulse as to what he would like to think is the matter with the patient or what diagnosis would be popular with the family. He knows he will find out the nature of the ailment sooner or later, either before the operation or at the autopsy. In international affairs, we have depended altogether too much on the autopsy. It might be as well to give more attention to diagnosis.

No matter how reasonable measures and remedies may appear to us here and now, we should never lose sight of the fact that they must take their chance of success with governments and statesmen who have been through the fiery ordeal and who will feel perhaps less trustful than we do. Ideas must be scrutinized with a view to determining what will be generally accepted and what will work.

We are inclined nowadays to consider foreign policy chiefly in connection with the problems of making peace and building a new world order after the war. But no matter how wise the measures decided on, their successful operation will be determined by the intelligence and knowledge brought to bear by the different governments in discharging their share of responsibility. It will not suffice for us to accept some form of world institution to preserve peace. No institution can do that. At best, it can be no more than a machine to be used by the member countries.

It is generally accepted that the League of Nations failed and that our problem will be solved by finding a more satisfactory form of machinery. This is not altogether justified. The League itself was no more than a piece of machinery. The machinery did not fail to operate. It was not operated. The member states did not live up to their obligations. In the light of this experience we must make up our minds that we are not going to find some miracle machine that will operate successfully, regardless of human actions. Our problem will be not so much to find a more effective machine as it will be to agree on measures and methods generally acceptable—and more likely to be carried out.

We Americans cannot decide these questions for others. There is no purpose in trying to coerce them into reluctant acceptance of some scheme that seems good to us. We tried that at Versailles, and the results were not successful.

The best we can do is to make up our minds as to what we are sure we can carry out. In the end we may have to content ourselves with something less—or even something else. For, regardless of our influence, we shall have only one voice among the nations. We shall not get our way by bringing pressure to bear on others to adopt our proposals. Any scheme that is reluctantly adopted cannot be made to work. It matters less to have our own way than to reach agreement on something that will work through the readiness of all parties to meet their commitments.

We in this country have not done our full part by adopting recent congressional resolutions expressing in purposely vague terms our readiness to join some world organization subject to senatorial approval. That action leaves things exactly where they were before the question came up. It is certainly far from being a blank check with a promise to the Executive that it will be honored when presented to the Senate for payment. Such resolutions are helpful in showing a readiness in principle to accept a proper place in world affairs, but despite the ecstatic gurglings of some political writers such resolutions do not equip our government to play its part in the world. It will be so equipped only when we have formulated a clearly recognized national policy based on understanding of our national interests, for that includes understanding of the role we can play in international collaboration. The reader might do well to turn to the Appendix and read the texts of these resolutions and try to conclude for himself just what they mean in definite terms—to just what form of international organization they commit us.

We are often irritated when foreign critics say that we are not dependable in foreign affairs; that they have had their disappointments in dealing with us; and that in the future they must have some binding guarantee as to what we can be expected to do. We are unhappy about charges of this sort, and seek simple, convenient explanations. For instance, as we didn't join the League of Nations, we explain it to ourselves on the ground that a small group of evil men who hated President Wilson defeated the Treaty.

But if we are honest with ourselves, the real explanation is entirely different. We refused to join the League of Nations primarily because of a revulsion of feeling among the mass of our people. Between the end of the last war and the time when Mr. Wilson brought back the Covenant the American attitude toward Europe underwent a fundamental change. When the Armistice was signed, we were filled with enthusiasm for all the Allies. We believed that a new era had dawned, that this was largely due to our own intervention in the war, and that the countries of Europe were filled with gratitude and a desire that we should lead the way into a better world. Consequently, we were shocked when Mr. Lloyd George and M. Clemenceau began to point out our shortcomings; when Mr. Keynes explained to the American people how President Wilson had been "bamboozled," and the daily press was filled with criticism and with news of violence of all sorts, recurrences of war, revolutions and uprisings, land-grabbing exploits, and other lawless activities which disclosed to us that power politics was operating full blast and that the new era had not dawned after all. This brought disillusionment to the mind of the ordinary American and realization that in spite of our enthusiasms the people we so admired were only human after all. We were outraged to see them playing the old game of power politics. We knew we did not want to play that game ourselves and, in our disillusionment, we came to the conclusion that it was best to wash our hands of Europe and get along as best we could at home.

This change may have been inevitable, but the move toward

isolationism would have been much less pronounced if we had been more reasonable and realistic in our earlier attitudes. If we had been less enthusiastic and had not endowed our allies with qualities they never claimed to have; if we had been more realistic from the start, there would have been less room for disillusionment. Be that as it may, it is precisely these changes in the feeling of the people of this country that cause other countries to feel we are not dependable allies or associates.

This is not to say that other governments never change. They do, of course, but we can usually perceive more clearly the pattern of their change, the reasons behind it—not as a rule a deliberate movement in an emotional about face.

All this may appear highly self-critical, but in reality it is no more than a diagnosis of our real ailment. The ailment is there. We suffer from it and we shall not be cured unless we treat the real ailment and not another which we would rather believe we suffer from. We need a cure for uninformed and artificially stimulated enthusiasms.

The first rule of intelligent diplomacy is for a country to mind its own business. There is ample scope for its activity in settling its own problems. In the last few years we have had some glaring examples of how obnoxious governments can be when they meddle in the affairs of other countries, especially when they have carried on systematic intrigue for the promotion of their ideologies and for territorial conquest.

Only somewhat less objectionable is meddling on high moral grounds. Of course when we call upon other countries to mend their ways, when we admonish them as to their evil practices, we are acting on high moral grounds and for the promotion of justice. Strangely enough, this does not make the approach any more acceptable. On the contrary, there is nothing more irritating than the individual who indulges in admonishing his neighbors as to their shortcomings.

Things are happening abroad every day that outrage our sense of justice. Any normal human being yearns to do something. If we can really do something, if it is in our power to right a wrong, our course is clear. But in most cases we can do nothing to right the wrong. The most we can do is to give vent to our feelings, by speeches and mass meetings, by picketing embassies, and by denouncing foreign governments. Of course this is a relief to our feelings, but has little or no relation to the problem of correcting an injustice abroad. Indeed in some cases it serves only to aggravate the situation. Before embarking on campaigns for this or that we should do well to satisfy ourselves whether there is hope of achievement or whether it is just for the luxury of self-expression. If the latter, we should do well to keep quiet. Sometimes we can find comfort in the knowledge that another people is working out its problems as we are working out our own, and that perhaps the wisest course is to refrain from back-seat driving—recalling how we would resent denunciation and advice in matters where we have undoubtedly been remiss.

It is quite proper to feel righteous indignation at injustice and brutality; we should otherwise be lacking in human feeling. But these evils are not always corrected by public agitation, particularly when whole peoples are keyed up to a high pitch of emotion. No one has yet been made more reasonable by public attacks. We have only to recall how little foreign criticism has done to abolish lynching in the United States. If anything is to be accomplished in such cases, the best chance of success lies in action by the government agencies charged with the handling of our foreign relations. General denunciation does not help the efforts of the Secretary of State. On the contrary, popular agitation often creates an antagonism which precludes him from taking effective action.

American leadership in such matters, to be effective, must come from the recognized authority of the government.

CHAPTER VIII

Prescriptions for Peace, Past and Future

IN OUR EAGERNESS to get things done we are sometimes prone to oversimplification. We seize on some idea as a panacea and cling to the hope that if only adopted it will solve all the troubles of the world.

The simpler the plan the better. One of the current favorites is to reorganize the world on the American model—a world government operating under a revised version of the American Constitution, a World Senate and House of Representatives, a World Supreme Court handing down the law, with a World Army to enforce its decrees, keep the peace, crush aggression, and maintain justice. The advocates of this simple solution recall the man who at the time of the earthquakes in Portugal peddled anti-earthquake pills in the streets of Lisbon. When rebuffed by a man to whom he offered them with an expression of skepticism, he met the situation with the crushing query, "What would you take in their place?"

Others advocate arbitration as the solution of all our ills. If governments agree to arbitrate there will be no more wars and hence we shall have peace.

Disarmament has its advocates as a general solution.

Others see great virtue in suppressing the private manufacture of arms and turning the armament industry over to governments.

There are those, too, who feel that we, in America, know best and that perhaps under present conditions we had better take over and police the world, standing no nonsense from anybody.

However tempting these ideas may be, we may as well face the fact that there are no panaceas.

Many of the ideas that are being discussed nowadays have their value—some great and fundamental value—but not as panaceas. Many of them have a place in any general scheme, but we shall get more out of them if we take what they have to offer and do not expect the impossible.

Oversimplification has definite dangers. It keeps us from concentrating on methods that will work. It also keeps us from recognizing the real possibilities that are to be found in many of the ideas that are being advocated as panaceas.

Perhaps the worst form of simplification is the readiness to accept beautifully phrased aspirations as solutions. As an illustration, we may recall the organization recently set up to hold meetings throughout the country and "pay tribute" to the Atlantic Charter and the Four Freedoms. In the announcement it was confidently stated that never before in history had the people "been afforded such a firm and practical basis for peacemaking." Before accepting this statement it would be a fair test to take these two texts and try to translate them into specific treaty provisions —for until they are put in this definite form they are no more than generous aspirations. Further, it must be borne in mind that even specific treaty provisions are realistic only so far as they represent the will of the prospective signatories. Thus each provision, however admirable it may appear in itself, must be scrutinized according to such knowledge as we may possess regarding the readiness of the various governments concerned to adopt and observe it. Scrutiny of the Atlantic Charter on this basis in the light of subsequent developments reveals that we are faced by no simple and easy task of "adopting" the Charter, that there are many difficulties to be overcome if we are to put its aspirations into practical operation.

The most popular form of simplification is the assumption that some one panacea will put everything right in the world.

A few illustrations will serve to show that while it is possible to achieve great improvements in the conduct of our foreign affairs this cannot be through the adoption of some simple plan. It must be through drudgery and planning and in extracting from all proposals those elements that can be made to work.

ARBITRATION

Arbitration is an old favorite. Many people believe that peace can be assured if only all nations will agree to submit all disputes to arbitration.

We are justified in having high hopes of arbitration. It is undoubtedly one of the most effective methods developed for the peaceful settlement of disputes of any character. But it cannot be invoked until a dispute has come into being. It has definite limitations, and we should be on our guard against expecting the impossible—against looking on arbitration as the universal remedy.

Arbitration is not desirable in itself. And is less so when it assumes a compulsory character. It might be compared to a remedy which is invaluable in certain cases but harmful if used indiscriminately. Or, to put it in another way, arbitration may be compared to surgery. Admirable as modern surgery is for cases beyond the power of medicine, no one would advise resort to surgery for all ills. It is only when we have exhausted the possibilities of the medicine of diplomacy that we resort to the surgery of arbitration to save the patient from the death of war.

It is all too generally accepted that arbitration takes place in an atmosphere of complete trust and confidence. As a matter of fact, it usually takes place in the midst of acute controversy. There is no resort to arbitration until diplomacy has failed. The fact that the dispute is submitted to arbitration brings it to the knowledge of the public in the interested countries, and from that moment some heat is bound to be generated. Whatever the award, some animosity usually remains. Experience indicates that almost any agreement reached by diplomatic negotiations carries more promise of permanence than an arbitral award.

There are certain categories of questions no powerful government is likely to agree to submit to arbitration—at least at present. We have only to consider what our own attitude would be if another government made what we considered preposterous demands upon us—something involving use of our territory for military bases or our exclusion from the right to trade. Then there are questions involving what are vaguely described as matters of "national honor."

Our own official position is that we will decide in the light of the circumstances of each individual case—that we will not commit ourselves sight unseen to submit to arbitration controversies we may not consider susceptible of solution by that means.

In the last forty years the possibilities of arbitration have been developed greatly. The greatest hope for the future lies in the steady improvement of procedure and extension of the range of problems subject to arbitral treatment. But our hopes should be kept within these limits.

DISARMAMENT

Of all the panaceas, none in the past has had wider appeal than disarmament.

The word itself is misleading, as real total disarmament is advocated by only the more extreme advocates of drastic measures. The bulk of proposals on the subject can be more accurately described as for the reduction and limitation of armaments.

Total disarmament may appear a simple solution. Deprive all governments of arms and they would be unable to wage war. But we are hardly warranted in assuming that it would work out quite so simply in practice. On the contrary, there are grounds for believing that it would merely alter conditions, and not necessarily for the better. Proposals for total immediate disarmament must be based on the assumption that all governments are intent on peace and need only to be reassured that others are giving up the means of warfare at the same time. The present state of the world gives us little encouragement to believe that all countries are completely committed to the ideal of perpetual peace.

If at a given moment after the present war we were to have complete scrapping of armies, navies, and air forces in all countries—unless at the same time we did away with the nationalist, imperialist, and other ambitions of governments—the struggle would merely be resumed under different forms. We might find that an aggressor state deprived of armies was able, with improvised weapons, to overwhelm its enemy. If all navies were to be sunk, the power with the largest merchant navy would emerge as the greatest naval power and could deny the sea to others.

Quite aside from the inherent defects of any plan for total disarmament, it is not in the realm of reality, as governments responsible for the security of their territories and people are not going to give up their means of protection.

Through all the years of discussion in Geneva it was demonstrated that the direct approach to the reduction of arms was merely an attempt to deal with the symptoms rather than with the disease. We shall have to make up our minds to grapple with the deeper forces and, as justification for disarmament appears, seek to secure the logical measure of reduction.

The long years devoted to the discussion of disarmament in Geneva were largely unrealistic. They were certainly inconclusive. It soon became clear that no important results were to be achieved through negotiations limited to men and ships and guns. There were various attempts to find other approaches. One that had much to commend it was to seek to create a sense of security and thereby lessen the instinctive dependence on arms. Another was to take into account the potential war strength of different nations. Under this method, in determining the needs of each country account would be taken of all the elements, other than actual armed force, that contribute to make up its war strength—geographical position, topography, climate, population, industry, natural resources, food supply, and a host of others. The most ruthlessly logical of these plans submitted to the Preparatory Commission for the Disarmament Conference went into such detail as to win the label "Hogs, Fogs, and Bogs."

Both of these approaches had their merits, but they both ignored a fundamental problem. Over a long period a number of Great Powers had built up a whole system of national life and national economy based on huge military establishments. These had come to be a recognized way of dealing with the problem of unemployment. To begin with, there were large numbers of men absorbed into the military forces. To supplement these were government arsenals with another army of workmen, with a still larger number employed in providing supplies, food, clothing, and transportation. No government living under this system could undertake drastic reduction of armaments without disrupting the whole national economy. We may as well recognize the fact that there can be no more than fragmentary and regional reductions until the nations are prepared to grapple with this fundamental difficulty.

The idea of a universal agreement strikes the imagination, but progress will more likely be made through regional or group agreements. Argentina's disarmament is not rendered easier by a reduction of Russian armed forces. A reduction in British naval strength is no incentive to reduction of the Dutch Navy, as its function could not conceivably be to fight Britain. As among the principal naval powers, the problem—a difficult and intricate one—is to maintain such a nice balance of strength between them as will serve to discourage risking hostilities. We made some progress along these lines at the Washington and London Naval conferences, and there is no doubt that in due time we shall have to approach the problem again, perhaps more skillfully in the light of past experience and with a greater measure of success.

As regards land armaments: The problem which often seems so simple to the layman proves more difficult when methods of application are discussed. A first difficulty lies in the difference in military systems. Where some countries have universal military service through conscription, others depend upon smaller voluntary forces to be expanded in time of war. Even with good will, it is difficult to find a yardstick to measure forces so fundamentally different in character. Solution cannot be based on mere numbers, for a few years ago that would have involved reducing the French Army to 100,000 men to meet the system that had been imposed on Germany by the Treaty of Versailles in order to create for her a permanent status of inferiority. That would have been a measure entirely unfair to France, unless she changed her military system, for her 100,000 conscripts would have been no match for the 100,000 carefully selected German troops with intensive training over periods of ten years or longer who constituted a force of great immediate value and far greater potential value in expanding a large army.

So long as these radically different systems are maintained, it is difficult to see how any system of limitation can be devised which will inspire a sufficient measure of confidence to be accepted. It is obviously impossible to secure agreement for the universal adoption of either the voluntary or the conscription system, for these systems grow out of the needs and traditions of different nations. Perhaps there is something to be accomplished, however, through a different approach—through securing agreement to limit forces to a police component adequate for the maintenance of internal order.

It will be a long time before any such sweeping arrangements would be practicable on a universal scale. Somebody will have to keep the peace during the inevitable period of turmoil after this war. It is not a pleasant prospect to have to maintain large military forces after the war is over. It is a course that is particularly repugnant to the Anglo-Saxon. But if we want to protect the fruits of victory, it is difficult to see how the principal victorious powers can avoid assuming the burden on behalf of the United Nations. This is a role that will probably be imposed upon them by circumstances. But it would strengthen our moral and legal position if the United Nations were to ask us, that is to say, the United States, the British Empire, and Russia, to accept the task as a mandate from all—to serve as Trustees of Peace until such time as a world organization can be set up to take over. We need not be concerned at the idea of our assuming the role permanently. There is greater danger that in the after-war reaction we may not be disposed to carry on long enough.

World Court

There is a belief that all international conflicts could be prevented by the simple expedient of setting up a world court to settle all disputes according to law.

This is a clear case of oversimplification. There are many kinds of international conflict which cannot be settled by a court decision—just as there are many human conflicts, often tragic ones, which do not lend themselves to juridical settlement.

The assumption that all international conflicts can be settled by law is based on the premise that there is a single system of law throughout the world. This is not the case. If there were a single and uniform body of law applied in exactly the same manner in all countries, the problem would be simplified, but there are different systems of law that have grown up along different lines in different parts of the world. The whole concept of law is fundamentally different in some countries and, in such cases, which body of law is to be applied in regard to an international conflict?

As a general rule, neither party is ready to submit itself to the legal system of the other.

There is a broad field where an international court of justice can render great service. But it cannot settle everything.

OUTLAWRY OF WAR

In the last generation there has developed considerable support for the idea of outlawry of war—putting war itself outside the pale of law. The fundamental idea back of this has been to place the state on the same moral basis as the individual who is forbidden by domestic law, with police power behind it, from taking the law into his own hands and enforcing his own will.

The advocates of the outlawry of war feel that the attempt to control and humanize methods of warfare merely tends to recognize war itself as inevitable and almost respectable; that the evil will not be extirpated so long as war has a recognized place in the field of international relations. Their solution, which has at least the virtue of simplicity, is to destroy this recognized position of war and outlaw any country engaging in aggressive action against another.

Thus far the advocates of outlawry are in step, but there is considerable divergence of opinion as to how the outlawry is to be affected. There are those who feel that there must be an international tribunal to determine when a state should be outlawed, together with an international police organization to enforce the decree of the court. According to this school of thought, a national outlaw would have the same status and receive the same treatment as an individual criminal.

An alternative widely held view is that while there must be an international tribunal to pronounce the decree of outlawry, the decree must depend for enforcement upon moral force and enlightened public opinion.

The American Committee for the Outlawry of War adopted the latter point of view and in its draft treaty provided for an international tribunal "with power to summon a defendant nation at the petition of a complaining nation and to hear and decide the matter in controversy." It is further provided that the signatories "agree to abide by and in full good faith to carry out the decisions of such international tribunal." Under this treaty the decisions of the court depend entirely upon moral sanctions for enforcement.

On June 20, 1927, M. Aristide Briand, French Minister for Foreign Affairs, proposed to the American Government a bilateral treaty providing that the French and American peoples "condemn recourse to war and renounce it respectively as an instrument of their national policy toward each other."

The corollary to this embodied in the second article was that the settlement of all conflicts between France and the United States "shall never be sought by either side except by pacific means."

The American Government replied to this proposal on December 28 with the suggestion that instead of a bilateral declaration an effort be made to secure general acceptance of the project.

As a result, the Briand-Kellogg Pact was signed in Paris on August 27, 1928.

It was quickly discovered that there were difficulties impeding universal, unqualified acceptance of the declaration. For one thing, British acceptance was conditioned upon simultaneous acceptance by the Dominions and the Government of India. It was found necessary to be sure of the inclusion of all parties to the Treaty of Locarno in order to do away with any inconsistency between that treaty and the new declaration. In order to secure general acceptance, it was necessary to give the assurance that the obligation would not restrict the right of self-defense. By careful study it was agreed that no obligations under the Covenant were inconsistent with the Briand-Kellogg Pact.

France's obligations to neutralized states called for consideration. It was decided that if any of these states were attacked it would be in violation of the Pact and that France would be free to carry out her obligations. The discussions revealed that there was no ready acceptance that the Pact would be respected, for nearly all the questions raised had to do with situations created by war. There was inquiry as to what relations would exist between the law-abiding states and a state violating the Pact. In the note from the American Government transmitting the final draft of the Pact, this and other questions were dealt with. It was pointed out that it would be superfluous to recognize the fact that violation of the Pact by one party would automatically release the other parties from their obligations to the treaty-breaking state.

The essential part of this treaty was embodied in two articles as follows:

ARTICLE I

The High Contracting Parties solemnly declare in the names of their respective peoples that they condemn recourse to war for the solution of international controversies, and renounce it as an instrument of national policy in their relations with one another.

ARTICLE II

The High Contracting Parties agree that the settlement or solution of all disputes or conflicts of whatever nature or of whatever origin they may be, which may arise among them, shall never be sought except by pacific means.

There is room for honest difference of opinion as to the value of declarations of this character. One obvious advantage is that it brings home to peoples all over the world the infamy of war and the existence of alternative means for the settlement of international disputes. To those who object that it is fatuous to expect the abolition of war through statements of this sort it may be pointed out that it was through just such growth of moral sense that unrestricted private warfare was done away with in the Dark Ages. In more recent times the practice of dueling has been generally done away with, although two or three generations ago the practice, often recognized as wicked and absurd, was looked upon as just as inevitable as war seems to many people today.

On the other hand, there are dangers in seeking to do away with war by such simple means. For one thing, many people are disposed to feel that they have done their full part in approving the statement that there shall be no war, and that they are absolved from the duty of doing anything further. In the present state of the world we know if we are realistic that such a statement, while it may have an excellent moral effect when made, will inevitably be violated sooner or later, and then we face the danger that the whole idea of peace by self-denying ordinance will fall into disrepute.

Are we not justified in believing that there will be more progress by approaching the problem in a less sweeping way, by encouraging agreements for peaceful settlement and, above all, by doing away with causes of conflict? Under such a system the inevitable breakdowns do not bring a universal system into disrepute while the bilateral or regional successes would tend to build toward ultimate success.

It seems clear in retrospect that the fundamental defect of the Briand-Kellogg Pact was that governments agreed to forego resort to war without first securing some method for the peaceful settlement of their conflicts. All that they had was an undertaking that all signatories would settle their differences by peaceful means. That is almost as vague and general as the assertion that they would not resort to war.

The dilemma has been well put in the terms of industrial relations: That if the leaders of labor were to sign an undertaking to forego now and forever the right to strike without, at the same time, providing some machinery for the solution of conflicts, no one would expect organized labor to respect the signature. Public opinion would not expect them to forego the right to strike without, at the same time, being assured of a fair method for defending the rights of labor. Strikes, like war, are a wasteful method of settling disputes, but in both cases we cannot do away with the bad method unless we offer the alternative of a better.

INTERNATIONAL FORCE

There is a broad choice of plans for the preservation of peace by international action through a common force.

These range from an international army, navy, and air force, with an international General Staff to deal with evildoers all over the world, to regional forces and to even more limited membership.

Let us consider the more comprehensive plans first. The idea of an international armed force was considered when the League Covenant was being drafted. There was so little agreement on the subject that it was not adopted.

Since that time there have been repeated attempts to secure consideration for an international force.

The advantages of such a force are obvious—a central authority to direct a peaceful solution of international conflicts; a central force, stronger than that possessed by any single country, to deal with any power which refused to carry out the orders of the central authority, the mere knowledge of its existence to serve as a restraining influence.

In theory the idea is attractive.

But are we warranted in accepting the first step of the central directive authority? Experience gives us no such warrant. The League was supposed to perform just this function, but in practice it failed to do so. It may be objected that its failure was due precisely to lack of an army to enforce its decrees.

That objection will hardly bear scrutiny. The failure did not invariably follow wise decisions based on general agreement and dependent on arms for enforcement. On the contrary, the failure was usually in the preliminary stage of deciding who was at fault or what the offender should be asked to do. The League was never able to agree on the definition of an aggressor, even in general terms, save in specific cases in the light of events.

There is another assumption that calls for reflection. The rights and wrongs of a given controversy are not always clear cut. Even when they appear to the detached observer as a clear case of black and white, it is not always that simple to an international tribunal. And, on the basis of the same facts, different members of the same body may hold conflicting views, colored perhaps by national interests, alliances, sympathies, and antipathies.

The international force must not only be employed with scrupulous fairness—once it is set up, there must be no failure to use it. We have seen the League brought into disrepute through failure to deal the same brand of justice to all, both great and small. The same uniformity would be expected of an armed force. It would need, therefore, to be preponderant in strength so that an alliance of evildoers should not be able to defy the central authority.

And then we come to some material difficulties. To direct such a force there must be an international General Staff. As no international, non-patriotic animal has yet been bred for the purpose, we have no alternative to using army, navy, and air officers from national forces—men raised and trained in a school exacting a high degree of patriotic devotion and fidelity. They are not trained to critical examination of their country's conduct—they are taught to defend it against all perils. How are such men to adapt themselves to their new duties?

As its first task the General Staff must work out plans for action against every country. Not only must these plans be worked out in advance—they must be kept absolutely secret.

Let us assume an American officer or group of American officers are assigned to the International General Staff. They can collaborate with interest and zeal in preparing plans for the invasion of Japan or Germany. But what is their attitude if called upon to draw plans for invasion of their own country? And what if they are excluded from discussion of this subject?

Secrecy of all plans is essential in any General Staff. How is this to be achieved? As it would not suffice to deny an officer information about plans against his own country, what intricate system of concealment would be required? It would be necessary to extend the secrecy to alliances and groups, and even to personal sympathies. Out of this would grow one of the greatest spy systems in history, for it would become imperative for each government to know all possible plans. This would lead to all sorts of intrigue where intermediaries would be used.

Quite aside from plans—when the time comes for action, would not the officers of the offending state use all their knowledge and experience and contacts to furnish their government with full advance information as to what was coming?

However attractive an international force may look on paper, there is one fundamental obstacle to its success. No nation that is strong enough to resist is going to acquiesce in disciplinary measures directed against itself. We, for instance, might look favorably on the abstract idea of an international force. But our attitude might undergo a change if the idea were stated in terms of invading and punishing the United States. Some of us may feel this is not a practical test, as we could not conceivably do anything to deserve such action. That might not be the point of view of the countries with the power of decision; and no country would willingly acquiesce in punitive measures even if it was clearly in the wrong. No country would agree to reducing its forces to the point of impotence as against an international force directed by some foreign body. In practice such a force could be employed only against weak countries.

These are practical issues.

Unless powerful nations are to defy the central authority, they must be disarmed to the point where they have no alternative to obedience. Thus we see it is no simple matter of placing some ships and troops and planes at the disposal of the central authority. It means that the Great Powers would have to abdicate their superior strength. Is it probable that they would consent to surrender the force they have built up to defend their territory, their wealth, and their people in the belief that they will get a superior brand of protection from an experimental central authority? The first duty of a government is to assure safety to its people. Can the government assign this duty to another authority?

There have been a number of proposals in more or less detail providing that peace is to be maintained after this war by some form of police force. A number of them advocate simplifying the problem by having the policing done by three or four of the strongest United Nations.

Mr. Knox once expressed the view that Britain and America will police the world between them for one hundred years. One hundred years is a long time, and to most of us this is equivalent to advocating that a permanent world system be adopted based on Anglo-American policing. In discussing this, it is necessary to say that during the after-war period our two countries will probably be called upon to play a large role in keeping order in the world. We can look at this not as a privilege, but as a burden, one that our people will not wish to prolong during a hundred years.

We may as well face the fact that no American administration can make binding plans of this character. In our country we are given to drastic changes in public feeling, and we must recognize that any plan involving the use of American forces abroad is subject to change with changing circumstances. Both in America and in Britain there is an inevitable reaction after a war in the desire to get back to the pursuits of peace, to reduce military expenditures, and to take refuge in some degree of isolationism born of a sense of frustration in making a better world. While this is an excellent corrective for the forces of militarism, it may become a danger to long-range plans for the maintenance of order. We should not lose sight of this as bearing on hundred-year plans.

While the role of international policeman may well be thrust upon us and some other powers by events in such form that we cannot refuse it, we should not too readily accept the idea that we have some natural mandate for the function. As a people, we are conscious of the purity of our motives, and are rather prone to believe ourselves qualified to judge what would be good for others. But there is probably no nation more sensitive than we are to attempts by others to decide what is good for us, and we should be on our guard against our own tendencies.

PRIVATE MANUFACTURE OF ARMS

In the search for scapegoats after the last war, the makers of arms and munitions received a large popular vote. Public opinion felt the need for convenient villains, and the munitions makers took their place alongside the international bankers and diplomats who were denounced as warmongers with different motives.

There are defects in the private manufacture of arms and munitions, but there is also much nonsense talked on the subject. There have undoubtedly been abuses, but for the most part they have not been in the system of private manufacture but in the conditions under which it operated. It was bad in Germany, but there it was a tool of the government, and there are few people today who would maintain that the abuses would have been corrected by having Krupp's taken over by the Nazi Government. In France there was a deplorable situation. The country was undoubtedly victimized by a selfish group who systematically fostered war scares to keep up business in France and among her allies.

This being the case, a great many people went on to generalize and to denounce the whole industry in all countries as a threat to world peace. In our own country we had a senatorial investigation, with a great deal of sound and fury and a meager result in facts. Certain abuses were disclosed, it is true, but it is probable that similar abuses would have been disclosed if the foreign trade in washing machines or motorcycles had been approached with the same apostolic zeal and a readiness to read sinister significance into everything that was discovered.

It is always convenient to have a scapegoat ready to hand, and the view is widespread in our country that the threat of war could be reduced, if not done away with, by prohibiting the private manufacture of arms and limiting ourselves to what could be manufactured in government arsenals.

This sweeping solution is rather like burning down the house to roast the pig. This bringing into contempt of an entire industry has been a disastrous business for us. We have always tended to depend upon private facilities for manufacturing the arms we need, but if we make it a matter of moral turpitude to maintain these needed facilities, the nation is the chief sufferer.

There are several other ideas to be weighed: First, if private manufacture is to be done away with and we are to have an adequate national defense for the future, it will mean building up and maintaining even in time of peace a huge system of national arsenals to replace existing facilities. It will mean operating these arsenals as government agencies with a huge bureaucracy; it will mean taking away the competitive element which has helped to keep prices down and will lead to increased costs for everything we secure.

Second, as matters now stand there are many countries which depend for their arms and munitions on the manufacturing facilities of other countries—our own among them. If we suppress facilities for the private manufacture of arms in this country, we oblige a number of other countries, particularly in this hemisphere, to go in for building national arsenals and in order to meet some of the cost to go into competitive business of securing orders from abroad. The net result might very well be to create a huge competitive governmental industry backed with the power and influence of government in place of a private industry.

WORLD FEDERATION

Probably the most familiar form of simplification is that of federation, the purest form of which is a world federation of all nations.

Federation has its uses. There is no doubt that some regional federations are both desirable and useful. But the farther we go toward universal federation, the greater loom the problems to be solved before federation can work. This is not an argument in favor of discarding the idea. It is, however, to advocate discarding the emotional approach. It is to advocate getting away from the all-too-prevalent approach of reaching conclusions first and then resenting honest examination of the possibilities of success. Federation is not a matter of religious faith, to be accepted and defended against all unbelievers. It is a political expedient which in the most elementary prudence we should subject to critical scrutiny before adopting it. Either it is a common-sense, workable method that will bear up under scrutiny or it is no good for our purposes. If it is good in its universal form, we shall all want it. If it is unsuitable, what purpose is to be served by adopting it by acclamation?

As matters now stand, it is difficult to establish to everybody's satisfaction how far federation is desirable because the advocates of the extreme form do not take kindly to discussion. You will indeed be lucky if you emerge from a conversation on the subject without having somebody fire at you Tennyson's reference to "the Parliament of Man, the Federation of the World," as if there were no more to be said. And unless you want to be annoying, you will refrain from answering that a poetic aspiration is not necessarily a plan of action susceptible of immediate execution.

As a matter of fact, any form of federation is a serious matter. When you reach the broader form of an organization of countries separated geographically and, quite as important, differing in tradition and forms of government, the problems are multiplied. The advocates of world federation sometimes admit this but go on to say that the only easy solution is to include all the countries of the world under one government. That is a neat way of turning the conversation, but world federation is far more difficult than any less ambitious form.

For one thing, it is necessary to devise some form of world government that will be accepted by every country in the world —and accepted willingly, for otherwise there will be withdrawals and an end of world federations—or, alternately, wars to prevent secession.

The first problem is the amount of authority the world government is to exercise. Any such authority is composed of sovereignty surrendered by the member states—or "delegated," as the federationists say. That is a vital question and not one to be settled lightly. Among other things, it means surrendering or delegating to an international or supernational body the authority and power to discipline us if it considers we are in need of discipline. Before embarking on any such enterprise we should know how far it would take us and just who is to exercise the power.

If the world government is to be more than a central bureau for conciliation, it must have power to deal with such national matters as immigration, tariffs, and minority questions. How far are we disposed to accept regulation of such matters by a body in which we have a minority voice?

Many of the proposals involving surrender of sovereignty are defended in the name of liberalism. In reality, the fact that we seek to remodel the world according to our own blueprint by scrapping what we have won by such effort and sacrifice is not in itself proof of liberalism. A man can be just as generous in his desire to have America play her part in the world while wanting to be sure of what he is doing. He may want to satisfy himself whether we should surrender national sovereignty to some organization not yet devised or whether America can play her part more effectively by retaining some authority to back up what she believes in.

There is a final consideration to be borne in mind in discussing plans for a world government. We have yet to hear any important country express its readiness to enter such a federation. In fact we have heard Mr. Churchill and Marshal Stalin express themselves in terms that admit no prospect of surrendering any measure of national sovereignty.

We also have a tendency to simplify our own attitude in world affairs. Most Americans are convinced that a great part of the world's troubles arise from the practice of balance-of-power politics. To them this is a peculiarly European vice, and they are proud of the fact that we have never been tainted with it.

As a matter of fact, we have played our full part in the balance-of-power politics. We were glad to have France's support against Britain during the Revolutionary War. Not many years later we were considering changing sides on what seemed to us sensible grounds. In 1802 Jefferson wrote to Robert Livingston:

The day that France takes possession of New Orleans fixes the sentence which is to restrain her forever within her low-water mark. It seals the union of two nations who, in conjunction, can maintain exclusive possession of the ocean. From that moment we must marry ourselves to the British fleet and nation.

This situation was tided over by the Louisiana Purchase, but the problem presented itself again and again. When the Holy Alliance threatened intervention to secure the return of Spanish colonies, we met the threat with the Monroe Doctrine. Canning made his own declaration, but fundamentally it was an effective readjustment of the balance of power.

President Theodore Roosevelt brought about the Portsmouth Conference between Russia and Japan in order to avert a military victory that would upset the existing equilibrium. Again we came into the picture at the Algeciras Conference. After 1914 there could be no doubt that America determined the balance of power. The same is true of our entry into this war. In spite of the fact that we go into periodic retreat, we instinctively play the game of balance of power. We disguise it by talking of parallel action, by fighting as an associated power, but the results are the same as if we clearly wore the label.

There is no ground for simplifying things to the point of condemning all manifestations of balance of power. Whatever its results, it has more often than not been invoked to preserve the peace.

The Congress of Vienna, for instance, redrafted the map of Europe to establish such a balance that France would not set out on another career of conquest. To achieve this, violence was done to the new ideas of nationality and national rights. Races and provinces were no more than pawns in the game. But the fact remains that Europe was given a long period of peace. The balance of power served a purpose.

We must remember that the theory of the balance of power recognized the collective right of Europe to peace and freedom from aggression. It recognized a collective interest in preventing undue expansion by any nation. It is said that the system has not often been called into operation to prevent aggression. This is perhaps true, but it has a long record of successful resistance to aggression.

Military alliances are sometimes suggested as the one sure way to prevent aggression, defend our interests, and maintain world peace.

The history of military alliances gives us little ground for confidence that they can achieve these purposes or even contribute to them. On the contrary, they have consistently failed to produce peace. This failure is due to certain inherent defects in the system of alliances.

For one thing, a military alliance is never purely military. It invariably has a political objective. It commits the parties to future action in circumstances which cannot be foreseen. It follows that the parties tend to support the *status quo*, and in time such an effort is almost bound to lead to conflict. As the interests of nations change, any attempt to invoke the alliance for the preservation of the *status quo* leads to misunderstanding and distrust. There is no safeguard against this, no way of ensuring that military treaties shall continue to apply regardless of changes. There is, unfortunately, nothing miraculous about them. They last just as long as the common interest or the common fear that inspired them.

Another drawback is that an alliance is likely to arouse fear among non-signatories. The result is counteralliance which, although aimed at creating security, is more likely to lead to conflict.

This trend toward counteralliance leads to rearmament on a competitive basis. Rearmament, caused by fear, leads to increased armaments and increased fears. The system of European alliances after the last world war created unrest and turned the continent into an armed camp.

In considering proposals for military alliances in our time we should not overlook the fact that they are incompatible with the whole spirit of our various charters and declarations with their promise of a world where there will be no need to seek security in military alliances and power politics. If the Great Powers set the example of reverting to the old and supposedly outmoded system of military alliances, how can we expect other nations to pursue a more enlightened course? They will inevitably rush back to the old system of alliances, groupings of satellites, and economic barriers. If the world once slips back into this state, the hopes of better world understanding will be slight indeed.

This series of illustrations might be extended indefinitely, but these will serve to show that no single proposal can avert conflicts and assure good international relations. Each of them has perhaps some element of value, but we are forced to the conclusion that there is no substitute for the laborious workings of diplomacy seeking to derive benefit from all possible methods.

To scrutinize all these generous schemes is not cynical or destructive. For so long as we continue to believe in miracles, to pin our hopes to paper plans—so long as this goes on we shall not get down to brass tacks, all of us together, and concentrate on methods that will work. We must clear the ground before we can build the edifice.

We should approach all proposals in the desire to find what is good in them, and measure them against the experience of history. The very limitations and defects of some of these plans have their value in indicating where we can work with better hope of success.

It should be clear that there is no easy, simple way to secure the blessings of world-wide peace and justice. It does not follow that we must throw up our hands in despair. It does follow that we must seriously set about finding what can be done. The search is not a contest that can be won on points, and we are likely to get further faster if we turn our efforts toward collaboration—collaboration among ourselves at home and with other nations wherever we can find good will and reciprocity.

The best hope of the world today lies in building up international collaboration and the confidence that can grow only from the knowledge that collaboration gets better results than can be gained through sharp practice and force.

There is one lesson to be learned from the proposals for military alliances. It is advocated nowadays that we conclude alliances with Britain, or with Britain and Soviet Russia, or even with Britain and Soviet Russia and China. The fundamental purpose of these proposals is to ensure effective co-operation between the signatories to prevent aggression and maintain peace and order in the world. No one in his senses can disagree with this objective, but we may question whether it can be achieved through military alliances. If not, how can we hope to achieve it? If the will to collaborate exists, there is no need of signed documents. Unless it exists, no document will serve. A common course of action, based on community of interest, has all the advantages sought in a treaty of alliance, and is free of the disadvantage of provoking hostile combinations and counteralliances.

Despite all the talk we hear about the equality of states, the fact remains that the strongest powers are going to play a leading role in keeping order in the world. This in itself is no infringement of the equality of states; these powers, having the necessary force and resources, are alone able to assume this responsibility. It is to be hoped that they can operate together fairly and effectively, and if they have the will to do this an alliance is superfluous.

Collaboration must be spontaneous. It cannot be imposed unilaterally or on a world-wide scale. It manifests itself in operation, not in signed promises, charters, and declarations. We shall probably get the best results by concentrating on co-operation with those governments which manifest a real readiness to co-operate with us. It is obviously desirable that the United States, Great Britain, and Soviet Russia work together in good understanding. What the prospects are can be judged only by performance. Recently Russia has unfortunately shown a tendency to settle things by herself without consultation with her Allies. It is to be hoped she will realize that she has more to gain by collaboration, and if she does, she should be welcomed in recognition of what it means to our civilization for her to throw her weight into the scales on the side of order and justice. We cannot, however, ignore the possibility that she may prefer to go her own way, to make unilateral settlements and trust to her strong right arm. If Russia should choose this course, it would become all the more important that the other two Great Powers develop the most effective collaboration, for the burden they have to bear will be all the greater.

Our own will to collaboration is there. At present, however, we are not equipped for it on a long-range scale. That can be remedied as we develop a foreign policy, and then we should be able to play a far greater part in world affairs.

We shall doubtless hear protests against too close association with Britain. There is no valid argument against close association with anybody if it is for the purposes envisaged by us. We hear that the British always get the better of us, that they are always out for their own interests. It is true they always have an eye for their own interests and that they put up a good struggle to get their own way. Why shouldn't they? There is something unsportsmanlike in grumbling about this. The sensible course would be to put up as good a show of looking after our own interests, for even in collaboration there is need for constant adjustment. Those who complain that the British always get the better of us do not always offer proof. As a matter of fact, we seem to have had our own way a reasonable part of the time. On some occasions when the British have had their own way it is not difficult to discern that this was because they knew clearly what they wanted, they prepared themselves adequately for the negotiations, and then stuck to essentials. We are not always as clear cut in our views and as thorough in our preparation. If we accept the idea that the British always get the better of us, we seem to accept also the idea that we are hopelessly incompetent. In that case we should perhaps withdraw from the world. The self-respecting course would be to equip ourselves with the best possible diplomacy, make up our minds as to what we want by building a foreign policy, and then sit down and negotiate with the British on equal terms. It may even be assumed that they would welcome such an improvement in our methods, for we should be infinitely more useful partners in the great enterprises we shall probably share.

CHAPTER IX

Infatuations and Antipathies

THERE is a staggering lot to be done before we can embark upon a well-balanced course of defending our own interests and, at the same time, play a worthy role in world affairs.

We must devise a method for formulating policy.

We must find a way—and it can be found—for the Senate to play a positive and constructive role in foreign affairs.

We must rid ourselves of irresponsible and incompetent amateur diplomacy and put in its place a trained diplomacy that knows what it is all about.

We must put a stop to free-lance activities of many government agencies in the foreign field and establish a unified command.

We must free ourselves of legalistic diplomacy.

But the most important task ahead of us is to straighten out our national thinking. Lack of an informed public opinion is a major obstacle to intelligent conduct of foreign affairs, and we shall never achieve that public opinion until we first become conscious of some national weaknesses and then free ourselves of them.

We have a weakness for classifying nations and governments according to our likes and dislikes of the moment. This is so instinctive that we have little or no embarrassment in doing an about-face as our feelings shift with events.

If we are infatuated with another country, we are not content to approve it as it is. In order to justify our adoration, we remodel it in our own image. The process is simple. If we do not care for a government, we often dispose of it as being fascist. If we like it, it is a democracy just as we are. In fact, it is so simple that there is no such thing as all totalitarian governments being bad. Some of them are stalwart fighters for the right—that is, if they happen to be fighting on our side.

Washington's Farewell Address is a mine of wisdom on the dangers of this weakness.

. . . Observe good faith and justice towards all nations . . . nothing is more essential than that permanent, inveterate antipathies against particular nations, and passionate attachments for others, should be excluded; and that in place of them, just and amicable feelings towards all should be cultivated. The nation, which indulges towards another an habitual hatred, or an habitual fondness, is in some degree a slave. It is a slave to its animosity or to its affection, either of which is sufficient to lead it astray from its duty and its interest. . . . The nation, prompted by ill-will and resentment, sometimes impels to war the government, contrary to the best calculations of policy. The government sometimes participates in the national propensity, and adopts through passion what reason would reject. . . . The peace often, and sometimes, perhaps, the liberty of nations, has been the victim.

So, likewise, a passionate attachment of one nation for another produces a variety of evils. Sympathy for the favorite nation facilitating the illusion of an imaginary common interest in cases where no real common interest exists, and infusing into one the enmities of the other, betrays the former into a participation in the quarrels and wars of the latter, without adequate inducement or justification. . . .

The entire section of the Address bearing upon foreign affairs should be read and pondered by every American.

If we form an attachment for a country, it does not matter if it lays no claim to democracy. Russia, for instance, is hailed as a great democracy and for a time anyone who raised a question on the subject was denounced as a fascist intent on disrupting allied unity. In the last war we managed to fight the common enemy without hailing the Czar as a reincarnation of Thomas Jefferson. But in this war it has been different. And we have persisted in our point of view even if the Soviet Government disagreed with us. Stalin came out not so long ago with the forthright statement:

It would be laughable to deny the difference in ideology and social structure of the various states comprising the Anglo-Soviet-American coalition.

Nevertheless, whether he likes it or not, we insist on classifying him as a democrat.

Russia has pursued a consistent course. Our own has been less consistent. Only a few years years ago Russia attacked Finland, an orderly democracy commanding our respect and esteem. American public opinion was revolted. The President unlimbered his heaviest guns to denounce Soviet aggression. In doing so he justifiably claimed to speak for the whole American people.

Without warning Russia was plunged into the war and was found fighting on the side of the angels. She did not force her way into the conflict to support the Atlantic Charter and the Four Freedoms. But she was fighting on our side, and instead of being content with her gallant defense against the common enemy, which was enough for practical purposes, we insisted on revising our views. The mists rolled away and we discovered that Finland was a Fascist country, while Russia was a great religious democracy.

Having found the Russian Government good and democratic and religious, we push on a step further to accepting it as perfect. No, only right—infallible.

This sort of thing is deplorable for us and for Russia too. She lays no claim to heavenly perfection—in fact, she openly proclaims her intention of mopping up some of our associates in the war and embarking on a career of imperialism. Even the Moscow Declaration does not go so far as explicitly to disown such designs. One day we may be shocked and outraged when Russia does the very things she has been announcing for all to hear. In fact, some of us are shocked now.

Infatuations blind us not only in our dealings with the object of our affections but with others as well. As Russia can do no wrong, we are hard put to it to explain some things that are happening—her freely proclaimed aggression against Poland, for instance. But we make a gallant effort. Our way of doing it reveals a curious American weakness in that many of us, instead of examining the question on its merits and reaching our own conclusions, tackle it from the point of view of either Russia or Poland. There are two predominant trends of thought:

1. To espouse the Polish cause and demand that Polish integrity be respected.

2. To side with Russia and demand that Poland be sold down the river.

There is nothing very mature about either of these demands. The first is no more than an expression with nothing to back it up. The second is urging that we give the green light to the aggressor and cheerfully acquiesce in the scrapping of the Atlantic Charter and the Moscow Declaration.

There is another possible approach, from the American instead of the Russian or Polish point of view, which might lead to sounder conclusions:

1. To determine what solution would be just and desirable.

2. To consider what means are at our disposal, moral, material, and diplomatic, for contributing to a just solution.

3. To proceed from there to achieve as much of (1) as (2) permits.

There is nothing well considered in the present approach. On one side we hear demands for "support" of Poland, regardless of the means at our disposal. On the other are those who, not content with abandoning Poland to her fate, want the luxury of doing it on high moral grounds. It may very well prove that there is nothing we can do to protect Poland against unilateral action by the Soviet Government. But it does not necessarily follow that we must approve or even acquiesce, thereby renouncing all our principles. By doing so we stultify ourselves and scrap all our fine professions of the Atlantic Charter and the Moscow and Teheran declarations.

The present attitude of some people is reminiscent of Disraeli's remark when he said in a moment of exasperation that he did not so much mind Gladstone having the ace of spades up his sleeve, but that he did object to his pretending that it was God Almighty who had put it there.

We should be on more even keel if we took Russia as she is, thankful for the military role she is playing in the war, and directed our energies toward plans for getting along with her when the common military purpose is achieved.

There might be something to be said for infatuations if they were reciprocal. But so often we are doomed to unrequited love. Take our present passionate attachment for Soviet Russia. Our whole attitude, both government and people, is "you-great-big-wonderful-boy." Everything Russia does is right. We must not criticize. In fact, we must not even comment—unless undiscriminating praise is to be considered as comment. We can criticize the British. We can hold meetings and make speeches dismantling their empire in the midst of war. But nothing of that sort for our great-big-wonderful-boy-friend. It is a touching attachment. But is it reciprocated? It is not. Does Stalin call in the press and tell them we are a superior country, proving it with references to the American Constitution? We haven't noticed it. Does he encourage mass meetings of Soviet-American Friendship like those held in New York? They have never been reported in the press. Just how does he manifest his infatuation for us, aside from unpleasant articles attacking us for the lack of a second front and the insufficiency of Lend Lease?

But perhaps after all that in itself is the answer to the enigma. Perhaps we are the clinging-vine type of nation. Stalin is the international cave man, and the more he knocks us about the more we love him. Perhaps if he were to express admiration and approval we should turn our affections elsewhere.

For instance, if Mr. Churchill were to get really tough we might form an attachment for him. True, he did shake his finger at our reformers and say he did not propose to liquidate the British Empire. But he must do much worse than that. He might begin by criticizing our war contribution and sneer at Lend Lease and the effort of private-relief organizations. Then we might witness the dawn of a great passion. At last we should perceive Mr. Churchill as a man after our own heart.

This liking for being rebuffed is found only in our country. And the really clever statesmen understand and give us what we want. Even gentle Madame Chiang Kai-shek—for she, too, is a statesman—gave us a course of lectures on our shortcomings—that is to say, wherein we failed to do our full duty by China. And we reveled in it and thought her charming for pointing out our misdeeds. In fact, we were so under her charm that it apparently never occurred to anyone to rise up in the audience and make the obvious remark that nobody in the world could criticize this country with less grace than a Chinese guest of our government —that if at any time in the last ten years we had been willing to let China down we could have made a deal with Japan. It is quite possible we could have made a deal that would have avoided the present war in the Pacific at a considerable saving of American lives.

But by some peculiar reasoning we could not say anything of the sort without being denounced on every hand for disrupting allied unity. So nobody did say anything of the sort. Instead, we accepted all her reproaches and cheered her to the echo for her courage and frankness. One of our national magazines went into ecstasies over the fact that she had carried her differences with the President direct to Congress and the people and that she "tangled with the President to his cost." That was not disrupting allied unity.

There ought to be some recognized superiority to authorize somebody from another country to instruct us in this way. Is it that Madame Chiang represents a more enlightened democracy than our own and can thus adopt an older-sister attitude? This is not strikingly apparent. We fail to see some of the familiar forms of democratic government in China. Is there a Chinese constitution? Is there a Chinese parliament? Have there ever been any Chinese elections? Was the Generalissimo himself chosen by the Chinese people?

This is not to suggest any reproach because China has not adopted our form of government. We have always got along in the same world with governments of many kinds, and it is probable that we shall have to continue to do so. But it is a reproach that we delude ourselves as to the character of the governments we have to deal with. For if we persist in these delusions the day will come when they fail to react as we do and as we expect them to do. When that is brought home to us we shall be quite unreasonably outraged and our infatuation will give way to bitter disillusionment.

Stalin can criticize us for not producing a second front or for not sending enough supplies or almost anything else, and nobody suggests that that disrupts allied unity. It is only refreshing frankness.

But if anybody asks—not complains, mind you, but asks—why Stalin won't provide a second front against Japan or why he won't wait until the end of the war, like the rest of us, to settle his frontier disputes, as prescribed in the joint declarations he has signed with us, there we are at it again, disrupting allied unity.

This, of course, is merely an illustration, for nobody *would* say anything of the sort. You don't ask questions of the cave man.

This infatuation of ours for Soviet Russia is a serious obstacle to a wise approach to our problems. It is fostered by those clamoring for collaboration with Russia. But the clamor is for collaboration with Russia rather than for collaboration between Russia and the United States, which is an entirely different conception. The latter is vitally important, and we should bend all our efforts to achieve it. A necessary preliminary is to free ourselves of our infatuation and look at this problem of collaboration as it really is.

The problem is usually presented as the need to strengthen American help and support for Russia. It is rarely if ever in terms of Russian collaboration with us, and any attempt to discuss that aspect is denounced with the familiar phrase about disrupting allied unity. Even superficial knowledge of the facts suffices to show the extent of American collaboration accorded to Russia and the good will with which it was given. Our contribution is there to see, together with the will to extend its scope generously so far as there is any reasonable reciprocity. As matters now stand the Russian share of collaboration is of a curious character. When it suits her purposes, Russia insists on participating in matters of common concern. Otherwise she insists, with equal firmness, on handling things her own way and rebuffs any suggestion of common action.

The present situation is rather painfully reminiscent of the old story told by the Two Black Crows. One of them had a load of hay but no horse; his friend had a horse but no hay. His friend was a believer in collaboration and allowed his horse to eat the hay—"And now we got reciprocity."

Hanson W. Baldwin gave the picture clearly in the New York *Times* of March 8, 1944, as follows:

Russia plainly holds many of the cards in Europe and is playing them aggressively. She has demanded, on the one hand, a voice in the affairs of Western Europe; she is represented on the Allied Advisory Council (concerning Italian affairs); she is accredited to General Charles de Gaulle's Government; she is represented on the Three-Power European Advisory Commission in London.

But she refuses similar representation to Britain and the United

States in Eastern Europe; she apparently insists upon multilateral settlements of problems in Western Europe but unilateral settlement—her own—of affairs in Eastern Europe. And her great cards are military power, international communism used to forward Russia's national ends, and pan-Slavism.

If we can face these facts, we may have an end to our unreasoning infatuation without impairing our desire to co-operate with Soviet Russia. But we should clarify our own minds not only as to the precise nature of the Russian attitude but also as to its implications. It now looks as if Russia were embarking on a policy of regionalism and spheres of influence. General Smuts intimated in his speech of last November that such a trend would force Britain into building her own spheres of influence. If this does develop, we are back in the welter of power politics, and just where does that leave the United States? We do not meet the situation by clamoring for more collaboration with Russia. We meet it by formulating a clear conception of our own national interest and then, whatever that may be, collaborating with Russia so far as she manifests a desire to collaborate with us.

Infatuations for other countries are dangerous, but there is an equally obvious danger in the antipathies we develop and the way we express them. If another country adopts an attitude we disapprove, we put it on the black list. Any country that does not follow along with us is in for an expression of our displeasure. There are bound to be demands that it be disciplined.

This tends to overlook the fact that other countries are no more obligated to conform to our wishes than we are obligated to conform to theirs. Within certain limits they have a right to follow the course that seems best to them. Sometimes it may be possible to persuade them to reconsider and go along with us, but this is rarely if ever achieved by pillorying them as enemies of democracy. That is the one course that makes it difficult for them to mend their ways.

Worst of all is the cultivation of hatred for whole nations, for that is clearly calculated to obscure our vision in dealing with them, perhaps as greatly to our disadvantage as to theirs. This does not imply ignoring the evil they have done or condoning it. It does imply dealing with them with our intelligence, rather than with our emotion. For those who protest that this is the one sure way to let the evildoer off scot-free, it may be answered that history does not always bear out their contention. We need look no farther back than the Treaty of Versailles. The allied leaders were coerced by an angry public opinion clamoring for punishment of the defeated enemy. To satisfy these demands, they imposed what were supposed to be punitive terms. These were so ill considered as to be inapplicable, and it was not long before Germany had wriggled out of many of them. If there had been a cooler approach, more practical terms might well have been imposed, conceived not with a view to satisfying momentary clamor, but to devise measures that could be enforced. If this course had been followed, Germany might have paid far more adequately than under the emotional terms that could not be enforced.

We shall be faced with this problem again and in even more acute form at the end of the present war. It will be rendered more difficult by the number of countries involved, by the clash of ideologies, by the weakening of military discipline and governmental ties, by widespread disintegration, famine, pestilence, and chaos and, above all, by the infamous behavior of the enemy. In spite of all this, our governments may be able to do a better job of peacemaking, but only if supported rather than hampered by public opinion.

We cannot expect our representatives to make a good job of it if we send them to the peace table with no support beyond starry-eyed aspirations and vindictive emotions; if after giving three rousing cheers for peace we hamstring their efforts by clamoring for punishment and revenge. That way lies disaster. To see how true this is, we can recall what happened at Versailles.

President Wilson was bent on a peace of reason and laid down a program which was largely accepted as a basis for the work of the Peace Conference. The statesmen who had conducted the war realized that if our civilization were to be saved there must be a peace founded on some degree of moderation.

President Wilson's aims were loudly cheered at home and abroad as representing the people's hopes and aspirations for a better world. But by the time he settled down to negotiate their application, their support was conspicuous by its absence. We are told he was thwarted and defeated by a handful of cynical politicians. That is not an accurate statement of the facts. The little group of men who made the peace were not free agents. They were borne along by powerful forces they could not control.

Mr. Lloyd George set out to get a reasonable peace—securing in the process some of the things he wanted, but still arriving at a reasonable settlement. But it was not long before he was assailed by public clamor for punishment and revenge—clamor from the same people who had cheered Mr. Wilson's aims. Mr. Lloyd George had a difficult choice—either to ignore this emotional clamor, knowing he would be turned out of office and could have no hand in making the peace, or to change his course enough to stay in office in the hope of being able to accomplish something. He chose the second course—and who can sit in judgment on him? He won his "khaki" election on promises to hang the Kaiser and make the Germans pay to the last farthing. So, when he came to the Conference, he was already a prisoner of the forces he had sought to conciliate.

Clemenceau could hardly be accused of being a sentimentalist, but his practical mind was not closed to all the dictates of reason until he, too, heard the mob clamoring for revenge. He was faced with the same alternatives as Lloyd George—and he made the same choice. He remained in office only on a fervid pledge to be ruthless, to deal with Germany once and for all time. Every allied country was equally clamorous for punishment and shared in responsibility for the result.

History shows what these men and their associates did to Mr. Wilson's program—a program which, if adopted, would have given us a better chance at least of lasting peace.

Yet it is too simple and easy to blame the bad peace on these individuals, just as it is too simple to blame the war on any one man. But it is undoubtedly a more popular explanation than to accept the blame and charge it to our own stupidity.

The real blame lay on the people themselves, or, to put it more tactfully, on the lack of an informed public opinion. The peace was not consciously sabotaged by the people. They wanted a good peace, most of them something substantially like the Wilson peace they had cheered so lustily. But after four years of nervous tension and suffering and anxiety they also felt a human desire to lash out at the cause of all their troubles. They did not stop to realize that they could not have a peace of reason and justice and at the same time gratify their yearnings for revenge. In other words, there was no informed public opinion to guide and support the peacemakers. On the contrary, there was clamorous public emotion which did effectively sabotage the efforts of the peacemakers.

Our troubles are sometimes aggravated by the fact that large and well-organized racial minorities create a problem for America that does not exist for other countries. In most European countries such minorities have two courses open to them: Either they are extremely circumspect in their actions and utterances, or they are in active revolt against the government and take the consequences. In our country we have gone very far in tolerating political activity by these groups. They are not even tempted to rise in revolt against the government because it is so much easier to gang up on the government and bulldoze it. The result is that the foreign minorities are far better organized than the American majority and they have far more than their share to say in the conduct of our affairs. Sometimes our decisions are dictated not by American but by foreign interests.

This calls for careful thought, for it is an aggravation of some of the evils foreseen by Washington in his Farewell Address. He foresaw the danger of American interests being subordinated to American sympathies for foreign countries. He did not foresee the danger that foreign groups would determine our national action by intimidating or infiltrating our government.

Uncontrolled emotion wrecked the last peace and left the door open for the present war. But the dangers of hate and revenge apply all the time, and it is our interest to give short shrift to the preachers of hate.

We, as a race, are not inclined to lasting hate or revenge. But in time of war the preachers of hate raise up their voices and give tongue.

The Fundamentalists go all out for *extermination.* Nothing less. If we want to have peace in the world we must eliminate the cause of war. Germany, Italy, and Japan are responsible. They should be wiped out to the last man, woman, and child. And then there will be peace. Q.E.D.

There is also a group which is hard to distinguish from an American form of nazism. These people advocate not only extermination but the systematic teaching of hate to our people. They tell us we do not hate our enemies enough and that we shall not fight with all that is in us unless we are inflamed with hate for every German, Italian, and Japanese, unless we yearn to kill and to see blood.

This is as good a time as any to analyze these schools of thought with a view to determining how far they contribute to the making of a wise peace.

Of course we must admit that if we could kill all the people in the world we dislike it would be a solution of a number of problems—including overpopulation. But we choose such big countries to exterminate.

It is not workmanlike to plan for the brotherhood of man and at the same time for the destruction of certain races. Either presents a point of view, but we cannot have both.

There remains one problem to be considered. Although we are consistent and above criticism in our attitude toward other countries, the fact remains that over a given period of time we come to detest most of them in turn.

Another thing we must bear in mind is that we are not conspicuously constant in our likes or dislikes. Let's avoid being personal about it, but we all know countries we were emotionally enthusiastic about not so long ago who fell deep into our disfavor. Others we distrusted and disliked, and today we are starry eyed about them and their motives, ready to swear eternal friendship, and go through life together hand in hand with them.

Once we have exterminated the Germans, Italians, and Japanese are we to abandon the weapon of extermination for all time? Or, having found it good, are we going to keep it polished and in hand for use against future evildoers? And on what footing would that leave us with the rest of the world?

Before we adopt the policy of extermination we ought to make sure that a large enough part of our people believe in it to make it work. What a humiliation if we announced a policy of extermination and events proved that our people were such sissies they would not see it through!

We ought to begin with the advocates of this super-totalitarian ruthlessness and require them to make good as leaders in the great work of purification—not to be confused with similar purification enterprises conducted by Adolf Hitler and his associates.

The first test would be to line up a lot of men, women, and children of enemy nationality, hand a tommy gun to the exterminator, and tell him to go to work. There is no cause for alarm. Your exterminator has not expected to be taken so literally and will probably be more annoyed with you than with those for whose blood he was bellowing.

Put it in another way. Let us say there are some 80,000,000 Germans, 60,000,000 Japanese, and 40,000,000 Italians. Suppose we take one million of each—a mere sample—and instruct the Army to shoot them as a first installment. Even if the Army went at this with a right good will, how long would it be before the American people would clamor for the slaughter to cease? However fierce we may become conversationally in time of war, we have not yet sunk to the level of exterminating whole peoples.

Extermination is like some other things you either have or haven't. It may have its dangers, but there are perhaps greater dangers in starting it and then leaving the job unfinished. That leaves a people filled with yearning for revenge and ready to subordinate everything in life to achieving it.

We may question whether it is an exaggeration to say that today Hitler's greatest hold on the German people is to be found in their belief that they can expect no mercy from us; that if they are to avoid not only humiliation but blood and massacre they have only one chance—to fight desperately to the last ditch. This being Hitler's greatest argument, it is obviously our interest and our purpose to take it away from him.

And those who work systematically to strengthen this German fear come pretty close to winning themselves the glittering title of Collaborationist they have conferred so generously on others.

The justification of the Haters is that through inflaming our blood lust we shall more quickly bring the war to a victorious conclusion.

As a matter of fact, such a policy is better calculated to prolong the war. It is equivalent to serving notice on the German people that we are building for a peace of revenge. The only conclusion open to them is that our hate will still be burning fiercely at the end of the war and will manifest itself in sadistic measures of revenge. If they can be made to believe that they are going to be slaughtered in defeat, they will obviously sell their lives as dearly as they can and die on the battlefield in a last desperate stand.

It is pointed out to us what a fine driving force hate is and how effective it has been in the case of the Germans. That is a fine *non sequitur*. In all fairness, we must admit the Nazis had a reason, and a good one, for indoctrinating their people with hate.

They had nothing better to offer.

They could not very well appeal to their people to fight for the preservation of personal liberty, or freedom of conscience, or love of peace; they could not appeal for love of the blessings we enjoy. These are dangerous ideas tyrants do not like. They could hardly be expected to start their people thinking about such things. So they reverted to the oldest resort of the demagogue and sought to unite their people through hate and fear— fear of evil nations banded against them, and hate that flows from fear.

Those who advocate imitation or adoption of Nazi methods talk about how well they have worked so far. But before we pay Hitler the compliment of imitating him we would do well to consider how his methods will work when things are not going well.

There was an effort to indoctrinate the German people with hate in the last war. They had it cleverly mixed with fear. They were being encircled. The Great Powers were intent on their destruction. The government provided them with a mania of persecution. They were given a Hymn of Hate.

And the fires of hate burned fiercely in the days of military success while the Germans were trampling roughshod on their enemies. But what happened under the strains and stresses of military reverses and food shortage and cold?

Hate alone was not enough to keep them going. The shot in the arm died on them and they collapsed.

In this war they have reverted to the old methods. Hate is being used to whip them up to fight and sacrifice. And fear of those they hate is invoked to make them hold out.

But what of the future?

Isn't it probable that the day will come when disillusion will open their eyes to the fact that they have nothing to fight for? And that is the beginning of defeat—as it was in the last war.

We claim to be a Christian nation. It is hard to see how we can reconcile our Christian professions with the preaching of hatred and extermination. If our professions are sincere, we should be able to adhere to them regardless of temporal advantages. But in this case it does not require much insight to grasp that hate is just as wrong from the political as from the moral point of view.

There is yet another argument against a policy of hate. It is as dangerous to us as to the other fellow. Not on rarefied ethical grounds, but from intelligent self-interest. No man inflamed with blind hate and blood lust possesses the clear judgment and vision to make a wise and farsighted deal with the man he hates. If, on the other hand, he leaves his enemy a monopoly of these feelings, he is at a distinct advantage when the time comes for a settlement.

And the same is true for nations as well.

One of the chief arguments for hate is that the American people cannot fight with all their souls unless influenced with blood lust.

Of course this may be true, but most Americans have labored under the delusion that throughout our history we've fought pretty well without being jazzed up with emotional hashish. Perhaps all our galaxy of so-called heroes never knew how to fight.

It may be that we would fight better if we hated.

But who says so, and on what authority?

We are not all convinced by the fire-breathing people who are promoting hate—convinced that what they say is based on knowledge of what it takes to make men fight.

I have known some respectable and successful fighters in my time—among them Joffre, Foch, Pilsudski, and Pershing—and never heard one of them demanding that the civil population be inflamed to hate. On the contrary, there is little talk of hate at the fighting front. This sentiment usually increases in ferocity in direct ratio to the distance from the firing line.

One of the Apostles of Hate in a recent discussion is reported to have asked a question to which he thought there was no answer—"If we don't teach our people hate, what other incentive can we offer them to make them fight and sacrifice?"

That one is not difficult to answer. And it doesn't seem so difficult as to escape the ordinary American. Most of us can't help feeling that we have the best possible incentive to fight and to make every sacrifice—the preservation of our country and our freedom. We are fighting to preserve for ourselves and our children the precious rights for which we have often fought before —political freedom, religious liberty, freedom of thought and expression, and that host of other freedoms we are prone to take for granted until they are threatened.

Of course if we have lost our devotion to these precious things, we may have to adopt Hitler's methods as a shot in the arm to keep us going during the emergency. But unless we have undergone a deterioration, we have just the incentive we need—and a better one than Hitler offers his people—for it is precisely in days of adversity that we are driven to the greatest effort to preserve these precious freedoms of ours.

Any argument against hatred and revenge is likely to be distorted as a plea for letting the enemy off scot-free, in fact helping him to his feet so that he can prepare another attack upon us. There is no justification for this. We must, as a matter of elementary common sense, bear clearly in mind what the enemy has done and take all possible precautions to see that he does not do it again. This involves neither forgiving nor forgetting, but it does mean concentrating on our objectives. If we clarify our thinking on this subject, we will realize that our interests will be best served by intelligent political action, and that both hate and revenge should be relegated to the limbo of discredited political forces.

CHAPTER X

The Department of State

THE DEPARTMENT OF STATE has long been the target for free-and-easy criticism. Recently this criticism has become constant and sometimes shrill. The department is held accountable for almost everything that goes wrong in the world. Altogether we are given a picture of utter incompetence, indecision, and ineptitude. We are told that the department resolutely refuses to look ahead and never faces up to a problem until it has reached a critical stage. Alternatively the department has been criticized for *laissez faire*, consisting of bringing matters to a head and then letting them take care of themselves. In fact, it is open season for anything in the way of criticism or abuse.

There is no denying the existence of evils in crying need of correction. The men in the department were openly critical long before the press and radio joined in the chorus, and they would be the first to welcome needed reforms. But if we deal with realities it soon becomes clear that, disregarding current weaknesses of departmental organization, the worst evils are due to causes outside the control of the Department of State. Tinkering with departmental machinery will not remedy fundamental defects.

To get down to brass tacks, the evil is that under our system the department is unable to perform its essential mission. By any sane standard that mission is to look ahead, foresee developments, and plan for the future. Under existing conditions this cannot be done because there are no facilities for determining in advance what course the department can take.

Much popular discussion appears to be based on the assumption that if the Secretary of State approves an idea it thereby becomes a matter of national policy. There is more to it than that. The Department of State cannot determine policy by itself for the reason that policy and diplomacy are, in large measure, determined and put into operation outside its own halls. In fact, policy operates largely through the interlocking action of all the important agencies of the government, each with its own force and resources.

To take an obvious illustration, let us assume an outbreak or disorder abroad which constitutes a threat to American lives and property. The course we should take may be clear to the Department of State, but the possibility of taking it may be entirely contingent on the availability of adequate naval forces. The Secretary of State cannot decide what to do until he learns whether the Navy can give him necessary support. It may be that, for lack of previous consultation, the Navy does not have adequate forces at hand. In such a case the action of our country will be determined, not by the wishes of the Secretary of State or the Secretary of the Navy, but by our lack of equipment at the right place.

At each step the Secretary of State must secure help or at least counsel from other departments. He must also justify himself to Congress—if only to prepare for the future in the hope of securing later ratification of his actions.

Above all, he must try to keep himself square with the country, and, as we have no recognized policy as a yardstick for public opinion, he must do it step by step. In other words, he is judged not on policy but on the handling of current business.

All this adds up to the fact that the Secretary of State has a minimum of elements for securing needed help and approval as he goes along—a maximum of difficulties making for delay and confusion and obstruction.

Some will dismiss this with the statement that the President handles foreign affairs himself and that there is no difficulty in his securing co-operation among government departments. This overlooks the fact that whoever exercises authority and orders co-operation, the details of that co-operation must be worked out by somebody. It does not set to work in all its carefully considered details just because the President says: "Let there be co-operation!" Whoever handles our foreign affairs, we shall continue to labor under great disadvantages so long as we lack machinery for continuing consultation and co-operation. In our anxiety to achieve this in the international field we should not forget how much is still unaccomplished in Washington.

We hear a great deal of glib talk about our naval and military policy, the foreign policy of Mr. Morgenthau and Mr. Wallace and Mr. Jesse Jones, and even a lot of minor officials. This leads to a deal of confusion and conflict. The War and Navy departments cannot have policies of their own. They can have a part in a national policy, when we have one. These different departments are not maintained to carry out independent policies.

Theoretically, at least, the Treasury Department is not supposed to have a foreign fiscal policy of its own. Nor the Department of Commerce a foreign trade policy of its own. Nor the Interior Department a policy on Arabian oil. All these and many other organizations are no more than instruments of foreign policy so far as they participate in foreign affairs—for some of them, indeed, foreign affairs ought to call for only a minor part of their activity. If we know anything about the mechanics of government, when we speak of foreign policy we do not mean a free-for-all with departments and alphabeticals charging into the foreign field, every man for himself and the devil take the one responsible authority. We mean a national policy directed by the one responsible authority—the Department of State, with other government organizations contributing what they can to make the policy successful.

The War and Navy departments are clear-cut examples of what ought to be. Neither of them can conceivably have a foreign policy of its own. They exist solely as instruments of national policy. They have no other function. They cannot go into operation unless and until they are called upon to do so as a result of developments in our relations with other countries. They cannot even determine intelligently what they need as equipment, save in the light of knowledge from other quarters of what they are expected to be ready to do. Their part in policy must be determined by others.

Some of our new alphabeticals have gone all out on little individual foreign policies of their own. They have flooded other countries with money and employees, and have gone in for all sorts of enterprises in complete disregard of their effect on our national interests.

The effects of this may in time bring home to us the obvious fact that there must be some one final authority in foreign affairs, some authority that passes on plans before they are put into effect. Otherwise we must be prepared for chaos—sometimes we get a glimpse of it nowadays.

To put it flatly we cannot decide how big a navy or what sort of ships we need until we know what the Navy is expected to do. In other words, until we have drawn up a complete policy with a clear idea of the mission of every government agency. This lack of policy is unfair to the Army and Navy. Under normal conditions (that is, in time of peace) they are reduced to what might be described as living by their wits. They never know what they may be called upon to do, so they try to get all they can from Congress—and they have heavy sledding in times of peace. They should not be reduced to the indignity—they and other government agencies—of being obliged to go begging, hat in hand. Under our normal peacetime conditions the Army and Navy have no choice. They must have the tools to do their work, and if these tools can be secured only by stunts and publicity, however distasteful, our fighting men would be remiss if they did not do whatever was necessary to secure appropriations. In doing this, they constantly run foul of high-minded opposition, maintaining that if they are granted funds and men and guns they will not be able to resist the temptation to play with their new toys and start a war. Fundamentally, this is no less than an assumption that the Army and Navy have their own policies and are free to start wars whenever they like.

Those with a large acquaintance among responsible army and navy men are hard put to it to point out any who yearn for war. The critics say the yearning for war is based on selfish personal ambition for glory and promotion. Perhaps to the critics war seems to be made up exclusively of glory and promotion. Strangely enough, it does not look that way to professional soldiers. They know, better perhaps than their critics, the real nature of war, with its dirt and suffering, its maimed men and broken homes, and the doubt whether, even with victory, there is anything to be gained from war.

But nonetheless we have for years forced these men to go out and fight for their tools, and the burden of proof has always been on them that they really did intend nothing more nefarious than to defend the United States. When we come to think, it is just as grotesque as it would be to oppose appropriations for the fire department lest its forces might also want to play with their pretty new toys and thence be driven to committing arson on a large scale.

The Army and Navy have never been allowed a very clear idea of what they might be called on to do. So to be on the safe side they try to get all they can, so as to be ready to do anything. Even when the country is being told that American boys will not be sent to fight overseas, the War and Navy departments consider it their duty to be on the safe side and have their plans ready in case such promises are not kept.

If we had a real policy this problem would be greatly simplified. The War and Navy departments we have used as our illustration would not be reduced to begging for their tools. It would be a far more dignified procedure for the Secretary of State to appear before congressional committees as their spokesman. There would be a greater confidence than we have had heretofore if the Secretary of State were to appear with his colleagues the Secretary of War and the Secretary of the Navy and assert that the estimates submitted represented considered agreement on the real needs of their departments in the light of the tasks they must be equipped to perform. Congress and the departments have come in time of peace to adopt an instinctive attitude of giving as little as possible on the one hand and securing as much as possible on the other. This might be replaced by a feeling of reciprocal confidence that would benefit both the Executive and the legislative.

And it would surely work against waste.

What we obviously need is to have the work of all agencies dealing with any phase of foreign affairs so integrated that problems are dealt with jointly as they develop, rather than severally after they have arisen in acute form.

We often hear the Department of State criticized for failing to prepare for all eventualities like the War and Navy departments. There is some unfairness in this comparison with the War and Navy departments. In making their plans to deal with every conceivable situation they are dealing largely with tangibles—men and ships and guns and supplies. If they are making plans for what seems like the highly improbable eventuality of landing American troops in Persia, they start with a number of definite factors. This makes it possible to pull the right plan out of a pigeonhole and put it to work.

One reason they are able to draw the right plan out of a pigeonhole is that they have ample time and an adequate staff to study and work out alternative plans for all conceivable situations. The Department of State has never had an adequate staff for its work. As regards equipment for its task, the department has always been a Cinderella. It cannot be justly criticized for failing to follow the methods of the War and Navy departments. There will be ground for that when the Secretary of State is furnished with proper machinery and ample funds for his responsible work.

The task of the Department of State is far less simple than that of the War and Navy departments. It deals with intangibles and imponderables. To do this intelligently it should begin with a full picture of ascertained fact as to its problems and in addition a clear understanding of the support it can count on from other agencies of the government. To play with the hypothetical without this basis would be no more than ouija-board diplomacy and likely to have disconcerting results.

However anxious we may be to be reasonable in our dealings with other countries, there is no escaping the fact that the respect with which we are listened to is dependent in large measure to the knowledge of ultimate force ready to back up what we say.

To know how far force is behind a given policy, it does not suffice for the Secretary of State to telephone the secretaries of War and Navy, inform them of his intentions, and ask if they are ready to support him. In such intricate matters, hearty assurances or expressed agreement is not enough. Support calls not only for assurances but for long and intricate preparation. This cannot be made after a crisis has arisen. To give effective support and to reach wise decisions, our military leaders must "grow up" with each problem. Even then they cannot take action alone. Funds will be required, and money bills originate in the House. How can Congress take the right decisions unless congressional leaders have also "grown up" with the question it is called upon to deal with?

We have more than one bitter example of the results of inadequate consultation—and anything less than twenty-four-hours-a-day consultation is inadequate. The *White Paper* recently issued by the Department of State indicates that our diplomatic officials were adequately informed as to Japanese intentions, that our representatives in Japan and in the Department of State realized the extremely critical state of affairs. But, perhaps inadvertently, it is revealed that there was a tragic failure to use this information for its obvious purpose. The only purpose in sending in such information was to make sure that we would be prepared for a Japanese attack. That attack would not be made upon the building of the State Department, but upon our military forces in the Pacific, and yet the mere fact that these forces were taken by surprise is proof that there was failure somewhere along the line to make use of the information sent in by our diplomatic representatives. In other words, there was inadequate consultation.

Diplomatic unpreparedness arising from lack of systematic consultation is costly in lives and treasure. Let us hope we learned that lesson at least from Pearl Harbor.

Year after year the department is criticized for its lack of organization. In support of this charge it is pointed out that there is never adequate delegation of authority and that all the important work is done by a small number of responsible officers. It is true that these men are always overworked, even in piping times of peace. In fact, the ordinary Undersecretary would find it a rest cure to serve a term as a convict at hard labor. However, this is not due entirely to lack of organization. The department has been reorganized time and again with a view to remedying this evil, which gets worse as the years go by. The trouble is that these efforts have never been directed at the real cause, which is lack of policy.

If a national policy were clearly laid down for the guidance of the Department of State, it would be possible to delegate authority and for subordinates to deal with a great part of the work now done by the chief officers of the department. As there is no such plan, each day's problems must be brought to the Secretary, Undersecretary, or Assistant secretaries, who assume responsibility for dealing with them as best they can. This comes pretty close to being pure improvisation, and our people, working under such handicaps, have done remarkably well. If they could operate under a real policy they would undoubtedly do better still, for they could devote more time to thought and discussion on the inevitable current problems, instead of consuming their energies in a frantic struggle to keep up with what should be routine.

This is not mere conjecture, as we have practical examples of what a known policy does in other countries to facilitate deliberate working methods and to eliminate the feverish overwork that has long characterized our own Department of State. We may take the case of Brazil as an illustration of one country that has a foreign policy. In many respects Brazil's situation is similar to our own. She is a big country that covets no territory. Her interest is in peace and the opportunity for peaceful development. She has nothing to conceal. One result is that she can afford the luxury of frank dealing. As a matter of fact, frankness is the easiest course, but it is important to know what you are to be frank about. In a long and varied career I have never encountered such straightforward and open dealing as in Rio. This was rendered possible only by the fact that even subordinates knew what the national policy was and how far they were safe in going—and they were safe in going much further than would have been possible without a national policy.

Our problems are doubtless more intricate than those of Brazil, but the fundamentals are the same and suffice to show how much we have to gain from achieving a similar understanding.

Our lack of highly organized, full-time consultation has forced on the Department of State the inability to make comprehensive plans for the future. Long consciousness of this weakness has led to the growth of a curious defense mechanism, so that the department has come not only to acquiesce but even to refuse to look ahead. This attitude, forced on the department by conditions, has become a fundamental obstacle to our having a foreign policy.

There is no department of the government where foresightedness is more essential. Its job is to look ahead, to foresee what may happen, to be prepared for anything, and to avert trouble. Instead of that the department waits until trouble comes. We seem to have adopted the old proverb about crossing our bridges when we come to them as a guiding principle.

The Army and the Navy operate on an entirely different basis. They try to anticipate every conceivable contingency so as to be ready. They do not lull themselves to rest with the assurance that they will cross the bridge when they come to it. They know that in times of stress and turmoil the bridge may be destroyed or occupied by the enemy, so they work out alternative ways of getting across and are not thrown into utter confusion if some unforeseen contingency arises.

No matter how farsightedly you have made your preparations, the one thing you have not foreseen may happen. But it does not justify refraining from trying to foresee.

As diplomacy covers the relations between states and peoples, that means it covers the whole range of human activities and human nature. There is nothing about human nature that can be reduced to all-embracing formula.

In this lies the difference of diplomacy from most other forms of governmental activity.

A great part of our government activities can be conducted more or less by rule of thumb.

Much of the work of the Department of Justice, the War Department, and others, is governed by laws, rules, and regulations. The work is conducted by functionaries who know the laws and regulations that apply. Of all government departments, the State Department is least governed by a book of rules.

Ironically enough, in the State Department and the Foreign Service we have the machinery for anticipating future developments. Fundamentally, according to any reasonable estimate, that is what these services are there for. But instead of using them for the intended purpose, foresight is not encouraged. Prophecy is frowned upon. This does not mean the use of soothsayers or the ouija board. But the man in the field, with firsthand knowledge and the feel of things, is often in a position to give a pretty accurate idea of what is going to happen next.

Prophecy, in the sense of forecasting the probable course of events, is essential to help the government in Washington to decide on a line of procedure and not be caught unprepared. The newspaper correspondent goes in for this sort of prophecy by keeping up a steady flow of cables giving his estimate of events and probable developments. But there is a difference between the use made of his forecasts and those of the diplomat. When the newspaperman has filed his cable, his task is done. His paper publishes it, but does not have to decide what is to be done next.

There is a greater analogy between the diplomatic and military services. It is on the basis of intelligence reports that strategic planning is based. The more these reports facilitate the efforts of the commanding general, or the General Staff, to anticipate events, the greater the chance of victory. We often hear that the successful general is the one who is able to figure out what his adversary is going to do and anticipate him. The best of generals does not do this by retiring into his tent and drawing on his inner consciousness. He does it in the light of the fullest information he can get as to enemy intentions, and this information comes largely from intelligence reports.

The neglectful man has to deal with accomplished facts and aggravated situations. That is the penalty of his neglect. The far-sighted man has the advantage of being able to think things over before they happen and of being ready to deal with them. Therefore, the hypothetical is his field.

But the State Department will have none of this. There is a standard telegram we have all received more or less often, according to the incorrigibility of our optimism, couched in these words: "It is not the practice of the department to deal with hypothetical questions."

It seems incredible, but that is the comfort dished out to grown men in the field who telegraph in that such and such things are happening, that such and such a situation may arise in a matter of hours or days, and seek guidance as to the course they are to pursue. The man at the front may be faced with a situation where he has to cross his bridge, and perhaps, as he foresaw, the bridge is not there. To put it in different words, he may find himself in a position where his action—whatever he does or does not do—will affect his government's position. But the decision does not rest with him. Should he endeavor to block some movement, or acquiesce, or even encourage it? Should he accept or reject a proposal which is likely to be made? He knows that these questions must be decided by those responsible in the light of facts and considerations perhaps unknown to him.

Obviously, it is a strain for the man in the armchair in Washington to give orders for which he will later have to accept responsibility, perhaps before a congressional committee.

But that does not justify sending off the standard telegram: "It is not the practice of the department to deal with hypothetical questions."

True, this is usually softened—at least in the eyes of the man who sends it off—with a little comfort to this general effect:

"The department is fully mindful of the difficulties of the situation with which you are faced. It is desired that you keep the department fully informed as to developments and that you cooperate closely with your French and British colleagues. We are in close consultation with the interested governments, and, as occasion requires, shall be prepared to send you appropriate instructions for your guidance!"

This is not fanciful, but a faithful paraphrase of standard practice. At least it was standard practice until a few years ago.

All of which is of very little help to a man responsible for American lives and interests.

It is easy to laugh at such instructions, but to be entirely fair there have been occasions when with the best will in the world the department was hard put to it to draft anything that made sense.

Once—and once only—when I was a young secretary I made the radical suggestion that a telegram be sent the man in the field that the situation was one that could not be dealt with from ten thousand miles away, and that he must be left a free hand to meet the problems as best he could with assurance of support in anything he felt obliged to do.

This suggestion nearly caused some of the old-timers to have a stroke. For the Foreign Service is, and always has been, driven from the back seat.

This matter of back-seat driving may seem to have nothing to do with our lack of policy. As a matter of fact, it is a clear manifestation of that lack. If we had a policy, we could outline a general plan for the guidance of our representative and then leave him to deal with matters of day-to-day negotiation, as we leave our doctor to his own devices in the operating room. We fail to do this simply because we have no policy—we cannot see ahead more than twenty-four hours at a time and the representative in the field has to report every detail back to Washington, where everybody goes into a huddle and issues fresh and often inapplicable instructions.

This hand-to-mouth diplomacy is not only a manifestation of lack of policy. It is one of the clear disadvantages under which we labor. Our representative in an international conference operates under a handicap in his dealings with the delegates of other countries. It is like seeing two men turned into the boxing ring —one foot-loose and free, the other with a rope around one arm, to enable his seconds to pull him back into his corner for coaching.

We choose a man after examinations. We train him in the department. We watch him grow in the field. He eventually reaches a point where we expect foreign governments to listen to him with deference and respect. In the letters of credence the diplomat delivers to the Chief of State, the President of the United States calls on the foreign government to give "full faith and credence" to everything he may say on behalf of his country.

But we retain the parental complex that our child has never grown up. We remember the days when he could be made to eat his supper only with the ritual of "Now one for Mummy; one for Daddy; one for Nanny," and so on. How can we treat him with respect? So we continue to instruct him in the minutest details, and the idea of authorizing him to use his own judgment throughout a crisis is more than we can bear.

This tendency is seen at its most acute in international conferences. Other nations send their delegates with general instructions for their guidance as to what they should seek to achieve. Within the limits of these general instructions they are free to act in their own discretion. They can do this because they have a policy, a plan; but with us it is different.

There is no way in which a man or group of men thousands of miles away can direct operations in a conference room. Situations develop quickly and change as quickly. A decision or proposal that would be excellent at noon may well be premature at eleven and futile at one o'clock. Only the man on the ground is able to size up the situation and act in the light of comprehensive knowledge.

Our government alone has always been given to sending elaborate day-to-day instructions, not only as to aims and purposes but also as to what is to be said and even what words are to be used. The result is to place a greater handicap, a greater burden on our delegates than is borne by any others. In the first place, there is the time and energy expended in keeping Washington informed on superfluous details and persuading distant people to reconsider instructions that do not apply. In the second place, there is the difficulty of dealing with other delegates when your hands are tied and theirs are free.

Life is full of minor disasters caused by this practice of ours. Someday we may have a major disaster, and then we may decide to trust the people we send into the field to do the best they can, even allowing for a reasonable margin of error, as is done by other countries.

This is not to advocate that our delegate shall be his own boss, free to do anything he likes—only that he shall be on the same footing as the lawyer in court and on the same footing as the delegates of other countries. He should be given clear instructions as to what his government desires, with distinction between the essential and the desirable that is subject to modification. Our delegates have rarely had such instructions. The Department of State has usually clung to its preference for crossing bridges when it comes to them. This leads inevitably to improvisation by men far away from the conference room—a method no better than directing a lawyer in the courtroom by summoning him to the telephone throughout the proceedings. In my own experience, extending over many years, I seldom had any adequate instructions unless I came home, wrote them myself, and secured their adoption.

The Department of State has a monopoly of this strange practice of not trying to plan ahead. In times of peace the Army and the Navy devote an unbelievable amount of study and hard work to planning for every conceivable contingency. Indeed, some of the plans seem so utterly preposterous that there has been criticism of wasting the public funds on drawing up detailed plans for landing and provisioning American troops in such places as

North Africa, Iceland, and the Southwest Pacific. This was looked upon by the Army and the Navy as perhaps hypothetical but prudent. To the layman, it was less charitably described as absurd. But when the absurd hypothetical situation presented itself as a reality, all the work that had gone before appeared in the guise of foresight and wisdom. We did not have to lose precious months in drawing up plans from scratch. This readiness on the part of the Army and the Navy has doubtless saved countless American lives in this war.

Not only is life complicated for an incoming Secretary of State by the necessity for changing policies, he must assert his independence by bringing in his own assistants, and by doing this he deprives himself of the help and counsel of the experienced men who served his predecessor. This is serious for both the Secretary and the men themselves, but in different ways.

The men in the State Department, like those in other foreign offices, used to be almost entirely non-political appointees who, like officers in the Army and the Navy, serve the government as a permanent and honorable career. No one would think that a change of administration called for a wholesale purge of army officers. But it was different with the Department of State, and it may be still more different in the future.

Nothing is of greater advantage to a Secretary of State than to be surrounded by a group of trained men in whose loyalty and ability he has full confidence. But the advantage is nearly all on his side. For it is not always helpful to a career officer to have it whispered that he was "very close" to the last Secretary of State. There seems to be some implication that this renders him unfit for service under the new chief. So we often have the spectacle of able men being relegated to obscure posts for no other reason than having rendered distinguished service under another administration.

This is probably an unconscious survival of the old spoils system —the slogan of "turn the rascals out"—in the days when the rascals had nothing to keep them in but the memory of political services to the outgoing party.

We cannot have a properly implemented policy without a competent trained career service, and we cannot build up the sort of career service we need unless men are rewarded rather than penalized for having won the esteem and confidence of their chiefs. We must come to realize the value of men recruited and trained as our diplomats are, having dinned into them day after day and year after year the fact that they are serving the country—that mixing party politics into our relations with other countries is a form of treason. Anyone who has had a close-up view of this question is bound to have the highest admiration for the loyalty and devotion of the successive groups of career men who have surrounded our secretaries of state. Many a Secretary comes into office prejudiced against the idea of a career diplomacy. He goes through a period of enlightenment, and in nearly all cases reaches a point where he wants to do something about it all, but this is usually toward the end of his term of office with the result that he gives the kiss of death to the very men who, by loyal service, have demonstrated their value to the department. And these men are marked for the slaughter as the incoming party considers that the endorsement of the outgoing Secretary makes them suspect.

Nowhere in the service of our government have we a higher standard of ability, loyalty, and integrity than is to be found in the Department of State. The machinery of the department is antiquated and defective and the operation of our diplomacy leaves much to be desired, but we have no right to blame this on the officers of the department. If they were properly equipped and organized, they would give an excellent account of themselves. In view of the handicaps under which they labor, the lack of adequate recognition, it is surprising that we have been able to attract to our service so many men of ability and character. Even today they stand as a group second to no foreign office in the world. If we are willing to forego our national indulgence in running down the men who conduct our foreign affairs and equip them for their job, we can recruit within a reasonable time the best group of its sort in the world.

CHAPTER XI

Amateur Diplomacy

FOREIGN POLICY is not like an eight-day clock that can be wound up and left to run itself. The only way that it can operate is under the direction of diplomacy, and there we come to the human problem of the kind of diplomats we need to make our policy tick. America is the only country in the world where there is widespread belief that ignorance is the best qualification for diplomats, that the man trained in diplomacy is necessarily unfitted, and that only 100-per-cent, he-man, grass-root representation is to be found among Americans straight from business life, with no knowledge of foreign affairs, foreign languages, history, geography, or the methods of diplomacy.

By some curious quirk in our upbringing there is always an outcry at any suggestion that foreign affairs need professional handling. There is no similar outcry about monetary or tariff professionalism or the conduct of military operations, except that something of the same complex is found in those who proclaim that the General Staff needs prodding to force it to do something costly in American lives, which its knowledge and sense of responsibility tell it is unwise. For the most part we are willing to trust our military leaders to fight their battles when and where they expect to get the best results.

We have never in our history had such a debauch of amateur diplomacy as we have experienced in the current war. It is troubling to think about the inevitable hangover.

We have always made some use of amateur diplomats, but at least we have for the most part put them in harness so that we had some control over their actions. At the present time, however, when even Nazis and Communists secure the best qualified men they can get, we have put many of our professional diplomats on the shelf and seem to be going out of our way to recruit new representatives on the assumption that the more disqualified they are the better they will represent us. We don't even put them in the diplomatic service, where we can hold them subject to a certain amount of discipline and control their utterances. We send them careering around the world by land, sea, and air, on personal missions trumpeting irresponsible promises and advice to all nations. Most dangerous of all are those who occupy no governmental position and consequently cannot be held responsible, no matter how outrageous their antics.

We have lumped all these people together as amateur diplomats. Perhaps that is too charitable and not altogether accurate. We might do better to classify them as follows:

The Crusaders.

The Reformers.

The Spenders.

The Exhibitionists.

Of course there is nothing rigid about this classification, for many of our current exhibits cover more than one classification. There are Exhibitionists who come under none of the other classifications, but some of the Crusaders belong to all four categories. Reformers and Spenders are often Exhibitionists as well.

Let us begin with the Crusaders. We have a lot of those charging around just now, and we should do well to take a look at them. Although a Crusader may be an irresponsible individual, impatient of achieving his ends by drudgery and give and take, he should certainly know where he is going and what he wants to do when he gets there. We may disapprove of his methods and his behavior, but at the very least we ought to be able to identify his objective. Unless we know that, it is difficult to find justification for his existence. Many of our present-day Crusaders seem all too obviously to have no specific objective. They are just crusading. With considerable expenditure of public money, they are imitating the late Stephen Leacock's knight in shining armor who rode out of the castle on a white charger and galloped off madly in all directions.

Now and then one of our Crusaders, after enjoying his canter abroad, comes to the realization—disconcerting to a Crusader—

that there are no infidels to be found, that he has to come home again to find the pagan hordes and rout them. These pagan hordes are the people who fail to agree with the Crusader, and their punishment is to be denounced as "reactionaries," "Fascists," "Isolationists," and what-have-you. Listen to Mr. Wallace.

Curiously enough, most of these Crusaders are quite unconscious of the fact that they themselves are adopting the methods of fascism. Some of them, it is true, have consciously adopted the technique of Berlin and Moscow and seek to muddle public thinking, to destroy those they dislike by smearing and by statements which are easily to be distinguished from the truth.

Then we have the Reformers. They are out to reform the whole world as soon as the smoke of battle blows away. In the meantime they are ready to content themselves with indicating to other countries the path they should follow. For instance, having clamored for us to get into the war in order to save Britain, they are now intent on picking the Empire to pieces, always in the name of the same high principles of human freedom.

They also have plenty of time to decide what form of government is suitable for almost any disorganized, distracted, and war-ravaged country—France or Italy, for instance, after we have formally declared they are to be free to decide their own form of government.

Most of the more vehement Reformers call themselves Internationalists, and we unquestioningly accept the tag they have pinned on themselves. As a matter of fact, some of them are among our most pronounced Imperialists. Of course all their ideas are propounded in the name of brotherhood—what might be called elder brotherhood. But the fact remains that they propose to order and direct, support and educate—in short, take over the control of the world to rebuild it in our own image—or at least the image into which they would like to distort our own national features.

If you disagree with this sort of thing, you are told at the least that you are no liberal. Now your self-defined "liberal" is often the most intolerant animal to be found. His self-defined liberalism confers on him some illiberal prerogative to impose his views and to excommunicate those who disagree. If he is sufficiently shrill in his denunciation of Hitler and Mussolini, he can adopt their methods and be ruthless and unprincipled in suppressing opposition without realizing that he is at heart a Fascist.

Such a volume of preaching, exhortation, advice, and promises pours from these amateur diplomats that there insensibly grows up abroad a belief that the United States will indefinitely back up these conflicting ideas with action. For the most part, other countries fail to recognize that the bulk of this advice emanates from people who have nothing to do with the conduct of public affairs, whereas action must come from the responsible agencies of government. Therefore, there is a frequently recurrent disillusionment abroad about America's failure to live up to her obligations. It was well expressed by a foreign diplomat some years ago at a time when America had been extremely vocal about the course that should be pursued by his country; when the time for action came and our support was sought, the American Government contented itself with some platitudes about right and wrong —and this disillusioned diplomat remarked how curious it was that although full of good admonitions and advice, when the time for action came the American Government could be counted upon to retire into a bombproof pulpit.

Many of our Reformers are convinced that salvation is to be found only through making the world over on the American model.

A super-government must be set up with a streamlined version of the American Constitution. There is to be an American Bill of Rights. Any regulation that is needed is to be according to our methods. Any part of the world where people do not think right is to be given appropriate treatment, that is to say, they are to be educated by Americans with an American educational system.

By what right? Our secondary education is not necessarily a model for all the world. There is a good deal to be said for much of our university education, but when we see the crackpot ideas it has fostered we may have certain reservations to make about turning our teachers loose to re-educate the world.

This is quite aside from the question that will arise in the minds of many people, particularly in other countries. By what right does America arrogate to herself the educational control of European peoples? If there is any arrogating to be done, why should not some of the victorious European powers have a go at it? An attempt to superimpose our ideas upon the ancient traditions of Europe would result in mental and political chaos. It would be very much like asking the Chinese to reform our colleges and schools. Incidentally, it might be objected that this is just the sort of thing we are fighting against. If our Crusaders feel that they are going to spread love of the United States by taking over the re-education of conquered peoples, they are making a ludicrous mistake. There is nothing so calculated to make us abhorred.

If it is our aim to get the world reorganized on the model of the United States, there is one course—and only one—that holds out hope. If, as a preliminary, we put our own house in order, develop a faultless and smoothly working government, find a solution of labor and unemployment problems, straighten out the tangled and tragic problems of Negroes and sharecroppers and Okies and slums—if we do all these things and establish a system that is the envy of the rest of the world, other nations may come to us humbly and beg us to show them how they can do as much for themselves.

The American Spender is also at large along with the Crusader and Reformer. His kind are for the most part moved to put all nations on the pay roll and keep them in the manner to which they would like to become accustomed. Some of these people operate in sheer love of unrestrained spending. For the most part, they have shown themselves incompetent in private business, so they glory in the fact they don't have to worry about balanced budgets. There is a whole school of amateur diplomacy that seems bent on building us a position of leadership through buying international affection—what might be called a policy of *largesse oblige*. America has a monopoly of that childish approach. Even the least advanced countries understand that the international affection you can buy is no more dependable and lasting than the personal affection you could secure by the same means. Naturally, governments are less likely to antagonize us, and are more likely to abound in expressions of affection, so long as we pour out the money, but we may well feel some misgivings as to how long they will continue when supplies are shut off. In the meantime, we must find what comfort we can in Governor Smith's assurance that nobody is going to shoot Santa Claus.

But the day our giving ceases—and someday it will have to cease—where shall we look for eternal friendship? We have already had some experience to guide us. Most of us should be able to remember when we were pilloried as Uncle Shylock. This is not to advocate that we should ever abandon our instinct for helpfulness, but only to recall that this helpfulness should be directed to some definite purpose and not just to gratify the urge to exuberant spending.

Many an amateur diplomat assumes that the first function of diplomacy is to make everybody happy—that is to say, everybody outside the borders of the United States—so he is lavish with promises, both for the present and for the distant future. He is gratified to see the smiles that greet his promises—an immediate satisfaction is quite sufficient for him, for your amateur diplomat will probably no longer be there when the time comes to make good on his promises.

We are now indulging this weakness in a grandiose way. We are promising not merely to feed the rest of the world and keep it in luxury for all time but also to preserve "freedom from want" for all time. This sort of talk would be deplorable but not really dangerous if other peoples realized, as we do, the utter foolishness of the amateur diplomat and his promises. Unfortunately there is a very human tendency abroad to accept these promises as national obligations.

Your career diplomat is, of course, hidebound in certain particulars. He has certain inhibitions about making easy promises. In fact, before making a promise on behalf of his government he likes to make sure that his government will be able to keep it. Your high-minded ambassador-at-large has no patience with such moss-grown, outmoded timidity, so he barges up to the mike and promises to feed the world out of our surplus. Of course even one of these people should have enough sense of responsibility to make sure of the existence of his surplus before broadcasting. There is no surplus. There will be none for a long time, and we shall be hard put to it to provide needed help to our numerous Allies. In other words, while we know we cannot keep our promises we are freely discussing the methods of distribution of nonexistent food.

All this is good, clean fun for those who enjoy it, but when we fail to make good on these promises, we shall incur the wrath and resentment of those who feel they have a claim upon us. The role of sugar daddy to all the world has its drawbacks.

Many of the Global Planners have adopted a new yardstick worthy of Alice in Wonderland. They judge an enterprise not by what is accomplished, but by the amount of public money spent and by the number of people employed. Others attach importance to these questions, too, but in a contrary sense—to the result achieved by a minimum expenditure and a minimum force of men. But this is old-fashioned, and some of our more enlightened gentlemen-at-large boast of their expenditures as if there were special merit in getting rid of our money. The new idea appears to be that if we can keep other nations awash in seas of American money everything will be lovely.

Recently one of our more enthusiastic spenders in a South American country expatiated to a friend on the vast achievements of his organization, although, according to his statement, the achievement appeared to consist in spending hundreds of millions with no mention of any return. In an effort to understand, the friend asked whether this great expenditure of American public money had brought about a change in the national attitude toward the United States. Our official almoner replied enthusiastically that there was indeed a great change. Asked to specify more definitely the nature of the change, he pondered a moment, and then, without any sign that he was being consciously humorous, he answered: "I should say it was a change from an attitude of dislike to one of suspicion."

Expenditures that serve our purposes in war are justifiable, but there is no justification for expenditure beyond our war efforts to buy affection or to carry into foreign countries our social ideas or those of some clique in power. It is these latter expenditures that create the suspicion that so gratified our official spender.

There is nothing very abstruse about this. We can imagine our own feelings if some foreign government were to invade the United States with an army of functionaries and unlimited funds and set out to improve the condition of our people according to its notions. Might we not develop some suspicions?

Most of these amateur diplomats fall in the final category of Exhibitionists. Most of them have always yearned for celebrity, or at least for notoriety. They know their hold upon the microphone is precarious, and the spotlight may be switched off at any moment. Therefore, their chief concern is for stunts that will keep them in the public eye and the national welfare seems to fall into second place. Our ambassadors-at-large seem to live before the movie camera and the microphone. They shoot off impassioned outbursts of nonsense.

Centuries of experience have proved the desirability of having diplomats work without the handicap of publicity. It is not their function to make speeches or public appearances. These can safely be left to the spokesmen of the government. It is the diplomat's task to negotiate agreements acceptable to all parties, and the function of our government spokesmen to make the agreements known.

If the problem is complicated, the diplomats seldom succeed at the first try. If they are trying to negotiate over the radio, this is a serious setback. In private negotiation, a first failure merely means that you cast about to find some other way and that you are free to try and fail, and try and fail until some solution is found. We are now suffering from the plague of these free-lance representatives with an itch for publicity—publicity in speech and radio talks; publicity in books; publicity in movie form, so as to get before the eyes of the whole people.

This is a far cry from old-fashioned diplomacy. A few years ago most Americans could not, on pain of death, have given the names of two American ambassadors abroad. They were not supposed to be in the public eye, like great controversial figures, protecting all foreign countries, promoting foreign ideologies. They were supposed to stay at their posts and attend to their professional duties without self-advertisement, and until we get back to that type of diplomacy we are going to suffer from this plague of people who are raising Cain with American thinking and preparing inevitable disillusionment and resentment for other peoples.

Some people find amusement in the sort of misrepresentation we suffer from abroad. At least they look on it as innocent foolishness. There is nothing funny about it if we consider the effects of all this clowning and irresponsibility on our national interests. We find nothing here calculated to enhance respect for our country. In the end, they may prove costly in lives and treasure. There is nothing amusing about all this—rather ground for concern and disgust.

If we don't eliminate our amateur diplomats-at-large we shall before long be the most disliked nation on earth.

One obstacle to the development of a proper foreign policy is our persistence as a nation in putting all our faith in myths.

For one thing, many of our people are convinced that while other nations deal with foreign relations through highly trained diplomats, we have a better system, and believe that these intricate questions can best be handled by people without experience or knowledge—those who bring to these effete questions the fresh viewpoint of American life and business.

There is one classic myth always brought forward to prove the superiority of ignorance—a wholly untrained man who made a brilliant success in diplomacy—Benjamin Franklin.

There is urgent need to explode this myth, which is based on vast ignorance of American history.

Far from being ignorant and untrained, Franklin was the most highly trained career diplomat we have ever had. He succeeded because of his special qualifications and training, and not because he wore homespun breeches.

This can be adequately driven home by a brief account of his diplomatic work. The mantle of the Prophet seems to do something for his successors, but we may question whether any one of our more conspicuous current exhibits would become a Benjamin Franklin if he put on those homespun breeches.

From an early age Franklin concerned himself with political and diplomatic languages: French, Italian, Spanish, and Latin—a remarkably good equipment. In 1757 he was sent to London by the Pennsylvania Assembly to negotiate a broad range of questions with the English Government. This was purely a diplomatic mission, involving questions of great importance, and lasted for five years, until 1762. From 1764 to 1775, a period of eleven years, Franklin represented in London not only Pennsylvania, but also New Jersey, Georgia, and Massachusetts, and handled a wide range of subjects calculated to develop his powers of negotiation and persuasion. He had to develop these powers, for he had nothing else to help him achieve success in his mission. These two missions, extending over a period of sixteen years, are really Franklin's period of training, although it is the custom to look upon his service in France as his only diplomatic experience. Upon Franklin's return to America, at the outbreak of the Revolution, he was entrusted with several diplomatic missions, such as that to Canada, to invoke support in the Revolution, and again when he was appointed by the Congress to negotiate terms of peace with Admiral Howe.

In 1776 Franklin was appointed Commissioner to France. He was chosen for this highly important mission precisely because he was the most experienced and successful negotiator who could be found—in other words, because he was our most highly trained diplomat. He was chosen for exactly the same reason we should choose our men today. Franklin remained in France until 1785. There is no one in our service today who has had such a background of experience and training as Franklin had when he went to France, and it is wrong to speak of him as an untrained diplomat. Furthermore, it should be borne in mind that quite aside from the question of training or the lack of it, he was Benjamin Franklin, that is to say, one of the ablest and most resourceful men our country has ever produced. If we could find enough trained Benjamin Franklins to staff the diplomatic service, we might be able to stop worrying, but there seem to be few Franklins available today.

Once the Franklin myth disappears nothing remains to support the idea of the value of ignorance. On the other hand, we have a long series of disastrous examples of barefoot boys who failed to make good in diplomacy.

Except for some of our more spectacular exhibitionists, few of them are known to the American people. The ordinary diplomat enjoys a charitable obscurity, and the American people seldom hear about the antics and absurdities of many of the unfit people we send abroad. They are keenly alive to shortcomings that do not exist, but the form of our mythology leaves our people convinced that if only our representative is untainted by training in diplomacy he can do little wrong.

It is high time the people realized the amount of harm done to our interests by many of these incompetents, the discredit that is brought upon us in the eyes of the rest of the world. The weaknesses of all the trained diplomats in our service have not done us half the mischief that has been worked by any one of twenty amateurs.

When the American people outgrow the superstition that it is all right for the President to pay off political obligations with embassies and even provide for his friends by entrusting delicate posts to them, they will realize that it would be a matter of good economy to have a duplicate service of purely honorary posts to satisfy these personal and political demands, so long as the real job could be handled by people who know what they are doing. Recently there has been a manifestation of discontent with obviously improper appointments of this sort.

Nothing less than an alert public opinion can protect us against the appointment of the wrong sort of people. There are evidences that we are making progress and that if the case is sufficiently clear cut public interest can be counted on to intervene. Not long ago Mr. Nelson Johnson, Minister to Australia, a recognized expert in Far Eastern affairs, read in the papers that he had expressed a wish to retire and that he was to be succeeded by Mr. Edward Flynn, a gentleman who, by the wildest flight of the imagination, could not be looked upon as qualified for the important post in Australia—a key position in the Far Eastern theater of war. There was little credence for the report that Mr. Johnson, a conscientious career diplomat, would down tools during the war, with Australia facing the threat of invasion. Public opinion was ruffled by Mr. Flynn's action in announcing his own appointment, not only as Minister to Australia, but as personal representative of the President with the rank of Ambassador and a roving mission. People who had hitherto been indifferent to diplomatic appointments were struck by the contrast in the qualifications of the distinguished public servant who was being booted out and those of the local politician who was slated to succeed him in a crisis where we had need of the best ability we could procure. The outcry was so general that Mr. Flynn's name was withdrawn and Mr. Johnson was asked to reconsider the resignation he was reported to have tendered. There was something wholesome and encouraging in the public reaction to this whole episode, and it is to be hoped it will serve as a warning that there are limits to the people's indulgence in such matters.

We might consider having a complete duplicate service with two ambassadors for each post. As an illustration, there would be two ambassadors to Great Britain, one to go there and do the work, the other to stay in this country and enjoy the prestige and publicity. It should be stipulated that the latter would lose his job, emoluments, and privileges if he left the continental limits of the United States. Of course by staying in the United States he would be deprived of some of the amenities of life in London particularly attractive to the amateur. On the other hand, he would have a wonderful chance to be important all the year round in the United States. On the whole, it might gratify his ambitions quite as well—and think how much better it would be for the interests of the United States!

But we must get over our superstitious belief in the superior virtues of ignorance.

The amateur diplomat often feels the temptation to proceed through stunts, but this practice seldom gets him anywhere. He resents any deliberate pace and feels it can and should be accelerated. According to his temperament he usually adopts one of two simple attitudes:

He demands everything we want on the ground that if the United States wants something there is no more to be said, and no need to consume time in negotiation.

He gives way on all essentials in the interest of agreement.

Both these courses are wrong. The first, because nobody can have his own way 100 per cent; agreement can be reached only by each contributing his share of concession. The second is wrong, too, for it is the duty of our representative to get a fair break for our country. That is what we hire him for, and he is not authorized to sacrifice our interests for the luxurious feeling it gives him of being generous.

Many of our people fail to realize that diplomacy, whether it be conducted through an international conference or otherwise, is a struggle—no less a struggle because of the courtesy with which it is conducted. You do not kill your opponent; you expect him to live to negotiate with you for years to come, and you deal with him courteously to avoid arousing animosity against the day when you will want to wring further concessions from him.

Before the present dispensation we seldom heard of diplomats making speeches. Now they are at it most of the time, and are filling the air with things that were better left unsaid. It is not the function of diplomats in the field to make pronouncements on foreign policy, except on special occasions as decided by the government. We should put an end to this free-for-all of speeches, magazine articles, newspaper columns, and the like, by which the amateur diplomat projects himself before the American people and conducts propaganda for his personal ideas—and even for foreign governments.

The personal ideas of most of these people are of no interest to anybody else. They would never get a hearing but for the accident of their occupying a public office, or even the still more deplorable accident of their having some family connection with public office. This last results in a vicious situation, inimical to democratic government, where an individual enjoys all the power and privilege of public office but cannot be called to account for his actions.

The view that diplomats should refrain from publicity stunts is frequently contested on the ground that "times have changed" and that "the people have a right to know." But does this prove that the diplomat is necessarily the one to tell them? After all, we do have a Secretary of State.

There are speeches the diplomat should make, and they are the hardest of all to make. Almost anyone can heave to his feet and loose off his ideas on world movements if he is accountable to no one. But just try to say something new and interesting on Washington's Birthday or the Fourth of July, and the ghosts of Webster and Clay and Jefferson rise up from the grave and sneer at you.

Aside from these set ordeals there are many occasions each year when the real diplomat is expected to make a speech. He is not free, like his amateur colleagues, to promote good understanding by denouncing countries disliked by his audience. Neither is he free to make promises of political and financial support which produce such a happy immediate effect and leave such a disastrous hangover. His is the difficult task of promoting understanding by interpreting our country, its standards, character, and aims. That calls for both knowledge and a sense of responsibility in utterance, knowing that anything he says will be weighed and interpreted as representing the views of his government.

Yet that is the field of the diplomat, and in the public interest he should be confined to it. There is plenty he can do to promote understanding without charging into policy. It is his task to cultivate friendly feeling for his country, and that is an ample field for anybody.

Of course from time to time the diplomat is used to make an important statement. A recent instance is Mr. Grew's "straight-from-the-horse's-mouth" speech in which he conveyed a considered warning to Japan. But to have effect it should be known that the diplomat is speaking with the full authority of his government behind him. There is no such effect if it is known or suspected that the diplomat is merely suffering from a call to preach.

One disadvantage in the use of political appointees—that is men appointed solely because they are active party workers—is that no matter how outrageously they behave they cannot be held accountable. If a career diplomat fails to conform to the wishes of the President and Secretary of State, he can be disciplined like an insubordinate army officer. There is no need for hesitation in dealing with him. In the case of a political appointee, however, disciplinary action is rarely to be considered. Indeed, his mistakes or indiscretions are seldom brought to his attention. He must be handled with gloves. Discipline or even admonition might drive him to indignant resignation or to raise Cain in the press or become troublesome in the party organization. So while the career man is very properly kept toeing the line, the political appointee is left free to disregard the views of Washington and indulge his every whim.

Our history is bristling with examples—some hilarious and some serious.

During the last war a Chicago brewer of foreign birth was appointed Minister to a European country. He traveled to his post through the Austro-Hungarian Empire with which we were then at peace. He had the unhappy inspiration of stopping at Prague and making a speech advocating the overthrow of the Empire and the establishment of a free Czech state, with promises of American support. There was a considerable upheaval but no action was taken beyond sending a telegram urging him to proceed to his post without delay. For several years this gentleman regaled us with a series of ridiculous and outrageous actions, but in spite of all he was kept in office for fear that if dismissed he might make trouble in Chicago.

The question here is not so much why he was not disciplined. The real question is why was he ever made a Minister?

The most dangerous of all is the American of foreign origin, or even of foreign descent, who goes back to the land of his fathers as American representative and speaks for this country. It should be laid down clearly that no American of foreign birth or descent should be sent back to the old country in any such capacity. It is a thoroughly unsatisfactory arrangement, unfair to both governments and doubly unfair to the individual. Many people assume that this is an excellent way to pay a compliment to the old country and to a racial element in the United States; but it has never worked out that way. We quite rightly expect him to act as a 100 per cent representative of the United States. He may play his role loyally, but the American community will have certain reservations and suspicions and he will rarely enjoy the full confidence of his countrymen which should be his as a matter of course. On the other hand, the people of the country to which he is accredited will welcome him as a long-lost son returned to the bosom of the family and will instinctively expect him to see their point of view better than somebody of alien blood. If he fails to give them the break they expect, they are likely to be resentful. Both countries will be watching him jealously to make sure he lives up to their contradictory expectations, and he will be lucky if he returns home without having antagonized both.

It is impossible to escape the conviction that we have the worst system that could be devised for appointment to high office. In any country, when a man has amassed a fortune, he is likely to want something more lasting in the form of recognition that he can hand down to his children. So he goes in for public service or public benefactions. This has the advantage of securing for the state services money could not buy. In most cases, this service is rendered without occupying public office, thus avoiding the costly evil of disrupting the machinery of government.

The British are more practical about this than we are. Every so often there appears in the Honours List the statement that Mr. John Smith has been made a peer, and it is made known that this is in recognition of distinguished services to the party in office. It is proper that a citizen should contribute to the conduct of party affairs provided he does it as a matter of public spirit and not with a view to buying something. If he is given a peerage or a pretty piece of ribbon, everything is aboveboard and everybody benefits. He achieves recognition and a step up in the world. The party has had its support. The taxpayers have no complaint, for there is no expense involved. The government is protected against a disruption of the orderly conduct of business. There is no question of making a place for him by entrusting to him vital matters he is unfitted to handle.

It has long been our practice to give an embassy to a lawyer or manufacturer or businessman as a pleasant interlude in a busy life. The new Ambassador sometimes explains that he is not particularly tempted by the idea himself but has accepted in order to afford his wife and daughters the advantages of life and travel abroad.

As this is accepted practice, why not carry it a logical step further? Many of our career diplomats, after long service abroad, would welcome an opportunity to give their wives and children the advantages of life in America. Why not adopt a system of reciprocity? When Mr. Snooks, the eminent banker, is sent as Ambassador to Megalomania, let Mr. Jones, the retiring Ambassador, take over the bank for the duration of the mission. There would be no logic in the possible objection that Mr. Jones doesn't know anything about banking. If we let Jones have the bank to play with, no matter how much of a mess he makes of it he cannot conceivably involve our country in war by his mistakes.

We sometimes have eminent professors representing us abroad. The trained diplomats they displace might welcome a few years of academic calm—perhaps in a chair of Sanskrit. Of course the new professor is hardly likely to know the first thing about Sanskrit—but just remember that diplomacy is Greek to Professor O'Prune. And even the complete collapse of the chair of Sanskrit is hardly likely to have international repercussions.

This sounds grotesque—too grotesque to be considered seriously. But it is not half so grotesque as our recognized and accepted practice of entrusting the affairs of our nation to utterly unqualified and untested men, some of whom have nothing to commend them beyond a generous check to the campaign fund of the victorious party. If the American people once grasped the dangers of confiding our destinies to such men, there would be an end to the practice. There should be jealous scrutiny of every appointment with a view to securing men fit to uphold our interests.

The man who wants recognition has the alternative of piling up more money or occupying public office. The first course, with the trend toward keeping private fortunes within limits, offers little beyond a reputation as the man who pays the largest income tax, and while this is certainly a public service it lacks glamor.

Consequently, the trend is more and more toward public office. The drawbacks about this in the field of diplomacy are many. First, the individual has seldom had any experience to fit him for handling intricate international questions. Second, it means foregoing the use of trained people. Third, more serious still, it prevents the growth of a trained service because you cannot expect young men to devote their lives to diplomacy if they know that all the rewards are reserved for the "Check Ambassadors." Fourth, it is bad for our reputation abroad. It often happens that a man who has contributed heavily and must be taken care of is so inept that he cannot be used at home. All right—send him abroad. This has the virtue of getting him out of sight, and after all it doesn't matter what foreigners think of us, because they are only foreigners, and while Mr. Buggins may be a complete noodle, his staff of career diplomats may be depended on to keep him from making too big a fool of himself.

This system has come to be accepted. But if it were in some other line of business, it would be coarsely described as the buying and selling of public office. How else can it be accurately described? But it is so taken for granted that when the news of Mr. Buggins' appointment is published, the papers carry, as a matter of course, a statement of how much he contributed to the campaign fund, not as a criticism, but as an explanation of why he got the job. There is no pretense about his getting it because of any experience or any innate distinction.

We are illogical. If poor old Silas Brown pays somebody seventy-five dollars to help him get a postmastership, there is the devil to pay. Even if he isn't very good at it, he would not endanger American lives and property, and in the wildest stretch of the imagination he could not involve us in a foreign war.

How about a law? Why not decide that a contribution of more than a thousand dollars to party funds shall disqualify the contributor from holding any high diplomatic post? It is desirable and laudable that citizens help support the party system by which we maintain our liberties. It is probably inevitable that there be "recognition" in the form of appointment to public office. However, that recognition has seldom been accorded by appointment to the General Staff. It is quite as important that our appointees to high diplomatic office be free from suspicion. No Ambassador is going to enjoy the prestige he should have if he is looked upon as having bought his job; and however we feel about the system, other countries often look upon it as a polite form of recognized corruption. If it were known that an Ambassador could no longer buy his embassy, our national stock might rise.

CHAPTER XII

The Senate and Foreign Affairs

WHEN our government was born there were twenty-six senators. Whether in New York or Philadelphia or Washington, the capital was a village. In the nature of things it was assumed the Senate would be aware of what was going on. The daily gossip of those in the know included what was going on in the State Department, then called the Department of Foreign Affairs. As a result senators were kept pretty well up to date in regard to foreign affairs. In addition the President and Secretary of State discussed their current·problems with perhaps a smaller number, but still a larger proportion, of the Senate than is done in our day. The result was that when a treaty came before the Senate for its "advice and consent" there was more general knowledge of the actual negotiations leading up to its conclusion. They had more knowledge of why we had foregone this advantage and why we had consented to something else—a more general understanding of the reasonableness of the bargain. This being the case, it was not unreasonable to assume that there would be a two-thirds majority for any sensible agreement.

It was maintained that Congress, and particularly the Senate, should exercise a large measure of control in foreign affairs as a brake upon impetuous action by the Executive. This is made clear by the provision that ratification of treaties should be by and with the "advice and consent" of the same body. The same proviso was attached to the power of the President to appoint ambassadors and public ministers.

The word "advice" has since become meaningless, but it was put there for a purpose. It was intended that the Executive should consult with the Senate as to the best choice of our representatives abroad. When we come to the matter of ratifying treaties, it was assumed that there would be consultation. It was, therefore, not unreasonable to prescribe that a treaty should be ratified only by and with the advice and consent of two thirds of the senators present as, having had their share in shaping the treaty, they would be normally ready to approve the result.

There is general recognition today that there is something unsatisfactory in the relations between the Senate and the Executive and that something should be done about it.

Many solutions are proposed.

It is suggested that we adopt the methods of parliamentary government to the extent of having the Secretary of State appear from time to time before the Senate and the House to answer questions and to make statements.

A variation of this is that an Undersecretary should have a seat in both Senate and House and be on hand to answer questions.

Still another suggestion often brought forward is that the Secretary should make periodic appearances before the Committee on Foreign Relations, in order to keep its members currently informed on matters which might call for senatorial action.

It has recently been proposed to set up a council on foreign relations, composed of representatives of the Department of State and the Senate, to hold frequent meetings and thus facilitate relations between the two institutions.

None of these suggestions really gets to the root of the problem.

It is no mere question of satisfying the curiosity of the Senate and keeping senators supplied with current international gossip —not even a matter of securing periodic senatorial guidance and approval. It is far more fundamental than that—a matter of integrating the authorities having to do with foreign affairs so that they can operate as one.

Most of this discussion is carried on in complete disregard of the original intent of the Constitution and of subsequent developments. For our immediate purposes it will suffice to recall that the conception of the Founding Fathers was that the President who was entrusted with negotiation should be above parties and that the Senate would be something in the nature of a privy council on foreign affairs. There have been great changes since that time and we must, as a practical matter, discuss the problem in the light of changed conditions, with the President acting as head of the party in power.

Aside from the question of appointments, this special relationship was confined to foreign affairs. The provisions of the Constitution were clearly based on the conviction that special measures of prudence were required for questions involving our relations with other countries.

There is no doubt that the Constitutional Convention intended to prescribe a close relationship between the President and the Senate. It seems clear that the "advice and consent" were intended to be, not those of an independent, jealous branch of the government, but rather the help of a council. The decline of this relationship is to be attributed, in some measure at least, to the unforeseen rise of the Cabinet and to the growth in numbers of the Senate. Thus was undermined the original intent of the Founding Fathers and the Senate's role evolved from one of support into that of a check upon the power of the President.

There is a reason in support of the two-thirds rule which is often overlooked. A treaty becomes the supreme law of the land and, once ratified, abrogates any domestic law which may be incompatible with it. A treaty can override the laws and even the constitutions of the states, and is thus a matter of special and legitimate interest to the senators as representatives of the several states. A treaty operates at the same time as a contract with a foreign government and as a municipal law.

This brings us to an aspect of the problem that is seldom considered in present-day discussion. If a domestic law proves unwise, Congress can repeal it by majority vote. However, when the Senate consents to ratification of a treaty, it has taken an irrevocable step. If the treaty proves unwise or harmful to our interests, there is nothing further the Senate can do about it, even by unanimous vote. We are bound for the duration of the treaty—in some cases for an unpredictably long time. The only way in which our government can be released from the terms of such a treaty is by negotiating a new treaty with the consent of the other party. If the other party is not amenable to the idea of foregoing advantages it secured by negotiation, there is nothing we can do about it. This constitutes another fundamental reason for being very sure before we take an irrevocable step.

Quite aside from legal considerations, there was a reason for the two-thirds rule based on human nature. It was felt that if treaties could be put over by majority vote any President controlling a majority could play fast and loose with such important matters, and that knowledge of the two-thirds requirement would have a sobering effect on the Executive in the negotiation of treaties.

It is generally overlooked that the two-thirds requirement is a direct brake on drastic changes of policy. Without this provision the lack of continuity would be even more pronounced than it is now. It would seem unwise to allow a single party to determine a course of action solidly opposed by the opposition party. Sooner or later the other party would come into power with reversal of everything that had been decided. In binding the country for the future there is much to be said for making obligations contingent on the assent of both parties if we are to hope for continuity of policy.

The two-thirds rule is frequently attacked as undemocratic on the ground that there is no democracy save under majority rule. But even under a purely democratic process we sometimes consider it wise to be far more exacting than that. For instance, where the life or liberty of a single man is at stake, we require not a majority vote, not a two-thirds vote from the jury, but unanimity. Is that democratic? Would it not be better to hang him by majority vote? No, we feel that in cases where such precious things as justice and a human reputation are at stake, democracy is best upheld not by counting noses but by being very sure of wise and just decisions.

We often hear the criticism that by the two-thirds requirement a minority of the Senate is made master of our fate. It might be put in another way—that in matters of such moment we should be prudent enough to require preponderant approval. We see nothing tyrannous in the fact that a single member of the jury can block a verdict carrying the death penalty.

Much of the discussion assumes that the Senate operates solely according to its own whims and caprices, regardless of the feeling and wishes of the country. This is hardly borne out by the facts. And we might even go so far as to believe that any treaty that does not command a two-thirds majority in the Senate would not command the amount of popular support to justify its ratification. There should also be some assurance that this popular support will continue, regardless of changes in party control.

One stand-by in these discussions is the rhetorical question: "Why, if we can be taken into war by a majority vote, should a two-thirds vote be necessary to establish peace?"

This is supposed to end the argument and demonstrate something or other, anything from the sufficiency of a majority vote to the wisdom of turning over the treaty-making power to the Executive.

This question, however, does not give us an entirely accurate picture. Neither part of it is strictly true. There is no analogy between the two votes. First, as to Congress "taking us into war" —this presents a picture of a war-minded Congress voting a peaceful country into war, regardless of public will. It overlooks the fact that the role of Congress is usually something of a formality. The resolution usually does no more than take note of an already existing state of war. Indeed, it often expresses itself only when hostilities are already under way and then not in the form of a declaration of war but rather of a formal recognition that a state of war exists. In such cases the vote has in practice exceeded the two thirds needed for a treaty. We remember the "eleven willful men" who voted against the resolution in 1917. In 1941 there was an even smaller vote of those who refused to recognize the fact that we were at war.

In view of this we might well raise the requirement on declaration of war to two thirds or four fifths, but that would not seem to imply the need for reducing the two-thirds requirement for the ratification of treaties. The two subjects are not interdependent.

We hear so much about the need for a two-thirds vote to permit the return of peace that many of us have accepted it as true. As a matter of fact, peace can come without a two-thirds vote—or a majority vote—or even one single vote. Peace often comes when firing ceases by agreement among the military leaders.

A treaty of peace is something very different—a binding, far-reaching agreement. It establishes not only peace but mutual agreements, which bind us perhaps for generations. It becomes the law of the land. It becomes a binding contract with other nations—perhaps many other nations. Once accepted, we are irrevocably bound. We must be sure it does not conflict with obligations under other treaties.

The conviction of the Founding Fathers that Congress must play a powerful role is shown by the fact that the war-making power is confided to Congress alone. The intent of this was to make the declaration of war a subject of sober discussion and not to leave it to the judgment of a single man. This is what we have on paper, but as a matter of fact, congressional power is considerably less conclusive than was originally intended. The Executive can readily outmaneuver a reluctant Congress by creating a situation where a declaration of war becomes inevitable.

We have come a long way from the original intent of the Constitution. Little by little the Executive has taken over the field, partly by intent, but perhaps even more through inevitable development. The fact remains that the vital word "advice" no longer has any meaning. The Senate is not consulted about appointments of our representatives abroad. There is left to the Senate only the negative power of withholding confirmation of a presidential appointment. It has become a frequent practice, however, to get around even this difficulty by appointing "personal representatives of the President with the rank of Ambassador." In early times Congress had a check on little games of this sort by its hold on the purse strings, but now these personal ambassadors are financed from ample funds at the disposal of the Executive, and the Senate is disregarded with impunity.

It is much the same as to the Senate's role in regard to treaties. As a rule, there is nothing in the nature of consultation to elicit advice from the Senate during the negotiation of a treaty. That is a change from earlier days—a material change in the relationship between the Senate and the Executive—brought about by the growth in the number of senators from twenty-six to ninety-six. The demands upon the time and energy of the Executive grew in even greater proportions; uninterrupted contact between the two branches was no longer possible. There is, as a rule, some hasty last-minute coaching of strategically placed senators, in order that they may be in a position to support the Administration during the hearings on a given treaty. This, however, is not so much to secure their advice as to make sure of their support.

The President has always, regardless of the intent of the Constitution, *exercised* full authority in the recognition of other governments and in breaking off diplomatic relations. In these steps, sometimes of great importance, he acts in his own discretion. Congress seeks, on occasion, to assert itself by calling upon the Secretary of State for information on a given matter, but it has no power to secure this information. Any unwelcome inquiry is disposed of by a letter from the Secretary of State to the effect that transmission of the desired information is not deemed to be "compatible with the public interest." And Congress is estopped from going any further.

The Senate, although deprived of its role of adviser in the conclusion of treaties, still feels its constitutional responsibility; but to discharge that responsibility it is thrown back upon its function of "consent." As a rule, the Senate sees the text of a treaty for the first time when it is submitted with a request for consent to the exchange of ratifications. It is too late to offer "advice," except by the heroic method of insisting upon reservations or even revisions of the treaty as a condition of senatorial consent.

There would seem to be no doubt as to the clear right of the Senate to specify its own reservations in consenting to the exchange of ratifications. In the case of the Versailles Treaty, to take the most striking example, there would seem to be no doubt that the other nations would have agreed to the reservations which President Wilson refused to accept. And it should be borne in mind that these reservations would not have conflicted with the character of the League of Nations as it actually developed. If the Senate has serious misgivings that a treaty is harmful to American interests, it has only one recourse, and that is to withhold consent to the exchange of ratifications.

Even so, there is a good deal of exaggeration in this criticism of the Senate. Most of it centers around its refusal to consent to the ratification of the Versailles Treaty. There were many other elements involved, and this was not typical of the senatorial exercise of its treaty-making powers. Whatever the misdeeds of the Senate may have been in this particular instance, we should do well to recall that fewer treaties have been rejected by the Senate than those which the President has failed to ratify after securing unconditional approval from the Senate. The Senate acts far more often to promote and implement presidential purposes than to thwart them. We might also recall that most of the amendments about which so much fuss has been made were moderate, and even insignificant, and that, for the most part, they might have been obviated if there had been some facilities for securing the advice of the Senate. Whatever the opinions of excited critics, the Senate is not constantly obstructive. Its present setup, however, does not afford the Senate scope for constructive action, or for the exercise of its constitutional powers in the field of Foreign affairs.

The fault lies neither with the senators nor the Executive, but primarily with our system—to put it more accurately, with changes in our system. If the negotiators could know the difficulties any given treaty was likely to encounter in the Senate before they set out, they would be guided in their negotiation. If, on the other hand, both majority and minority in the Senate understood just what the State Department was trying to accomplish and why it was adopting a given course, word would get around that the agreement reached was reasonable, and in a majority of cases there would be no difficulty about ratification. It is fashionable to picture senators as making trouble for the Administration for the joy of obstruction, but experience does not bear out this impression. Senators have a definite responsibility under the Constitution. When instruments are brought before them which they do not understand or of which they disapprove, they properly show a disinclination to accept anybody's say-so for the performance of their constitutional duty. Taking them as a body, they show a high sense of responsibility for the best interests of the country.

It may be added that there is an increasing tendency to resort to the conclusion of executive agreements which do not have to be submitted to the Senate. While such agreements are sometimes justified, any wholesale use of them is a clear evasion of the intent of the Constitution.

There has always been a field for executive agreements, but in the last few years this field has been dangerously extended with clear intent to evade constitutional checks. A striking indication of this encroachment upon the functions of the Senate is to be found in a book entitled *International Executive Agreements* by Dr. Wallace McClure, an official of the Department of State. In this volume we find this rather startling statement: "The President can do anything by executive agreement that he can do by treaty, provided Congress by law co-operates, and there is a very wide field of action in which the co-operation of Congress is not necessary; indeed where Congress possesses no constitutional authority to dissent."

This would appear to be a daring statement to come from an officer of a government department. The Supreme Court has often upheld executive agreements, but has never gone so far as to declare obsolete or superfluous the provisions of the Constitution on the subject of treaty making.

The line of demarcation between treaties and executive agreements has never been precisely defined. It is this very lack of definition that has made it easy for the Executive to use the latter as an expedient to sidestep the Senate.

There is one common-sense distinction that can be made, despite Mr. McClure's contention. A treaty is not valid until it is approved by the Senate. An executive agreement, according to established usage, is valid on signature and need not await approval by Congress.

There is another aspect to the distinction between the two forms of document. As we have already seen, a treaty, once ratified, abrogates any domestic statute inconsistent with it. It overrides state constitutions. An executive agreement can do neither of these things.

However, the excessive use of executive agreements may lead us into disastrous complications.

Let us take, as an illustration, the United Nations Relief and Rehabilitation Administration, set up by the agreement signed on November 9, 1943. This document was clearly an executive agreement rather than a treaty, because it became effective on signature, without need for senatorial action. The only call for such action would come from a request for appropriations which Congress would have full freedom to grant or to withhold.

It would seem that the voting of appropriations would imply approval of the agreement itself. This suggests a convenient way of securing congressional approval by indirection. It boils down to the fact that the President can sign an agreement with the proviso that it is "subject to the approval of the Congress" and thereby relieve himself of the obligation of making a treaty and submitting it to the Senate for approval by a two-thirds vote. If that can be done in any matter where we assume obligations, the question arises whether he could not follow the same course for an agreement taking us into a league of nations or a world federation or a military alliance. The only guarantee against this would be the determination of the Senate to keep its constitutional power, even in a matter commanding approval of a majority.

There seems to be general agreement that there is something wrong with this picture of relations between the Executive and the Senate but wide divergence of opinion as to what should be done.

On one hand, there is the demand that the Senate be deprived of the power of "advice and consent," which we have already dealt with. At the other extreme, the contrary demand for extension of senatorial jurisdiction to share in the negotiation of treaties.

We may well consider whether this latter suggestion is not based on a fundamental misconception, whether it would not tend to lessen rather than augment the role of the Senate in foreign affairs. The clear intent of the Constitution was to entrust the handling of actual negotiation to the Executive with the benefit of senatorial guidance and advice. It was intended that the advice of the Senate should have behind it the sanction of "consent"—in other words, that the Executive should always have in mind the knowledge that the Senate was in a position to withhold consent to the exchange of ratifications; in fact, it went further than this. It was assumed that the President would be above parties, and that any question of ratification would be decided on its own merits and not as a partisan matter.

The field of each branch of the government was clearly defined. If the Senate descends into the arena of negotiation, it inevitably abdicates a part of its constitutional power. If it sits at the peace table and participates in negotiation, it assumes a share of responsibility. By what right can it later dissociate itself and refuse approval of arrangements it has helped conclude? It cannot play both sides.

What the Senate desires and needs is a fuller knowledge of the reasons behind the agreements reached, the processes followed, and the justifications for demanding this or conceding that. The Executive needs advance knowledge of senatorial views. Such knowledge in advance and during the actual negotiations would help to avert a host of misunderstandings. But neither of these requires senatorial participation in the actual negotiation. There is no reason for this and a number of reasons against. The real need might be met by having adequate representation of the Senate in an advisory capacity, both in the studies preliminary to the treaty negotiations and during the negotiations themselves. Our problems are not solved by having the senators participate in the daily grind of discussion with foreign powers. It is, however, highly desirable to have them constantly available for advice and as witnesses to the reasonableness of the agreements reached. If any such expedient is adopted, it should be borne in mind that if we are to escape partisan handling of foreign affairs the Executive must set the pace. Both the major parties should be represented in an attempt at co-operation. If this is undertaken in the right spirit, we may hope for good results.

There is undoubtedly ground for the uneasy feeling that the Senate is not playing its part in foreign affairs, but the remedy does not necessarily lie in embarking on activities for which the Senate is not equipped. It would seem to lie rather in getting back to the intent of the Founding Fathers.

There is agitation to deprive the Senate of its treaty-making powers. It is a serious matter to tamper with the provisions of the Constitution. Particularly so when there is no general and continuing purpose in view. Most of the current discussion is aimed at assuring the adoption of the agreements to be concluded at the end of the present war. This is based on a double-barreled conjecture—that the Executive will conclude desirable agreements and that the Senate will adopt an obstructive attitude. These are rather bold assumptions and offer meager grounds for tinkering with the balance of the Constitution.

There is more to this question than a single transaction. We should not lose sight of the fact that treaties can be momentous in their effects. Treaty making is not purely a matter of negotiation with foreign governments. There is a broad legislative field that cannot lightly be abdicated and turned over to the Executive.

In order to make a case for scrapping the provisions of the Constitution, we are edified with much loose talk about "the long record of senatorial sabotage" with lists of the treaties that have been rejected or mangled out of all recognition. That is, of course, one way of describing the record of the Senate. Another would be to call it the record of the Senate's action in discharging its constitutional obligation of advice and consent. According to the first view, any refusal to consent to the ratification exactly as it is submitted by the Executive is sabotage. That is an assumption that will not bear scrutiny. We may well recall that the Constitution conferred on the Senate an important share in the treaty-making power. It was given the final say as to whether a treaty was to be put into effect or rejected. It could temper its power of rejection by the formulation of reservations or by demanding amendments as a condition of approval. It is difficult to see on what grounds all exercise of these powers can be condemned as reprehensible abuse of power. Any such position is less a criticism of the present Senate than of the Founding Fathers for having inserted in the Constitution provisions suited only to sabotage.

Those who want the Senate shouldered aside have also produced some figures to show how the will of the overwhelming majority of the people can be thwarted by senators from a third of the least populous states. If the necessary thirty-four negative votes came from the seventeen states in this category, a treaty desired by some one hundred and twenty millions of our people could be rejected by those representing only some ten millions. According to this method of calculation we must assume that all the people in seventeen states are against the treaty and the other one hundred and twenty millions unanimously in favor of it. That sounds bad enough, but it can be presented even more alarmingly. Suppose a treaty involving the future of the world were to be brought to a vote when nobody was looking and there was a bare quorum (half plus one of the senators being on hand), it can be worked out that three and a half millions of the population could, through their senators, defeat the desires of the rest of the nation. Variations can be played on this theme until it seems as though we might as well give up the idea of having any treaties. There may, however, be some reassurance in the fact that never in the wildest flight of the imagination can such an alignment be looked upon as a possibility. There is nothing in the entire history of the Senate to give color to such hysterical figuring.

To be logical, however, we might see what happens in legislation adopted by majority vote. There we might well find cases where the majority of senators did not represent a majority of the population. The only remedy for that would be to scrap the whole conception of senatorial voting and give each senator a vote based on the population of his state. And when we have got there, where are we?

Most of the current criticism gives the impression of the Senate as a body that flouts the will of the nation and imposes its own on us. Often the critics seem to take as their starting point that their will is the will of the nation; that if they do not get their way violence has been done to democracy and that the Constitution ought to be stood in the corner. It is difficult to see how the Senate, however evil its purpose, can thwart the popular will and go on doing it. After all, if the country is displeased with the Senate it can change the entire membership in six years. If the Senate persists in flagrant disregard of the popular will, either the people can be depended on to exercise their privileges or we must admit that they attach so little value to their rights that they have surrendered to an oligarchy. We ought to carry this discussion a step further. If it is true that we are living under the tyranny of one third of the Senate, the evil is far more serious than we are given to understand even by those who call for remedial action. Abuse of power in the matter of treaties is no more than a symptom. If the intent of the Senate is sinister in this one matter, what reason have we for assuming it is less evil in other respects? If we accept the idea that the Senate is hostile to the popular will and bent on frustrating it, the only logical remedy is to do away with the Senate altogether.

Perhaps the real solution lies in something other than depriving the Senate of its role in foreign affairs. Possibly it lies in the contrary course of giving the Senate a larger role—more nearly what it was intended to have under the Constitution.

We hear a good deal of agitation in the name of democratic control of foreign policy, that the Senate should be eliminated from any share in the treaty-making power. This comes pretty close to being a contradiction in terms. Democratic control must be—and can only be—exercised through the elected representatives of the people. At least no one has as yet put forward a plan to short-circuit the people's elected representatives and thereby secure something more democratic. The solution of this problem would, therefore, appear to be found not in eliminating the Senate, but in equipping it to resume the discharge of its constitutional function.

CHAPTER XIII

Suggestions for Building a Foreign Policy

MARK TWAIN once remarked that everybody grumbles about the weather, but nobody does anything about it. This comes uncomfortably close to describing the American attitude toward foreign policy.

We can go on for years criticizing the Department of State and the Senate in the conduct of our foreign relations; we can continue to advocate tinkering with the Constitution or changing our machinery without getting any nearer to our goal.

But we can have a foreign policy if we want it enough. To achieve this we need not amend the Constitution. We need nothing more spectacular than a well-thought-out plan for a great deal of hard work.

It is the purpose of this chapter to outline such a plan to serve as a basis of discussion.

No such plan will be accomplished without a radical departure from stereotyped methods.

The Department of State has recently gone through one of the periodic reorganizations with which we have been familiar for a generation. Each of these is heralded as a daring change to do away with old evils and provide more effective handling of our foreign affairs. Unfortunately there has never yet been a reorganization that was more than a reshuffling of men and offices and duties according to some new chart.

In the latest reorganization notice has been taken of the growing public feeling that something ought to be done about foreign policy. But it has been done by the time-honored method of creating another bureau and adding it to the rickety structure that has been growing in this way for over a generation. One of our weaknesses is the assumption that almost any problem can be dealt with by setting up another bureau with an appropriate name. This is sometimes advisable, as in creating a bureau for the press service or a visa bureau, or some other form of departmental routine.

But it is an entirely different matter when we come to dealing with one of the most important and intricate problems confronting our government. Even if staffed by the ablest men in the country, another bureau as such cannot conceivably meet our needs. It cannot deal with fundamentals. The State Department alone can neither formulate nor implement a policy. In reality, it can do no more than offer advice as to the conduct of current business.

That is exactly what is provided in the newly created Policy Committee announced on January 15, 1944. The organization is described in the *Foreign Policy Bulletin* of the Foreign Policy Association of March 3, 1944, in the following terms:

The foremost single achievement of the reorganization was the creation of a Policy Committee, composed of Secretary Cordell Hull, Undersecretary Edward R. Stettinius, Jr., the four Assistant Secretaries, Legal Adviser Green H. Hackworth, and Special Assistant to the Secretary Leo Pasvolsky. On February 22 Michael J. McDermott, Special Assistant to the Secretary in matters concerning the Department's relations with the press, was added to the Committee, which meets regularly three times a week to discuss current questions. Thus top officials of the Department participate in all decisions on high policy (although the final word in political matters often rests with President Roosevelt or the Combined Chiefs of Staff Committee). Before January 15 the casually run Department reached high policy decisions only through conference among those officials immediately interested.

Exploration of the Bolivian recognition problem, for instance, was monopolized by the Secretary and officers concerned with Latin-American affairs, although its implications touched the whole range of American foreign policy. On the petroleum question, however—which has become acute since the reorganization—the higher officials have been contributing to the ultimate decision through their exchanges at Policy Committee meetings. Officers immediately concerned with whatever problem is before the Committee share in its discussions. When the Committee discusses Arabian oil, Charles D. Rayner, adviser on petroleum policy, is present, with Wallace S. Murray, Director of the Office of Eastern and African Affairs, and John D.

Hickerson, Chief of the Division of British Commonwealth Affairs. When it discusses Russia, Charles E. Bohlen, Chief of the Division of Eastern European Affairs, participates.

It is evident even from this approving account that the new machinery does no more than prescribe consultation among the responsible officers of the department and their advisers in regard to current developments. It is not unreasonable to assume that this should take place as a matter of course, without need for such publicity and back-patting.

We are told by the press that the bureau is to have the benefit of advice from several eminent citizens, few with more than a brief flier in diplomacy to their credit. They are busy men, and it is obvious they can be expected to do no regular work, to be available for no more than occasional consultation. This is to ignore the importance and urgency of the task that confronts us. The questions of policy that demand wise solution are stupendous and call for all the wisdom and ability we can mobilize. We shall not get these by designating a few gentlemen to help out in their spare time. Such occasional consultations have a value, but they are inadequate for solving fundamental problems; and again it looks as if we were falling back on providing more and more advice for the conduct of current business.

But the whole setup fails to come to grips with the real problem of any policy-making body.

We have never outgrown the idea that foreign policy is the exclusive preserve of the Department of State. This is far from being a fact. Policy must be determined and put into effect by a surprisingly large number of government agencies. The department not only has no authority to decide for them what they are to do, but it does not possess the expert knowledge on which to base a decision as to what they can and should do.

Its essential task, therefore, is to elicit from them all such information as they can give as to the nature of our problems, and the contributions they can make to solving them, and then take the lead in formulating policy and conducting our international relations.

No State Department bureau can suffice for this task. No bureaucratic functionary is going to settle our most vital problems no matter how much advice and assistance may be given him.

If we recognize the importance of the problems to be faced we begin to realize that they need far broader and more imaginative treatment than they have ever had.

We might consider the establishment of a Council on National Defense, for that is exactly what an adequate board of policy would be. It would be under the chairmanship and direction of the Secretary of State as the official chiefly responsible for the implementing of foreign policy and the conduct of our international relations. It should be a sort of Siamese twin of the Department of State, for it would draw upon the information and personnel of the department and formulate plans for its guidance.

This would not be merely a new piece of machinery. It would not be merely a modernization and streamlining of diplomacy. It would be aimed at bringing about an effective co-ordination of all government activities having to do with foreign affairs.

While the Secretary of State should perhaps be titular head of the Council, in practice he could give only a part of his time to its activities and there should be a working head who devotes his entire time and energies to the work. To be effective he should have Cabinet rank or at the very least be an Undersecretary, for he must at all times have ready access to all heads of the government, including the President.

The work of the Council could not be achieved by the occasional meetings envisaged for most of the committees which have been proposed from time to time. It would operate uninterruptedly, like any federal department.

The staff would be largely composed of officials of the Department of State and the Foreign Service. In addition, there should be permanent, full-time, high-ranking representatives of the various government departments having to do with foreign affairs—Treasury, War, Navy, Commerce, Agriculture, and those alphabeticals which operate to any extent in the foreign field, each of these officials supported by his own staff of experts.

This would be calculated to bring about continuous day-to-day co-operation between all these branches of the government, instead of the hand-to-mouth consultations now undertaken when emergencies arise. It would mean the establishment of an organization to work all the time, year in and year out, in peace and war, to build a common fund of knowledge on which alone co-operation can be based.

The membership of the Council should be further extended—and this is a vital part of the scheme—to include majority and minority members of the Senate Committee on Foreign Relations and of the House Committee on Foreign Affairs.

This, of course, is to advocate a radical departure from present practice. Various objections will be offered. First of all, that the House has no role to play in the conduct of foreign affairs and that this would constitute a legislative invasion of the executive power. It is difficult to see how such objections can be maintained. The House plays an essential role in spite of the steady encroachment on its powers by the Executive. For one thing, it originates all money bills which permit the operation of the Department of State and the Foreign Service and fulfillment of our international obligations. Is it not reasonable to suppose that this role would be more wisely performed if the House were afforded greater facilities for understanding the problems of the Department of State and for putting in its word as to how they are to be solved? And there would be no invasion of the executive power, for the whole purpose of the Council would be to support the operation of the Executive.

There is something even more than this. The House has a vital role in the declaration of war. It might not be a bad idea—although perhaps a radical one—for the House to discharge this responsibility in the light of knowledge.

We tend to disregard the role played by the House—to overlook the fact that the actual conduct of our foreign affairs is in no small measure determined by laws passed by Congress by majority vote.

We should disabuse our minds of the idea that Congress has only an occasional perfunctory duty to perform in regard to foreign affairs. That is as ridiculous as it would be to say the same thing about the Secretary of State. The members of the Senate, for instance, cannot take a wise decision about the ratification of a treaty unless they know why it was negotiated, why we failed to obtain this, why we conceded that, whether our negotiators were competent and secured a fair bargain. They have a right to satisfy themselves on such matters before taking a decision.

The granting of such information is not a favor or a concession made to the Senate. It is a positive advantage to the Department of State to have the Senate fully advised, for this affords the best facilities for keeping the country informed. The State Department is not equipped to inform the country directly, save through an occasional speech or statement.

If, however, we had a couple of senators known to be thoroughly informed through continuous work on the Council on National Defense, they would be able, without any change in our governmental structure, to meet the need perceived by those who advocate having the Secretary of State appear and answer questions in the Senate. There is a definite need to keep the Senate informed, and this can be met by modernizing our practice.

As matters now stand, speeches on foreign affairs in Congress are not impressive to the nation. The statements made in such speeches are so often contradicted by the Department of State that we know that a senator or congressman is usually expressing no more than his own opinions, at best with some hasty last-minute coaching from the State Department. How different if there were certain members who were recognized as being informed on foreign problems and whose statements would therefore be accepted as wholly responsible. Their speeches would be listened to with great respect and would be pondered outside the halls of Congress.

The other members of the Council should be of rank and authority to deal with the Secretary of State and the senators. Appointment of junior functionaries to represent the different departments would inevitably result in the Council fizzling out as just another half-baked piece of reorganization. For instance, the officer representing the General Staff should be an experienced general, perhaps an assistant chief of staff. Otherwise he would be no more than a liaison officer. Those representing Treasury, Commerce, and other departments should have the rank of undersecretaries and be men who speak with authority for and to their departments.

Each of these members would have as his sole task to keep himself posted as the recognized authority on his own department, its resources and needs, and to study the general program so as to be able to inform his department of its place in the scheme of things. These men should make the offices of the Council their head-quarters. Any tendency to carry on from widely scattered government offices would merely start the trend toward disintegration. There would be no lack of work to justify this whole-time operation.

There would be several phases of the work. The chief members would be called on for discussion and review of our methods and for formulation of suggestions for the Department of State. This gives little idea of the amount and importance of this work. For the first time in our history we would have a full-time operation to co-ordinate our conduct of foreign affairs and there would be work for a considerable staff.

But when we approach the question of formulating foreign policy, we realize that the problems involved extend pretty much over the whole range of human activities. The amount of drudgery called for is staggering. That is no reason for failing to undertake it any more than it would be an argument against the huge amount of drudgery, research, compilation, and analysis carried on by the General Staff of the Army.

This would involve building up a large research staff. Many of the men could be brought in from the Department of State and other government agencies. In addition, it might be necessary to import outside talent and even to farm out research on special subjects to unofficial agencies like the Brookings Institution, the Carnegie Peace Foundation, the Chamber of Commerce of the United States, and universities and colleges.

Our task is to clarify our minds as to the exact character of the problems confronting us abroad, as to just what we want to do about them, and what means are at our disposal. And with all this clearly in our minds, we must decide how to use those means, which aims are essential and which can be sacrificed in order to concentrate on essentials. In other words, it is a gigantic job of cutting our garment according to the cloth.

There is a rich field here for public discussion. Lots of good ideas can doubtless be brought forward for the improvement of our methods.

How this Council would work is open to discussion. One thing is certain—we must do a vast amount of preliminary work before we are ready to discuss policy. It is fatuous to debate the relative merits and advantages of any given course unless we have before us a clear picture of the *situation*. We have never had this picture. We have great masses of information about conditions and developments and events, but they are only pieces of a jigsaw puzzle that have never been fitted together into a clear, understandable picture.

So the first task of the Council—and a titanic one—would be to plot out in some coherent form a chart or statement of all the problems facing our government. A mere statement of the task shows its encyclopedic proportions. Work would have to be done both according to countries and according to problems, for we have both sorts of questions to deal with. There are some problems that are universal and some that arise out of special or even local circumstances.

By way of illustration let us single out the study of the Mexican situation.

As a preliminary we must take the general state of the country, the character of the government in power, its attitude toward the United States and toward other countries, its attitude toward resident foreigners and toward private property, the character of the constitution and the sort of legislation voted and projected, the character and attitude of the press and of public feeling. These and many other background questions.

All the departments represented on the Council would bring their contributions toward building this picture.

The results of this study—probably of long duration—should be boiled down into not too bulky form, giving as fact what has been established, as opinion conclusions that have been reached, together with the views of recognized authorities in a position to understand the questions under review.

With this in hand the members of the Council would begin to see a more accurate and comprehensive picture. But it would be no more than a basis for further work. It would enable the Council to begin specializing on Mexican problems specifically affecting the United States. There are many of them. By way of rough illustration we might enumerate:

1. Political relationships.
2. Frontier incidents.

3. Protection of citizens and their property.
4. Anti-American feeling.
5. Oil cases.
6. Mining cases.
7. Expropriation of other properties.

All this, of course, is a purely one-sided approach. We examine everything from the American point of view—from the point of view of our own interests. That is the way everybody else does it, but it is not highly imaginative. We would often understand our own problems better if we got to know as much as possible of the other fellow's point of view. And the better our understanding, the better our chance of getting our own way.

Still using Mexico as our illustration, we should do well to remember that there are problems created for the Mexicans by conditions and behavior on this side of the frontier. Whether we can agree with it or not, the more we can grasp the Mexican view, the more substance there is for our approach to policy.

Of course it is unorthodox to ask foreigners to sit in on the formulation of policy, but it might be intelligent to do just that— at least to the extent of asking some of them to sit in and discuss with us matters of common concern.

Let us single out one of these, anti-American feeling. There is no record that we have ever made an effort to dig into this problem. We deplore it, we are bewildered and sometimes indignant. Lately we have been inclined to ascribe any such irritations to Nazi or Fascist machinations. Again, it is like the weather. But why not try to do something about it? Let the Council try to get at fundamental causes—seeking information from our own people in Mexico, from Mexicans, and from anybody who may have something interesting to tell us. And then try to formulate some ideas as to what can be done about it; where well-founded grievances can be remedied; how misconceptions can be dispelled, and how active good feeling and confidence can be promoted. It is obvious that this is the real task of diplomacy.

And once this particular study was completed, it could be laid aside until all other Mexican questions were ready for consideration. For it is only when we have a clear understanding of the character of all our problems with Mexico that we are able to sit down and discuss intelligently the general range of our relations and how we are going to distribute the application of our influence.

Once we have all the reports brought in and co-ordinated, so that we can evaluate them, we have, for the first time, a preliminary estimate of the situation—at least as far as relations with one country are concerned.

On the basis of such an estimate we can proceed to the next step, that of considering our mission—that is to say, what we should seek to achieve in our relations with Mexico.

The same method would have to be applied to all countries and from another angle to all regions. Then there are over-all problems, like tariffs, which call for careful study and shout for co-operation with Congress. Under this method they would get it.

In the first step of estimating the situation, the representatives of other government agencies would co-operate with their own special knowledge and the work of their experts.

In the second step they would make an even more vital contribution. Under the old practice, when a situation arose, the State Department consulted other departments as to what help could be given, but that was usually last-minute consultation of the hand-to-mouth variety.

What is here suggested is something better. We cannot even make up our own minds as to what we ought to do about Mexico unless we know what means we have at our disposal. But in the sittings of the Council we are able to have daily discussion as to what help could be counted on from Treasury, Commerce, Interior, Agriculture, War, and Navy, and such other departments as might be brought into a given situation.

The Senate members could give their views at any time as to what the reaction of the Senate would be to any course under consideration, and many delays and uncertainties could be eliminated. Past experience of previous consultations with senators has left a memory of helpful contribution—of suggestions that never would have occurred to an executive department. These seldom require a change of substance, usually some adaptation of form that would facilitate senatorial approval.

The members of the House would by this stage have reached a new understanding of what we were seeking to accomplish and why, and they could begin to play a useful role by suggesting how to secure legislation, appropriations, and other help needed from the House.

These intricate discussions should end with the formulation of a coherent statement of what we are trying to do and by what means we propose to do it. This we have never yet had in all our history.

Once we reach agreement on these points we have got something very important. To begin with, the men in the Department of State are clear in their own minds as to what we really want to accomplish and what instruments we can count on. For the first time they are in a position to tell our representatives in the field that this is our policy and that within clearly defined limits they are free to go ahead and use their own judgment—thus doing away with the back-seat driving on details which is the curse of our diplomacy.

It is not advocated that a committee should formulate a policy covering our relations with Mexico or as regards some general problem facing us all over the world and then consider it frozen for all time. Nothing of the sort. Diplomacy is not static. It is constantly changing, and the committee would have to deal constructively with each and every problem constantly under review. Any new situation, or even a request for instructions, may call for reconsideration, and often for readjustment.

At first we could begin no more than the application of restricted and tentative plans, for there could be no question of putting into operation a policy for China, or a policy for Germany, or a policy for the protection of American property by itself. Those would be scraps of policy of another sort, and might often be applied only at the cost of sacrificing something more important. It is only when we have completed the first general survey that we can begin the second task of co-ordinating our views on all the different questions, our relations with all the countries of the world, our relations with them singly and as groups or alliances.

And, as if this were not intricate enough, we have another whole category of questions we must deal with, bearing upon our relations with various countries—questions like disarmament, international debts, trade agreements, and a host of others.

And after we have all these problems formulated in a tentative way, the delicate and fundamental task of deciding relative importance begins.

The ideal system would be to rush to the help of our people anywhere and at any time. But we are not living in an ideal world. If we rush off to the aid of Americans in Asia Minor, we may thereby forfeit the possibility of rendering an even more urgent service to Americans in China. All those things must be thought out and discussed and weighed, and general decisions reached as to where we are going to concentrate, how we can achieve a maximum result.

At this stage we might take another unprecedented step.

It does not suffice for the Secretary of State to make up his mind as to what he ought to do. It does not even suffice to secure the acquiescence of the other government departments and assurances of support from Congress.

With all this, if we venture into the field we may know what we want, but we still lack knowledge of what other governments want and what they propose to do about it. And our troubles are only beginning. It would be a new departure if, when we have made up our own minds, we were to sound out other governments and seek to learn how ready they are to go along with us. If we find ourselves in agreement, we can go full steam ahead. If they are not in agreement, we may find that we can get better results by reconsidering our course and adapting it to the views of others.

Our present practice is to discuss with other governments little beyond current day-to-day problems. That is inadequate. Once we have some idea of what our country is able to accomplish for a more abundant life as well as what we should like to achieve, we are in a better position to discuss broader aspects with others. That would be a real modernization of diplomacy—far more important than the adoption of some new form of machinery.

There is nothing more important in the development of our diplomacy than building up slowly and patiently a fund of common interest, common understanding, and common purpose with other governments. Co-operation in daily tasks is all to the good, but there is far more to be accomplished by working out agreement on lines of conduct for the future. There should be nothing exclusive about this, but we should build the co-operation wherever the basis for it exists. There may be found matters in which we can extend the offer of co-operation to all comers. But there may be others where we find community of interest and purpose exist only for a limited number of countries. Others where the problem exists only for ourselves and one other country, whether it be Britain or Iran or Paraguay. There is a great field here to strengthen the operation of our diplomacy.

If we had a definite policy, say about Mexico again, one essential step would be full consultation with Mexico herself, with all countries having direct interests there, and with various American countries to make sure that they realized the reasonableness of what we were seeking to achieve. We are usually in a state of mind about the attitude of other American countries. We are hurt and bewildered by their distrust of our motives. To be quite honest, some of them are also in a state of mind about us, hurt and bewildered by some of our actions. They don't understand what we are trying to do. No wonder! But whereas we know that our ignorance is often due to the fact that there is little to know, other countries are sometimes convinced that we are being deep and devious, that we are pursuing sinister aims, and that they are all threatened—the idea being that if we succeed in present enterprises their turn will come in time.

It would be a great advance if we could reach a point where we could call in foreign representatives and give them a frank and convincing statement of our aims and policies. Experience indicates that in many cases there would be reciprocal frankness, a fading of suspicions, and an automatic easing of international tensions. It would not be the dawn of the millennium, but other countries would often be able to meet us halfway if they knew what we were driving at. On our side, we might be able to take their views and misgivings into account in such a way as to reassure them.

Our hope of better foreign relations lies in winning the confidence of other nations in our sincerity and honesty and our ability to keep our commitments. They are more fundamentally interested in our observing our obligations than in our showering them with affection and promises.

Other nations would grasp the significance of congressional participation in the building of policy. They would be quick to sense that this might be the beginning of a new era of non-partisan conduct of foreign affairs—and the end of the old system of broaching a new policy for each administration.

There is a great deal more to international collaboration than assertion that we will work together with other nations. The nature of the collaboration differs with each nation and must be worked out by people who know what it is all about in practice. The collaboration varies in importance—and even in reality. There may, for instance, be perfect collaboration between the United States and Tibet, but compared with our relations with a number of other countries, it is hardly likely to have much effect on world affairs.

Take, on the other hand, the question of our collaboration with a country such as Britain. We both need it every day. The better the quality of that collaboration, stretching as it does to every corner of the world, the better for all of us.

There is much loose thinking on this subject of international collaboration—the assumption that there is something inherently noble in an expression of our readiness to collaborate with others while they should collaborate with us as a matter of course. This sense of nobility and high idealism is enhanced when we collaborate for world peace. There is no ground for this condescending attitude. We have the same interest in peace as everybody else, and our collaboration is nothing nobler than working together to get something we all want. We may develop international collaboration when it is discussed on a more matter-of-fact basis.

And there are even more obvious decisions to be made. The Council might even decide not to try to please everybody. For instance, we might be urged to satisfy the noble aspirations of some of our people by reducing the Army and Navy, and, at the same time, to satisfy the equally noble aspirations of others by adopting a hectoring attitude that would lead to war. This has happened before. It will call for careful study and courage and a great effort of popular education.

The final responsibility in diplomacy and policy lies with the President, and obviously he could not be relieved of it by any such organization as is here suggested. The duty of the Council would not be to determine policy and adopt it. Rather to do the necessary work preliminary to determination of any policy and to submit to the President the background material and carefully matured recommendations on which he can base a decision.

Such a plan calls for no elaborate legislation. It is no more than a tightening up of existing agencies in better collaboration. An executive order would probably suffice to specify the setup and methods.

The foregoing outline is not offered as a definite blueprint but rather as a line of thought that may lead to constructive action. There is a broad field for discussion here—alternatives, improvements, and variations.

There have been a number of proposals put forward as solutions for our problems which we might profitably re-examine. No one of them suffices as a cure-all, but one or more of them may fit usefully into a more comprehensive operation.

First we might consider the proposals that have been made for establishing contact between the Department of State and the Senate. It is important that these two institutions be as closely integrated as possible, for the closer we get to a working relationship the farther we get from the conception of two antagonistic authorities bent on thwarting each other.

There have been a number of proposals for providing a seat in the Senate for the Secretary or Undersecretary of State in order to secure some of the advantages of the British parliamentary system. We must as a starter set aside the idea that we would achieve the same identity of purpose as in Britain, for that is achieved, not by having ministers sit in Parliament, but rather by the fact that the Cabinet is in the last analysis no more than the executive committee of the House of Commons, subject to dismissal whenever it ceases to command the support of a majority. Having ministers in attendance is merely a device for facilitating the flow of information that will maintain the confidence of the House as long as possible.

For that limited but important purpose we might consider adopting the device in some form.

The Secretary of State is perhaps the obvious man to appear

before the Senate to answer questions and justify the course of the government. But under our system he is an overworked man and we should be chary about adding to his burdens. There is not the some compelling reason for him to attend and participate in debates. In Great Britain or any other parliamentary country the fate of the government is at stake in every debate. With us the life of the Cabinet is not at stake. No matter what the Senate may vote or resolve the Cabinet goes on to the end of its term. Constitutionally the Cabinet does not exist. We do not have a responsible ministry in the constitutional sense. In the everyday sense the Cabinet is responsible only to the President and not to the Congress or the electorate.

If we accept this fundamental distinction between our system and that of parliamentary government it becomes clear that the attendance of any representative of the Executive is for the limited objective of conveying information, ironing out misunderstandings, and promoting collaboration. For this limited objective accurate information and frankness are required more than official position.

There have been many proposals that the Undersecretary of State be charged with this task. This might well be considered. However, the same end might well be attained by entrusting this duty to an official of the Council on National Defense. In fact, he might be better qualified for the task. The Undersecretary of State is kept busy dealing with the conduct of current affairs and this requires his full time. The Council on National Defense, on the other hand, is concerned with laying down the general lines of policy, and this is of greater interest to the Senate. We might consider confiding to the Secretary of the Council on National Defense a function analogous to that of the Secretary General of the League of Nations, and having him report from time to time to the Senate, as the Secretary General reported developments to the League Council. There would be much logic in this, for our senators have the status of ambassadors from the sovereign states to the federal government. The Secretary of the Council on National Defense would be responsible for the co-ordination of research and interdepartmental co-operation and would thus be in a unique position to keep the Senate informed.

It is also suggested from time to time that the Secretary or

Undersecretary meet frequently with the Committee on Foreign Relations to keep that body informed and to seek guidance as to senatorial views. This in itself is not enough, but anything that brings about more intimate exchange of views between the Executive and the Senate is an undoubted improvement and is worthy of serious consideration.

The work of the Council on National Defense would of course be a full-time operation for its regular members, but we might also consider giving them the benefit of much experience not available on a full-time basis. There is much to be said for a consultative body of elder statesmen to give opinions on matters of moment. As a rule we make little use of experience acquired in public service. Once a man retires from active service we have a way of turning him out to grass. We are the only grown-up country to make so little use of available experience. We utilize their services during the long years they are acquiring experience, and just as they acquire their maximum usefulness in wisdom and experience, we scrap them.

To take Britain again as an illustration: When public servants return home to settle down after long careers as ambassadors, viceroys, and governors, some useful occupation is usually found for them. They are used on commissions or inquiries of various sorts and render valuable service. Those who go into Parliament fill a definite need. Some are put into the House of Lords for the purpose of retaining their experience without requiring them to go into politics. A few years ago I listened to a debate in that body on reforms in the diplomatic service. The quality of the debate was striking and prompted me to make a rough calculation with one of the participants which disclosed that the speakers had a combined diplomatic experience of some one hundred and eighty years in the field and the Foreign Office.

We have nothing of this sort, but there is no reason why we should do without it. To indicate the possibilities it might be suggested that there be a consultative committee on call for consideration of important problems. There might be some ex-officio members—any former President of the United States, any retired Chief Justice, Secretary of State, or Chief of Staff. In addition the President might designate any retired Ambassador or other public figure who might be a valuable addition to the membership of the committee.

It would not be the function of such a committee to meddle in the activities of the Department of State. Rather to give thought to difficult problems where their opinion would be of value to the Council. This does not imply that they should decide what was to be done. That responsibility is one of which the President cannot be relieved. But recommendations carefully thought out by men of experience and prestige should be of great value to the President in reaching his own decisions. At times it would strengthen his hand with the country if he could say that his decision had been reached after consultation with a body of such prestige.

All this has been long in the telling, but would be much longer in the doing. It would take years of hard work by many able men even to get things started. But able men are glad to work hard on far less important and less hopeful tasks. Hard work is no argument against this plan, although it is the one most often encountered when advocating it.

And if we ever progress this far we shall have achieved a number of things.

First of all, we should have for the first time a coherent idea of the world pattern, where we fit into it, what our interests really are, where we can concentrate our national effort to the best effect.

Second, our negotiators—that is to say the President, the Secretary of State, and their agents—both at home and abroad would, for the first time, have a clear understanding of what they can actually accomplish.

Third, we should have an end of the ostrich diplomacy we have suffered from so long. Equipped with a policy, we should begin to look ahead and plan.

Fourth, we should have an end to the free-for-all, catch-as-catch-can attempt of government departments to deal each with its share of the foreign field. They would all be stronger operating under a single plan. They would secure their individual objectives more easily together than separately. And there would be elimination of waste—both in money and effort.

Fifth, we would terminate the amateur diplomacy that has been such a costly handicap. If there were a foreign policy and it were made known to the American people, it is a fair assumption they would begin to take a real interest in the character and qualifications of those sent abroad to represent them. We would begin to see the present sort of representation in its true light as a highly unflattering reflection on ourselves.

Sixth, the Senate would be better equipped to exercise its constitutional responsibility; for if majority and minority members sat through all this preliminary work and realized the grounds for the decisions reached, they would be in a position, in the vast majority of cases, to satisfy their colleagues that there was nothing antagonistic to the national interest in the instruments sent them for ratification.

Seventh, we should have a sounder basis of co-operation with the House, with recognized representatives qualified to keep the House informed on matters of concern to it. We should also do away with much of the current distrust and antagonism. If decent Americans sit in on the formulation of their country's foreign policy and are satisfied as to its reasonableness, are we justified in believing that they would make capital of their confidential knowledge for partisan advantage? On the contrary, may we not hope that this sharing of responsibility with both the Senate and the House would prove the shortest road to a nonpartisan and continuous foreign policy, without which we can never exercise effective international leadership?

There can be no doubt that the adoption of a system for maintaining a continuous foreign policy would do much to bridge the gap between the Executive and Congress, as regards the tremendously important field of foreign affairs.

Membership on the Committee on Foreign Relations is one of the highest distinctions that can now come to a senator. If the Council on National Defense were built up to its proper importance, the Council would be a step higher for the members chosen, who would represent the entire committee and indeed the Senate in dealing with the whole range of foreign affairs.

This prestige could reasonably be expected to develop a new sense of responsibility. Senators of both parties, working together year after year on the foreign problems of the country, could reasonably be expected to see things from a national point of view. They would presumably develop into the spokesmen of the government on foreign affairs—not spokesmen of the Administration, but of the government. Here the Senate would benefit from informed statements and speeches, and we might get back to the sort of debates that once served to enlighten the country and to focus our political thinking on a level comparable with that of our early history.

Eighth, we would enlarge the area of possible collaboration with other countries. With a clear picture of our problems and our purposes, we might go further. As matters now stand we devote most of our effort to disposing of the daily run of difficulties as they arise. This energy is concentrated on dealing with conflicts of interest. With the growth of an American policy we should be able to give an increasing share of our energy to community of interest with other countries. There is no doubt that we shall always confront conflicts of interest—it is far more constructive to discover and strengthen community of interest. And as we build up this side of our relations there is reason to believe that we shall find steadily increasing strength and skill in dealing with the conflicts.

This is a whole phase of international relations that has been sadly neglected by all countries.

Ninth, we should be working our way toward a genuine democratic control of policy. With simplified and co-ordinated leadership it should be possible to concentrate public interest on fundamentals—on our aims, our international undertakings, our obligations to other countries and their obligations to us. These are things the people have a right to know. It is also in the interest of the government that they should know in order that there may be effective and understanding support in international affairs. There is also a secondary but important advantage. As public knowledge of policy grew, there would be less feverish anxiety in regard to current negotiation and current events. The negotiators would be less harassed in carrying out their duties.

Tenth, if the day comes when we have a comprehensive, well-considered, reasonable policy, the chances of our exercising effective leadership in the world will be considerably increased. For one thing, other countries will understand far better what we are aiming at, and if our aims are reasonable, there will be an increased chance of their endorsement. We cannot, without grave danger, feel our way by improvisation in the postwar world. We may be sure other governments will be all set with their schemes for getting their own way, and we shall not be working on equal terms unless we have ready prepared plans for what we want, both for our national interests and in the common interest where we hope to play a worthy role. As it is, our country plays an important, often a dominant, part in world affairs by dint of its power and resources, rather than because of any well-considered policy. There is sometimes a tendency to feel that what we want should be done because we want it. Sometimes we are able to get our way on no better grounds. But we should be able to provide less childish reasons.

Eleventh, one result of a policy would be to build up a permanent service in the Department of State. Congress and the country would soon grasp the fact that a policy formulated by so much thought and hard work, so precious to the country, could not be turned over to new and inexperienced hands every four years and that we must have an experienced crew to keep it in order.

We know that professional diplomats will never have the final decision in matters of importance. Decision and responsibility belong together, which means that final decision rests with the President and Secretary of State. Both these men are bound to be amateurs in diplomacy, for it would be an extraordinary case where a career diplomat would occupy either position. But for that very reason both President and Secretary of State have all the more need for expert support and backing—both in Washington and in the field.

Finally, having once formulated what can be described as a policy, we should have continuity of policy. The reason for this prediction is that once we have a general plan which everybody understands, no normal man is going to scrap the work of years in order to substitute for it his own improvisations. Established continuity would survive changes of administration and would with time become non-partisan—a consummation devoutly to be desired. It is easier and more natural and safer for the individual to continue something that works than it is to change. And, above all, if we have a recognized policy—and only if we have one—we can hope that partisanship will really stop at the water's edge.

CHAPTER XIV

Democratic Control of Policy

ELIHU ROOT said in 1922:

When foreign affairs were ruled by autocracies or oligarchies, the danger of war was in sinister purpose. When foreign affairs are ruled by democracies, the dangers of war will be in mistaken beliefs. The world will be the gainer by the change, for, while there is no human way to prevent a king from having a bad heart, there is a human way to prevent a people from having an erroneous opinion. That way is to furnish the whole people . . . with correct information.

It may be hoped that some such organization as that we have discussed would bring about an improvement in the conduct of our foreign affairs and contribute to the building of a foreign policy with continuity. But no organization, however good, can by itself achieve the full measure of improvement we need. We cannot too strongly emphasize that in our country foreign policy will, in the last analysis, be determined by public opinion, or, in the absence of an informed public opinion, by public feeling. Our fundamental problem is, therefore, to devise measures that contribute to the building of an informed public opinion.

It is altogether too easy to blame all our ills and all our weaknesses on the government. It is the mark of enlightenment nowadays to berate the Department of State and demand that it "enter into relations with the American people." This biting phrase represents what is fast becoming a general attitude. The department has become the whipping boy of the critics. There is no denying that the whole machinery for handling our foreign affairs needs a thorough overhauling, but it is childish to accept the charge that our position in the world would be quite different if the Secretary of State had kept the American people more informed as to events.

Just what information did the American people lack that would have changed their course? Did the Secretary of State withhold from them the fact that Japan was on the rampage in the East and that we were in danger of war? Did he conceal from the people the fact that the Axis powers were arming and committing one act of aggression after another? What did he conceal from them aside from the details of day-to-day negotiation which it would have been folly to reveal? When we unload the blame for everything that goes wrong on the Department of State, we are merely side-stepping our own responsibility.

It is time we realized that "correct information," as the words were used by Mr. Root, means a great deal more than a flow of information on current events. That, of course, would be an improvement on our present state, but we need much more. In order to judge current events we need the yardstick of knowledge. We need first of all to know our own history, why we have grown and evolved as we have, the obstacles that have been overcome, and the sacrifices that have been made to secure and maintain our liberties. We need understanding of the process by which we have grown to our present stature—and why. We need also to know the history of other countries in order to understand their different outlooks and the need for the adjustment of our ideas and theirs; and last but by no means least we need, if we are to play a worthy part, to have leadership in understanding the moral issues and the moral values that confront us in so many of our problems. A purely political approach to world problems is not always enough. In many of them there are issues of right and wrong, of justice or injustice, of compassion or cruelty. Only if the American people bring to their problems this broader understanding can they do justice to themselves and make a maximum contribution to building the better world we all want. No government can by itself furnish this understanding, and we need to go far beyond the domain of governmental activity if we are to achieve not only democratic control of foreign policy, but intelligent, enlightened control.

There are three factors we should consider in this connection: the press, education, and the churches. It is within our power as a people to make each of these an effective instrument if we care enough to do the necessary hard work.

The press is a most important instrument for the building of public opinion on foreign affairs—an instrument for which there is no substitute. Most of us are pretty free in criticizing the short-comings of the press and blaming it for not giving us more adequate information. Few of us, however, realize the handicaps under which our newspapermen work or the remarkable results they get in spite of difficulties in their way. There is no press in the world more keenly conscious of its mission. It is bred in the bone of every newspaperman that the people have a right to know and that he is hired to find out and tell them. He does not feel that he is relieved of his duty by the fact that official sources are not forthcoming. That merely means that he is reduced to making bricks without straw—or with not enough straw. It is largely due to the efforts of the press that we are as well informed as we are.

The press is inundated by torrents of propaganda and handouts of various kinds. Fortunately the press does not content itself with this material but seeks to check it with independent information from other sources. Despite much undoubted good will in government offices, information is often scattered among many agencies, and it is not always possible for any one of them to facilitate the work of the news gatherers. This condition has led to sending men scouting around Washington—to the White House, executive departments, and a bewildering number of alphabeticals—to gather information. The bits of information that are brought in are fitted together to make the story to be given to the people. It often happens that no one of the officials they see is in a position to give the whole story. In such cases, the only prudent course is to say as little as possible. This is not so much willful secrecy as it is incomplete information among the officials who are the available sources of news and background material. This is not a reproach against the officials, but it is a criticism of the system. In many cases it is to the interest of the government to have its course known and understood, but there is often a struggle between the seekers for information and officials hampered by their own limitations. The fact remains that much of our news is put together in a makeshift way, and a great part of our editorial comment is based on inadequate material. It is not surprising that the results are unsatisfactory, for the press is working under unfair handicaps.

Parenthetically, it may be said that with all its shortcomings the much-abused Department of State is far more frank and forthcoming than is generally known. The Division of Current Information, under the experienced direction of Michael J. McDermott, has for many years done a brilliant job of providing news and background to the press. If we develop a real national policy to elaborate and explain, Mr. McDermott is fitted by training and character to do a superb job of streamlining our information services.

With all the handicaps under which it labors there is no doubt that the press has proved itself the chief safeguard of our liberties. Properly equipped, and with the right sort of co-operation, it could perform a still greater service of national enlightenment.

We hear talk about how the press is going to promote peace and international understanding after this war. There is no doubt this is desirable, but there is room for some doubt as to how well the press will be equipped for this mission in our own country or any other. There is an immense potential force for good, and we might do well to stop taking it out in talk and give thought to equipping the press for a useful mission.

There have been many proposals for founding a government school for training our diplomats. We have discussed that question elsewhere and indicated some reasons for having our diplomats trained in non-governmental institutions. But this suggests another idea. We might consider making use of the Council on National Defense as a school for correspondents and writers on international affairs. We might go so far as to establish as an integral part of the Council a special section where a number of correspondents could, under official guidance and with government help, participate in the fact-finding work—or, alternatively, go through a thorough training course in the methods of formulating policy. Such training would furnish invaluable background for newspaper work.

If some such scheme were to be adopted, it should not be as a patronizing gesture, a reward of virtue to the press. There would, of course, be great advantage to the press in sharing the same background as is given to our diplomats. But there would be a corresponding advantage to the government to have an understanding press—understanding in the real sense. And the fundamental advantage would be that we should have a better informed public opinion.

We have an ever-growing corps of correspondents serving overseas. Their dispatches are to the people what diplomatic dispatches are to the Department of State. These correspondents would benefit from a course in the press division before going overseas—and from a refresher course now and then. It would give them a yardstick they now lack in judging matters affecting their own country and that of their residence.

The last thing we want in the national interest is to have an alliance that will subordinate the press to the government. It is an entirely different matter to give the press access to information by which it can judge whether the government is on the right track. While this would be calculated to win support—and informed support—for the government if the press was satisfied, it would also equip the press to challenge the government on the strength of authentic information. This would furnish a double safeguard of great benefit to the country.

This does not mean that we should have an obedient press, reflecting only the government viewpoint. That would be a disaster. But it would mean that criticism would be better informed criticism and hence of greater value and effect. This would be no one-way operation of conveying knowledge to the press. Our press has sources of its own of value to the government. The correspondents, as a whole, are prolific in ideas, and many of them are real students of the problems on which they write. If they had a recognized place in the scheme of things, there would be a great deal of mutual advantage.

No government has as yet adopted such an attitude in its relations with the press—at least not on such a scale. When a really close relationship exists, it is usually that of the boa and the rabbit —convenient perhaps for the boa. And if not equally convenient for the rabbit, he is not in a position to complain.

The writer has always found that, given responsibility, the press can be depended on to do a thorough job of keeping faith. There would be great responsibility in such an assignment to the Council which should be looked on not as a favor to the press but as an arrangement for the general good. And we should have a real modernization of our diplomacy.

This has taken us far from the limited field of departmental organization—farther than we have previously gone even in discussion. If the public is to benefit from such changes, however, we may have to venture much farther afield before we achieve our objective. If the public is to benefit from changes in our handling of foreign affairs, we should consider not only an improvement in the sources of news but what happens at the receiving end. Better daily news and editorial comment would, of course, make for better public understanding, but public understanding itself needs fundamental improvement if it is to get full benefit from an improved press service. The hardest part of our task will still lie ahead before we can build the public opinion we want and achieve an intelligent, democratic control of foreign policy.

Any governmental reorganization and any improvement of newspaper methods are only means to an end—the development of wise public thinking on foreign affairs. There is a fundamental need to improve the equipment of the public for doing such thinking. We expect our public opinion to form wise judgments as to matters affecting other countries. We cannot form intelligent opinions about other countries—what they are likely to do and what we can expect them to do—without some knowledge of their background and traditions. In other words, their history. By that same token our first requirement is knowledge of our own history and understanding of the process by which we have grown to our present stature and character and, above all, why. Without the equipment of a sound knowledge of American history first of all, and of world history, we are seriously handicapped in grappling with world problems.

The urgency of this problem is obvious. In April 1943 the New York *Times* published a report on the teaching of history in the United States—a report which has something like the importance of a state paper. It made the shocking revelation that in some 80 per cent of our institutions of higher learning knowledge of American history is not required for the granting of a degree. This survey of the historical knowledge of some 7,000 representative freshmen is an alarming forecast of the understanding of public affairs that we must expect in the future unless there is a national drive to act upon the revelations made by the New York *Times.* We cannot do better than to quote an editorial appearing in the *Times* on April 5, 1943:

Highly discouraging is the report in this morning's *Times* based on a survey covering 7,000 students in thirty-six universities, indicating that American college students are appallingly ignorant even of the most elementary aspects of United States history. It is not a matter of failing to recall obscure dates or becoming entangled in insignificant details. Actually 25 per cent of these students did not know that Lincoln was President of the United States during the Civil War. In this bicentennial year of Thomas Jefferson, 84 per cent could not cite two of the contributions made by this great American.

Even more distressing than the lack of information is the astonishing amount of misinformation disclosed by the students. Many college freshmen apparently have not the slightest notion of what this country looks like. Portland, Oregon, is placed on the Atlantic Ocean, Hudson River, or Great Lakes. Illinois, Texas, California, and New Jersey are listed as being on the Eastern seaboard. Oregon, Mississippi, Wyoming, and Nevada are cited among the thirteen original colonies. Students are misinformed even on fundamental questions, such as the freedoms granted by the Bill of Rights. To many the Bill of Rights guarantees the right to work, to play, to happiness, or to choose one's own recreation. A large number believe it secures them against "want" or "fear." How can anyone study American history and not know that the Bill of Rights guarantees us freedom of speech, press, religion, and assembly?

Since most of these college students had only recently completed high-school courses in American history, the conclusion is inescapable that our high schools need better teaching in that subject. They need a course that will give them an intelligent picture of the growth and development of this country. Moreover, United States history should be required of all college students. When the *Times's* survey of last June disclosed that 82 per cent of all colleges and universities did not require their students to take this subject, the argument was raised that the students are taught American history in the high schools and therefore repeating it on the college level would be a waste of time. It would appear that this argument is fallacious.

There is no doubt that we must overhaul our whole system of teaching history, for without some knowledge of world history it is impossible to judge events, and without a real knowledge of American history we are seriously handicapped, even in judging our own interests. Without knowledge of our own history we can have no conception of the ordeals and the sacrifices which were the price of our present-day freedom. Without this understanding citizens can have no realization of the need for constant vigilance, and they are more readily amenable to proposals that we scrap our hard-won liberties and embark upon experiments of all sorts which are alien to our system and harmful to our interests. The ordinary citizen assumes that there is not much he can do about giving us a foreign policy beyond signing petitions and giving three rousing cheers for the Four Freedoms. There is plenty he can do. For one thing, he can work locally and demand the adequate teaching of history in our schools and colleges. Until this is done we shall never have the benefit of a really enlightened public opinion and a wisely conducted foreign policy.

If we are to play a great part in the world, to play it nobly and boldly, we need more than knowledge and organization. We need understanding both of the nature of diplomacy and the part the citizen can play in its operation.

There is a general impression that diplomacy is inherently crooked and that diplomats must gain their ends by trickery and shifty methods. This is as unfounded as an assumption that all business is inherently crooked. We know that no businessman can be successful on a large scale and for a long period unless he conforms to honest business practices.

The same is true about diplomacy.

In my own experience I have had to deal with all sorts of diplomats from every corner of the earth and have found a remarkable amount of straightforward, honest dealing—as much as in any other profession. There are dishonest diplomats, of course, but their usefulness is short-lived. We sometimes lose sight of the fact that the diplomat is much like the newspaperman in that his chief professional capital is the confidence he is able to inspire and maintain among the people with whom he deals. When a newspaperman rises to eminence in his profession, not notoriety but eminence, it will be found that he has proven himself trustworthy and that people feel free to talk to him frankly. No matter what the pressures and temptations, he can be depended on to keep confidence and play the game. One betrayal of confidence ends his usefulness to his paper, for people fear to trust him and his sources of information dry up. The better his reputation for reliability the greater his influence and the better the information he can gather.

This is true also of the diplomat, not only of the individual, but also of the government he represents. A rich and powerful country can muddle along after a fashion, for a period at least, regardless of accepted standards. But on the positive side it is difficult to exaggerate the importance of general recognition of national honesty and integrity. This is not proved by broadcasting of inspiring professions of purposes but by national conduct, from year to year and decade to decade.

Of course there are those who maintain that the standards of private life do not apply in international affairs. That is a school of thought that should be repudiated. We hear this sort of thing whenever there is talk of the role of the churches in world affairs or of the need for a Christian peace. We are almost sure to hear the argument that war itself is un-Christian and that there will be plenty of time for Christianity when we have defeated the enemy; that in the meantime we need something more practical. To this we may be permitted to reply that there *is* nothing more practical than eternal verities.

The churches of the country are concerning themselves as never before with foreign affairs. They are making an immense and much-needed contribution. It is important that they should do this and that they should increase the scope of their action, for there is a role that they alone can play.

Unfortunately, among much that is inspiring there is some waste effort through concentrating on aspects others are better qualified to deal with, through drawing up blueprints and promoting oversimplified solutions. The churches are not equipped by knowledge or experience to formulate detailed plans. They lose prestige when the man in the street examines their plans and comes to the conclusion that they are amateurish and no better than he could draw himself. On the other hand, they alone can give us leadership to discriminate between truth and untruth, and keep before our eyes the spiritual values which constitute the only true guide. As John Foster Dulles has said:

If the Church follows Christ's example, it will proclaim eternal verities in terms such that their practical significance is made plain, but it will avoid sponsoring specifics that necessarily must be compromises compounded out of worldly knowledge.

There are numerous examples of approach to this task of the churches. Some are directed to stating the moral issues in such a way as to afford a yardstick for measuring the value of the various solutions that are proposed. More of them tend to offer both moral and political guidance, and it must be admitted that in some cases the political solution follows logically upon the moral statement.

As an illustration we may take the report from the Commission of the Federal Council of Churches of Christ in America which met at Delaware, Ohio, March 3–5, 1942. This document, while it states the moral aspect of the problems we shall confront at the end of the war, does from time to time move over the border and advocate political solutions. With great respect for the statement of moral values which constitutes a valuable contribution to our national thinking, some parts of the report are given over to political solutions outside the province of the churches. For instance, we find under the heading "The Economic Bases of a Just and Durable Peace" a suggestion for "the establishment of a universal system of money. The money system should be so planned as to prevent inflation and deflation, in so far as this is possible through monetary means.

"The establishment of a democratically controlled international bank or banks to make development capital available in all parts of the world without the predatory or imperialistic aftermath so characteristic of large-scale private or government loans."

It is difficult to find in proposals for a universal monetary system and an international bank a religious issue the churches are qualified to deal with. A question arises in the mind of the ordinary citizen as to just how much expert knowledge lies behind these proposals. How much study by qualified people is represented in these categorical suggestions? And regardless of how sound they may be financially, just where is the moral issue?

This has its practical importance, for the influence of the churches is not enhanced by proposals of a purely political or economic character. The ordinary, level-headed citizen looks to the churches for spiritual, not financial, guidance.

To choose another illustration, under the heading "The Social Bases of a Just and Durable Peace" we find the following "principle":

"All men should be free to move over the surface of the earth, under international agreement, in search of the fullest opportunity for personal development."

This provision was currently described as a recommendation for "unrestricted world-wide immigration." This may not have been the intention of those who drafted the report, but the wording does lend itself to that interpretation. As the text stands we may pay tribute to its generosity of purpose and still question whether even the moral aspects of the problem were thought through before the report was drafted.

Without quibbling as to the intent of this particular report we know that some generous people have been advocating that all barriers to immigration should be swept away. This idea may be worth a brief examination, both as to the prospects of its being adopted and its effect if it could be put into operation.

An appeal for unrestricted world-wide immigration sounds generous and enlightened, but as a matter of fact there is no such thing, never has been, and probably never will be—certainly not so long as countries retain enough sovereignty to do their own housekeeping. No government in its senses is going to fling wide its doors to immigrants afflicted with disease, to the criminal, illiterate, and insane, to those likely to become a public charge, or to any others it may consider undesirable. Each government will decide for itself—as a vital part of its sovereignty—what is desirable and undesirable. And until governments renounce this right to pick and choose unrestricted immigration remains no more than a glittering and meretricious generality.

"Unrestricted world-wide immigration" has a fine, resounding ring of universal co-operation and conveys a picture of two-way streams of immigration crisscrossing all over the globe. But would it be that way in reality? Or would not the great bulk of this movement flow in one-way streams to the United States? This country is the first preference for the overwhelming majority of the people the world over who would like to move across the seas to better their lot. A negligible number of Americans seek their fortunes abroad, and these are not accurately described as immigrants because most of them bring capital from America to invest, or income or salaries from home.

If all the barriers were removed there would be streams of immigration flowing to this country, limited only by the transportation available. They would pour in regardless of our unemployment problems in the after-war readjustment. Without waiting for things to go that far we may consider how long we could maintain our American standard of living. We might do well to consider how organized labor would react to schemes to open our doors to competitive labor from all over the world. We might even consider how far this would constitute a solution for the impoverished millions coming to the Promised Land. Indeed we may well raise the question whether unrestricted immigration, if permitted, would not aggravate rather than solve the problem. We can recall "race riots" in this country arising from immigration of Chinese labor. Although called "race riots" they did not really stem from racial prejudice. The resentment was at the threat to the American standard of living. We have experience to show that the capacity to work for less than our own people is looked upon as a threat to our way of living. What warrant have we for assuming that the same threat on a far larger scale would provoke no reaction? There is neither kindness nor humanitarianism in adopting generous-sounding plans that lead to violence and misery.

This is perhaps a political question, but it is difficult to find a moral issue calling for the formulation of proposals by the church. Any such proposals ignore real obstacles that cannot be removed by sweeping measures; they ignore the fact that such proposed solutions merely substitute one sort of evil for another.

The question of immigration is one that will face us and one that will call for all the wisdom and leadership we can command. But real leadership will begin by clarifying the issues and not by offering conclusions.

The Six Pillars of Peace adopted by the Federation will be found in the Appendix. They deal with principles and offer the groundwork for the study of real issues. They are free from the weakness of advocating specific solutions.

We might do well to single out one example of a matter of policy involving a moral issue and calling for spiritual leadership. The question of food relief for the small occupied democracies of Europe stands out clearly in this category. When this question arose, the obvious starting point of the government should have been the desire of any decent person that suffering should be relieved if it could be done without hampering the war effort or helping the enemy. Any enlightened government should have adopted that approach. Instead, our government apparently took the position that as the British Government had expressed unwillingness to consider the question nothing could be done. Since 1940 all appeals for consideration have been met either with repetition of arguments ignoring known facts, or with blank silence. It might be remarked in passing that there is nothing sacred about a decision by the British Government or any other, our own included, and that if a great moral issue were at stake we had not only the right but the duty to seek to make our point of view prevail. Other governments frequently seek to persuade us to modify our position; we on our side do as much. It is part of the give and take of international life and need not have the slightest tinge of unfriendliness. And when there is a moral issue at stake there should be no hesitation.

The Turkish Government suffered from no such inhibitions. In 1941 it addressed to the British Foreign Office a request for permission to send food to the suffering Greeks. In reply it received a statement of the old arguments that have stopped us in our tracks. But the Turkish Government, instead of washing its hands of the Greeks, set us an example of human compassion by notifying the Foreign Office that on a specified date it was sending certain ships designated by name to certain Greek ports. This amounted to forcing the blockade, but it got food to the Greeks. Other Allied Powers decided to participate in the work, and food has been sent uninterruptedly to Greece from that day to this. Our own government has gone clearly on record in writing to defend the Greek operation, maintaining that the food reaches the Greek population, that the Nazi authorities do not take it, and generally advancing in support of Greek relief the very arguments put forward in vain on behalf of the other sufferers among our Allies.

It might be thought that the success of the Greek effort would have spurred our government on to re-examine the whole subject in the hope of finding out whether there was not after all some way of relieving the suffering of the other victims of Nazi occupation. Instead, with a cynicism that clashes strangely with our high professions, it has continued to reject the very arguments it continues to advance for the Greek case. This is a striking instance of devious official behavior in order to maintain an unfortunate obstinacy. A government can be wrong, and it is the right and duty of the citizen in such cases to press for change.

There is clearly a great moral issue involved in this—the issue of feeding the starving children of our Allies. Here is where the churches as a whole made a great effort, and even though their leadership has not led to success we can be proud of it. We can take comfort from the unanimity with which an imposing array of religious leaders and religious organizations of all faiths are demanding a moral approach to this question. What they have done gives us hope of what they can do.

There was enough popular conviction on this subject to lead to the adoption of a joint resolution by the Senate and House in which the Congress urged the President to examine the problem with a view to the relief of suffering in Belgium, Holland, Norway, and Poland. Although the resolution was non-partisan and in courteous terms, it was not honored with a reply. In fact, it was totally ignored—a strange spectacle in a democracy. This episode gives a curious confirmation to our earlier assertion that in this great democracy we have autocratic control of foreign policy.

This year the Senate passed another resolution—this time unanimously—again urging the President to try to do something about this tragic problem. At the time of writing there has been no reply. The only comment from the White House was a passage in "My Day" in which Mrs. Roosevelt took liberties with the facts, forgetful that she has been repeatedly apprised of them and that she gave assurance of her sympathy and that of the President. Not content with a curious misstatement of the problem, Mrs. Roosevelt dismissed those in favor of relief as "pacifists and church groups" and intimated that they were not intent on winning the war—a highly insulting and unwarranted charge against large numbers of good citizens, including the whole membership of the United States Senate, to say nothing of such outstanding "pacifists" as General Pershing and Admiral Pratt.

The arrogance of brushing the Senate and other leaders aside as irresponsible sentimentalists is startling coming from the White House. The intimation that a unanimous vote of the Senate can be set aside with a little gentle smearing in Mrs. Roosevelt's column on the ground that a great moral issue is in the exclusive jurisdiction of the military is a shocking assumption that in our country democracy has abdicated, and the military have taken over.

Mrs. Roosevelt brought out one of the stock arguments—that war cannot be waged in a humanitarian way, and that therefore nobody can be fed in the occupied democracies. This argument has nothing to do with the case. Relief is not a matter of waging the war. It is a question of alleviating unnecessary suffering and preserving a generation of children for the rebuilding of shattered Europe. Our whole national tradition is in contradiction to Mrs. Roosevelt's line of argument. We have never been willing to abandon innocent people to suffering and death on specious arguments. Otherwise we should have had no Red Cross, no conventions on the treatment of prisoners of war, no shipment of food packages to our own prisoners in enemy hands, and finally no UNNRA.

This subject has been stated at some length to indicate the great field in which we should look to the churches for leadership. They are the rightful custodians of the Christian virtue of compassion, and they have the right and duty to uphold it against the overpowering forces of cruelty and blood lust raging in time of war. This is not to advocate that they should prescribe methods of relief or the conditions under which it is to be administered, but there is a clear call for the accepted religious leaders of the country to insist that suffering civilians should not be abandoned to their fate without first exhausting all possibilities of coming to their help. We need this sort of leadership desperately in the fog of confusion and moral degeneracy where we wander today.

Confusion on this subject has been deliberately and systematically fostered. We are told that the Germans would take the food. We are told that the blockade would be undermined. We are told that we cannot spare the food. We are told that we have no ships to spare. We are told that the cost would be too great.

Although all these arguments have been refuted over and over, they are still dished up to us. To show how the problem is simplified by a little truth we may say:

According to our own government's official statements the Nazis have not taken the food in Greece. If they did take any, the flow of relief would stop.

The blockade would not be destroyed. A blockade is not a dyke to be washed away. It is a door you keep closed, and open only for those things you are willing to let through. A door is not destroyed by being opened.

We should not have to spare any food. If desired, it could all be furnished from South America.

We are not even asked for ships. The Swedish merchant fleet, now confined to Swedish ports, is available for this purpose and for this purpose only.

There would be no expenditures involved for us. The governments-in-exile have ample funds with which to pay the cost of all operations.

Thus stripped of misrepresentations, the problem is ready for solution. It could be solved almost overnight if the government would examine the facts. If examination of the facts revealed real rather than imaginary obstacles, we should at least have the knowledge that we had tried to do our simple, humanitarian duty.

We should also probably find that the dictates of humanity, strategy, and expediency coincide.

In the knowledge we have of wholesale starvation among our Allies, death from disease and malnutrition, of children doomed to death or lives of wretchedness, it is difficult to see how any human being can be at peace with his own conscience if he fails at least to press for some effort to be made to establish the real possibilities of relief.

The churches are in a unique position to keep clear in our minds and hearts the issues of national honor and morality. If they succeed in enlightening us, they achieve much more. For if they press for moral solutions with sufficient vigor, no government dare ignore them. It may well prove that it is not in the power of the government to adopt or enforce the moral solution, but at least this conclusion should be reached only after exhausting our efforts to do what we know to be right. It should not be reached as a matter of pure expediency. If they recognize their true strength, our churches have a far greater power than they have ever realized to influence our government.

Without being cynical it may be pointed out that a sound religious approach to world problems is also a sound political approach—that in the long run no policy that does not bear moral scrutiny is good politics. To give an unhappy illustration: when this war is over it is important that the countries overrun by the Nazis recognize the superiority of our system, that they turn unhesitatingly to our leadership, and collaborate confidently with us in building the peace. Has our attitude on relief done anything to bind them to us in this way? They are not fooled by our government's arguments, even if some of our own people are. They know it was possible to feed them, that it has been done before, and that it is being done elsewhere for others now. They do not recognize our right to settle this problem as a matter of American or British policy. They know they have a right to have it settled as a matter of allied policy where their governments would have a voice. They resent our arrogating to ourselves the right to doom them to starvation without a hearing. They are outraged by our patronizing and sanctimonious short-wave broadcasts, telling them how the President's heart bleeds for them in their suffering, how he grieves that nothing can be done for them without helping the enemy, and promising them that if they will only be philosophical about letting their children starve for the next few years there will be food for all after the war. This sort of thing is an insult to the intelligence of our wretched Allies. They know they will be fed after the war—and on no grounds of compassion—and as they watch their children wither before their eyes they know we are begging the real question and leaving them to their fate because in this great democracy no way has been found to oblige a reluctant government to face a moral problem. In a case like this if the churches bring their great authority to bear in the right way they can force the government to deal with the problem in a way that is consistent with the honor and dignity of our country.

The churches must be our defense against unmitigated expediency. We have a flagrant case of this in our own changed attitude toward Finland. In the early stages of this war we saw Russia in the role of an aggressor and Finland as an innocent victim. The President voiced the feelings of the American people when, in a series of utterances, he spoke of Russia's "wanton disregard for law" and of the bombings which "sickened the hearts of every civilized man and woman" and "profoundly shocked the conscience of humanity."

On February 10, 1940, he said:

Here is a small republic in northern Europe which, without any question whatever, wishes solely to maintain its own territorial and governmental integrity.

Nobody with any pretense of common sense believes that Finland had any ulterior design on the integrity or the safety of the Soviet Union.

That American sympathy is 98 per cent with the Finns in their effort to stave off invasion of their own soil is now axiomatic.

With Russia in the war on our side it naturally became desirable from our point of view to end the war with Finland. It would have been proper and sensible for us to seek to bring about cessation of hostilities on terms fair to the Finns—to use our new relationship with Russia to obtain such terms. Instead, we contented ourselves with admonishing Finland to make peace while disclaiming any responsibility for trying to get fair terms for her. As she was not ready for abject surrender we went a step farther and adopted an antagonistic attitude toward her. We continued this evolution to the point where Mr. Hull was able to tell a congressional group that he regarded the Russian proposals as fair and felt Finland should get out of the war on that basis.

Finland's attitude remains unchanged. Our interests have changed, and to justify ourselves we have reversed our high moral stand. Today we are as high-minded in looking upon Finland as a disturber of the peace as we once were in regarding her as a noble and gallant fighter against aggression. We can hardly expect clarity in public thinking when there is such confusion in governmental thinking. There is ample justification for demanding more clarity in the handling of our foreign affairs.

But the evil goes much farther. We need clarity, it is true, but we need consistency and intellectual honesty and integrity even more.

We have touched on only these examples of problems before the American people where they have need of guidance on moral issues. If the churches deal with them as political issues, they contribute little or nothing to helping us understand what we should do. If, on the other hand, they preach the fundamentals of right and justice and human brotherhood, they give us help that can come from no other source. This goes far beyond immediate problems, for if the religious leaders will keep ever before our eyes the eternal verities, they may bring us to realization of the fact that morality and compassion, far from being mere liturgical abstractions, something of concern only at the approach of death, are ever-present demands upon us as citizens. Nothing would give more reality to our beliefs or contribute more to the building of that living faith, without which all paper plans for lasting peace remain lifeless and meaningless.

We hear it said that democracies cannot be as effective as dictatorships, which command fanatical devotion. Without entering into the lasting character of that brand of devotion, we must admit that Nazis and Japanese are driven by a dynamic faith—a rotten faith, it is true, and one that has brought sorrow and suffering and ruin to the world, but still a faith that gets things done.

We complain of lack of religious conviction in this country, but there is no earthly reason why we should not have a positive and burning faith. We shall not get it from articles and sermons deploring our shortcomings. It must be brought home to us that in our daily life we have to deal individually with great problems of right and humanity, that eternal truth makes demands upon us every day, and that in its claims upon us we have the grounds for faith.

I have outlined an ambitious program—a real foreign policy, a professionalized diplomacy, an informed press, a vital spiritual leadership, and a public opinion fitted to exercise intelligent, democratic control of policy. Although ambitious it is not unattainable. There are no obstacles which render accomplishment of this program impossible. It would give us much more than the specific advantages we have enumerated. The development suggested would make it possible for our people to realize their generous desire to play a great and worthy part in the world. If we have the desire, we can hope in our time to take a real lead in enlightened international life.

Appendix

THE CONSTITUTION

Section 2—1. The President shall be Commander-in-Chief of the Army and Navy of the United States, and of the militia of the several States when called into the actual service of the United States; he may require the opinion, in writing, of the principal officer in each of the executive departments upon any subject relating to the duties of their respective offices, and he shall have power to grant reprieves and pardons for offenses against the United States except in cases of impeachment.

2. He shall have power by and with the advice and consent of the Senate to make treaties, provided two-thirds of the Senators present concur; and he shall nominate and by and with the advice and consent of the Senate shall appoint ambassadors, other public ministers and consuls, judges of the Supreme Court, and all other officers of the United States whose appointments are not herein otherwise provided for, and which shall be established by law; but the Congress may by law vest the appointment of such inferior officers as they think proper in the President alone, in the courts of law, or in the heads of departments.

3. The President shall have power to fill up all vacancies that may happen during the recess of the Senate by granting commissions, which shall expire at the end of their next session.

Section 3—He shall from time to time give to the Congress information of the state of the Union, and recommend to their consideration such measures as he shall judge necessary and expedient; he may, on extraordinary occasions, convene both Houses, or either of them, and in case of disagreement between them with respect to the time of adjournment, he may adjourn them to such time as he shall think proper; he shall receive ambassadors and other public ministers; he shall take care that the laws be faithfully executed, and shall commission all the officers of the United States.

THE MONROE DOCTRINE

In July 1823 John Quincy Adams, Secretary of State, in contesting Russian claims on the northwest coast of North America, informed the Russian Minister that the United States "should contest the right of Russia to any territorial establishment on this continent, and that we should assume distinctly the principle that the American continents are no longer subjects for any new European colonial establishments."

On December 2, 1823, President Monroe addressed a message to Congress in which he elaborated on the latter part of Secretary Adams' statement to the Russian Minister. After referring to proposals for amicable negotiations with Russia, he went on to say:

"In the discussions to which this interest has given rise, and in the arrangements by which they may terminate, the occasion has been judged proper for asserting as a principle in which the rights and interests of the United States are involved, that the American continents, by the free and independent condition which they have assumed and maintained, are henceforth not to be considered as subjects for future colonization by any European powers.

"In the wars of the European powers in matters relating to themselves we have never taken any part, nor does it comport with our policy to do so. It is only when our rights are invaded or seriously menaced that we resent injuries or make preparation for our defense. With the movements in this hemisphere we are, of necessity, more immediately connected, and by causes which must be obvious to all enlightened and impartial observers. The political system of the allied powers is essentially different in this respect from that of America. . . . We owe it, therefore, to candour, and to the amicable relations existing between the United States and those powers, to declare that we should consider any attempt on their part to extend their system to any portion of this hemisphere as dangerous to our peace and safety. With the existing colonies or dependencies of any European power we have not interfered and shall not interfere. But with the governments who have declared their independence and maintained it, and whose independence we have, on great consideration and on just principles, acknowledged, we could not view any interposition for the purpose of oppressing them, or controlling in any other manner their destiny, by any European power, in any other light than as the manifestation of an unfriendly disposition toward the United States. . . . It is impossible that the allied powers should extend their political system to any portion of either continent without endangering our peace and happiness; nor can any one believe that our southern brethren, if left to themselves, would adopt it of their own accord. It is equally impossible, therefore, that we should behold such interposition, in any form, with indifference."

THE TEXT OF THE FOURTEEN POINTS

President Wilson's Fourteen Points, as set forth in an address made before the joint session of Congress, on January 8, 1918.

1. Open covenants of peace openly arrived at, after which there shall be no private international understandings of any kind, but diplomacy shall proceed always frankly and in the public view.

2. Absolute freedom of navigation upon the seas outside territorial waters alike in peace and in war, except as the seas may be closed in whole or in part by international action or the enforcement of international covenants.

3. The removal, so far as possible, of all economic barriers and the establishment of an equality of trade conditions among all the nations consenting to the peace and associating themselves for its maintenance.

4. Adequate guarantees given and taken that national armaments will be reduced to the lowest point consistent with domestic safety.

5. A free, open-minded and absolutely impartial adjustment of all colonial claims based upon a strict observance of the principle that in determining all such questions of sovereignty the interests of the populations concerned must have equal weight with the equitable claims of the government whose title is to be determined.

6. The evacuation of all Russian territory, and such a settlement of all questions affecting Russia as will secure the best and freest cooperation of the other nations of the world in obtaining for her an unhampered and unembarrassed opportunity for the independent determination of her own political development and national policy, and assure her of a sincere welcome into the society of free nations under institutions of her own choosing; and, more than a welcome, assistance also of every kind that she may need and may herself desire. The treatment accorded Russia by her sister nations in the months to come will be the acid test of their goodwill, of their comprehension of her needs as distinguished from their own interests, and of their intelligent and unselfish sympathy.

7. Belgium, the whole world will agree, must be evacuated and restored, without any attempt to limit the sovereignty which she enjoys in common with all other free nations. No other single act will serve as this will serve to restore confidence among the nations in the laws

which they have themselves set and determined for the government of their relations with one another. Without this healing act the whole structure and validity of international law is forever impaired.

8. All French territory should be freed and the invaded portions restored, and the wrong done to France by Prussia in 1871 in the matter of Alsace-Lorraine, which has unsettled the peace of the world for nearly fifty years, should be righted, in order that peace may once more be made secure in the interest of all.

9. A readjustment of the frontiers of Italy should be effected along clearly recognizable lines of nationality.

10. The peoples of Austria-Hungary, whose place among the nations we wish to see safeguarded and assured, should be accorded the freest opportunity of autonomous development.

11. Rumania, Serbia, and Montenegro should be evacuated; occupied territories restored; Serbia accorded free and secure access to the sea; and the relations of the several Balkan States to one another determined by friendly counsel along historically established lines of allegiance and nationality; and international guarantees of the political and economic independence and territorial integrity of the several Balkan States should be entered upon.

12. The Turkish portions of the present Ottoman Empire should be assured a secure sovereignty, but the other nationalities which are now under Turkish rule should be assured an undoubted security of life and an absolutely unmolested opportunity of autonomous development, and the Dardanelles should be permanently opened as a free passage to the ships and commerce of all nations under international guarantees.

13. An independent Polish State should be erected which should include the territories inhabited by indisputably Polish populations, which should be assured a free and secure access to the sea, and whose political and economic independence and territorial integrity should be guaranteed by international covenant.

14. A general association of nations must be formed under specific covenants for the purpose of affording mutual guarantees of political independence and territorial integrity to great and small States alike.

THE SO-CALLED "FIVE-POINT PEACE PROGRAM" OF POPE PIUS XII

From Christmas Message, December 24, 1939.

First. A fundamental condition of a just and honorable peace is to assure the right to life and independence of all nations, large and small, strong and weak. One nation's will to live must never be tantamount to a death sentence for another. When this equality of rights has been destroyed, injured, or imperilled, the juridical order requires reparation whose measure and extent are not determined by the sword or selfish, arbitrary judgment, but by the standards of justice and reciprocal equity.

Second. That order, re-established in such a manner, may be tranquil and durable—the cardinal principles of true peace—nations must be liberated from the heavy slavery of the race for armaments and from the danger that material force, instead of serving to protect rights, become the tyrannical violator of them.

Conclusions of peace which failed to attribute fundamental importance to disarmament, mutually accepted, organic and progressive both in practice and spirit, and failed to carry out this disarmament loyally, would sooner or later reveal their inconsistency and lack of vitality.

Third. In any reordering of international community life it would conform to the rules of human wisdom for all parties concerned to examine the consequences of the gaps and deficiencies of the past; and in creating or reconstituting the international institutions, which have so lofty a mission and at the same time one that is so difficult and full of the gravest responsibilities, they should keep present before them the experiences which poured from the inefficacy or defective operation of similar previous projects.

And, since it is so difficult—one would be tempted to say almost impossible—for human weakness to foresee everything and assure everything at the time of the drafting of treaties of peace—when it is difficult to be entirely free from passions and bitterness—the establishment of juridical institutions, which serve to guarantee the loyal and faithful fulfillment of terms and, in case of recognized need, to revise and correct them, is of decisive importance for an honorable acceptance of a peace treaty and to avoid arbitrary and unilateral ruptures and interpretations of the terms of these treaties.

Fourth. A point which should draw particular attention if better ordering of Europe is sought, concerns the real needs and just demands of nations and of peoples as well as of ethnical minorities; demands which, if not always sufficient to form a strict right when there are recognized or confirmed treaties or other juridical titles which oppose them, deserve at all events benevolent examination to meet them in a peaceful way and, where it appears necessary, by means of equitable, wise, and harmonious revision of treaties.

Once true equilibrium among nations is thus brought back and the basis of mutual trust is re-established, many of the incentives to resort to violence would be removed.

Fifth. But even better and more complete settlements will be imperfect and condemned to ultimate failure, if those who guide the destinies of peoples, and the peoples themselves, do not allow themselves to be penetrated always more and more by that spirit from which alone can arise life, authority, and obligation for the dead letter of articles in international agreements—by that spirit, namely, of intimate, acute responsibility that measures and weighs human statutes according to the holy, unshakeable rules of Divine Law; by that hunger and thirst for justice which is proclaimed as a Beatitude in the Sermon on the Mount, and which has, as a natural presupposition, moral justice; by that universal love which is the compendium of and most comprehensive term for the Christian ideal, and therefore throws across also a bridge to those who have not the benefit of participating in our own Faith.

THE ATLANTIC CHARTER'S EIGHT POINTS

As promulgated by President Roosevelt and Prime Minister Churchill on August 14, 1941:

The President of the United States of America and the Prime Minister, Mr. Churchill, representing his Majesty's Government in the United Kingdom, being met together, deem it right to make known certain common principles in the national policies of their respective countries on which they base their hopes for a better future for the world.

1. Their countries seek no aggrandizement, territorial or other.

2. They desire to see no territorial changes that do not accord with the freely expressed wishes of the peoples concerned.

3. They respect the right of all peoples to choose the form of government under which they will live; and they wish to see sovereign rights and self-government restored to those who have been forcibly deprived of them.

4. They will endeavor, with due respect for their existing obligations, to further the enjoyment by all States, great or small, victor or vanquished, of access, on equal terms, to the trade and to the raw materials of the world which are needed for their economic prosperity.

5. They desire to bring about the fullest collaboration between all nations in the economic field with the object of securing, for all, improved labor standards, economic advancement, and social security.

6. After the final destruction of the Nazi tyranny, they hope to

see established a peace which will afford to all nations the means of dwelling in safety within their own boundaries, and which will afford assurance that all the men in all the lands may live out their lives in freedom from fear and want.

7. Such a peace should enable all men to traverse the high seas and oceans without hindrance.

8. They believe that all of the nations of the world, for realistic as well as spiritual reasons must come to the abandonment of the use of force. Since no future peace can be maintained if land, sea or air armaments continued to be employed by nations which threaten, or may threaten, aggression outside of their frontiers, they believe, pending the establishment of a wider and permanent system of general security, that the disarmament of such nations is essential. They will likewise aid and encourage all other practicable measures which will lighten for peace-loving peoples the crushing burden of armaments.

FRANKLIN D. ROOSEVELT.
WINSTON S. CHURCHILL.

August 14, 1941.

DECLARATION BY THE UNITED NATIONS

The governments signatory hereto,

Having subscribed to a common program of purposes and principles embodied in the joint declaration of the President of the United States of America and the Prime Minister of the United Kingdom of Great Britain and Northern Ireland dated August 14, 1941, known as the Atlantic Charter, being convinced that complete victory over their enemies is essential to defend life, liberty, independence, and religious freedom, and to preserve human rights and justice in their own lands as well as in other lands, and that they are now engaged in a common struggle against savage and brutal forces seeking to subjugate the world, declare:

(1) Each government pledges itself to employ its full resources, military or economic, against those members of the tripartite pact and its adherents with which such government is at war.

(2) Each government pledges itself to co-operate with the governments signatory hereto and not to make a separate armistice or peace with the enemies.

The foregoing declaration may be adhered to by other nations which are, or which may be, rendering material assistance and contributions in the struggles for victory over Hitlerism.

Done at Washington.

January First, 1942.

ORIGINAL SIGNATORIES

Australia	Dominican Republic	Luxembourg
Belgium	El Salvador	Netherlands
Canada	Greece	New Zealand
China	Guatemala	Nicaragua
Costa Rica	Haiti	Norway
Cuba	Honduras	Panama
Czecho-Slovakia	India	Poland

Union of South Africa
Union of Soviet Socialist Republics
United Kingdom of Great Britain and Northern Ireland
United States of America
Yugoslavia

LATER SIGNATORIES

Bolivia
Brazil
Ethiopia
Iran
Iraq
Mexico
The Philippines

THE MOSCOW DECLARATION

Joint Four-Nation Agreement of Foreign Ministers

The governments of the United States of America, the United Kingdom, the Soviet Union and China:

United in their determination, in accordance with the declaration by the United Nations of January 1, 1942, and subsequent declarations, to continue hostilities against those Axis powers with which they respectively are at war until such powers have laid down their arms on the basis of unconditional surrender;

Conscious of their responsibility to secure the liberation of themselves and the peoples allied with them from the menace of aggression;

Recognizing the necessity of ensuring a rapid and orderly transition from war to peace and of establishing and maintaining international peace and security with the least diversion of the world's human and economic resources for armaments;

Jointly declare:

1. That their united action, pledged for the prosecution of the war against their respective enemies, will be continued for the organization and maintenance of peace and security.

2. That those of them at war with a common enemy will act together in all matters relating to the surrender and disarmament of that enemy.

3. That they will take all measures deemed by them to be necessary to provide against any violation of the terms imposed upon the enemy.

4. That they recognize the necessity of establishing at the earliest practicable date a general international organization, based on the principle of the sovereign equality of all peace-loving States, and open to membership by all such States, large and small, for the maintenance of international peace and security.

5. That for the purpose of maintaining international peace and security pending the re-establishment of law and order and the inauguration of a system of general security, they will consult with one another and as occasion requires with other members of the United Nations with a view to joint action on behalf of the community of nations.

6. That after the termination of hostilities they will not employ their military forces within the territories of other States except for the purposes envisaged in this declaration and after joint consultation.

7. That they will confer and co-operate with one another and with other members of the United Nations to bring about a practicable general agreement with respect to the regulation of armaments in the postwar period.

MOLOTOV, EDEN, HULL, FOO PING-SHEUNG.

Moscow,
October 30, 1943.

STATEMENT OF SIX "POLITICAL PROPOSITIONS," FEDERAL COUNCIL OF THE CHURCHES OF CHRIST IN AMERICA, MARCH 1943

I. The peace must provide the political framework for a continuing collaboration of the United Nations and, in due course, of neutral and enemy nations.

II. The peace must make provision for bringing within the scope of international agreement those economic and financial acts of national governments which have widespread international repercussions.

III. The peace must make provision for an organization to adapt the treaty structure of the world to changing underlying conditions.

IV. The peace must proclaim the goal of autonomy for subject peoples, and it must establish international organization to assure and to supervise the realization of that end.

V. The peace must establish procedures for controlling military establishments everywhere.

VI. The peace must establish in principle, and seek to achieve in practice, the right of individuals everywhere to religious and intellectual liberty.

BALL, HILL, BURTON, AND HATCH RESOLUTION

Resolved, That the Senate advises that the United States take the initiative in calling meetings of representatives of the United Nations for the purpose of forming an organization of the United Nations with specific and limited authority—

(1) To assist in co-ordinating and fully utilizing the military and economic resources of all member nations in the prosecution of the war against the Axis.

(2) To establish temporary administrations for Axis-controlled areas of the world as these are occupied by United Nations forces, until such time as permanent governments can be established.

(3) To administer relief and assistance in economic rehabilitation in territories of member nations needing such aid and in Axis territory occupied by United Nations forces.

(4) To establish procedures and machinery for peaceful settlement of disputes and disagreements between nations.

(5) To provide for the assembly and maintenance of a United Nations military force and to suppress by immediate use of such force any future attempt at military aggression by any nation.

That the Senate further advises that any establishment of such United Nations organization provide machinery for its modification, for the delegation of additional specific and limited functions to such organization, and for admission of other nations to membership, and that member nations should commit themselves to seek no territorial aggrandizement.

March 16, 1943.

TEXT OF REPUBLICAN POSTWAR COUNCIL'S DECLARATIONS

The members of this council are aware of the gravity of the problems our nation faces. We are fighting a desperate war, which must be won as speedily as possible. When the war is ended, we must participate in the making of the peace. This puts upon the nation a triple responsibility.

(A) We must preserve and protect all our own national interests.

(B) We must aid in restoring order and decent living in a distressed world.

(C) We must do our full share in a program for permanent peace among nations.

At this time a detailed program for the accomplishment of these great objectives will be impossible and specific commitments of this council of the Republican party, or by the nation, would be unwise. We cannot know now what situation may obtain at the war's end. But a specific program must be devolved in the months to come, as events and relations unfold.

Therefore, we consider it to be our duty at the beginning of our work as an advisory council of the Republican party to declare our approval of the following:

1. Prosecution of the war by a United Nations to conclusive victory over all our enemies, including:

(a) Disarmament and disorganization of the armed forces of the Axis.

(b) Disqualification of the Axis to construct facilities for the manufacture of the implements of war.

(c) Permanent maintenance of trained and well-equipped armed forces at home.

2. Responsible participation by the United States in postwar co-operative organization among sovereign nations to prevent military aggression and to attain permanent peace with organized justice in a free world.

In making this recommendation we ground our judgment upon the belief that both the foreign policy and domestic policy of every country are related to each other so closely that each member of the United Nations (or whatever co-operative organization perpetuating existing unity may be agreed upon) ought to consider both the immediate and remote consequences of every proposition with careful regard for:

1. Its effect upon the vital interests of the nation.

2. Its bearing upon the foreseeable international developments.

If there should be a conflict between the two, then the United States of America should adhere to the policy which will preserve its constitutionalism as expressed in the Declaration of Independence, the Constitution itself, and the Bill of Rights, as administered through our republican form of government. Constitutionalism should be adhered to in determining the substance of our policies and shall be followed in ways and means of making international commitments.

In addition to these things, this council advises that peace and security ought to be ultimately established upon other sanctions than force. It recommends that we work toward a policy which will comprehend other means than war for the determination of international controversy, and the attainment of a peace that will prevail by virtue of its inherent reciprocal interests and its spiritual foundation, reached from time to time with the understanding of the peoples of the negotiating nations.

In all of these undertakings we favor the widest consultation of the gallant men and women in our armed forces who have a special right to speak with authority on behalf of the security and liberty for which they fight.

It is determined that this council make complete examination of the means by which these ends may be fully achieved with due regard for all American interests and responsibilities.

The council invites all Americans to adhere to the principles here set forth to the end that our place among the nations of the world and our part in helping to bring about international peace and justice shall not be the subject of domestic partisan controversy and political bitterness.

September 7, 1943.

FULBRIGHT RESOLUTION

The text of the House Concurrent Resolution introduced by Representative Fulbright of Arkansas and agreed to by the House on September 21, 1943, by a vote of 360 to 29 is as follows:

That the Congress hereby expresses itself as favoring the creating of appropriate international machinery with power adequate to establish and to maintain a just and lasting peace, among the nations of the world, and as favoring the participation by the United States therein.

CONNALLY RESOLUTION

The text of the Senate Resolution introduced by Senator Connally and agreed to by the Senate on November 5, 1943, by a vote of 85 to 5 is as follows:

RESOLVED, That the war against all our enemies be waged until complete victory is achieved.

That the United States co-operate with its comrades-in-arms in securing a just and honorable peace.

That the United States, acting through its constitutional processes, join with free and sovereign nations in establishment and maintenance of international authority with power to prevent aggression and to preserve the peace of the world.

That the Senate recognizes the necessity of there being established at the earliest practicable date a general international organization, based on the principle of the sovereign equality of all peace-loving states, and open to membership by all such states, large and small, for the maintenance of international peace and security.

That, pursuant to the Constitution of the United States, any treaty made to effect the purposes of this resolution, on behalf of the Government of the United States with any other nation or any association of nations, shall be made only by and with the advice and consent of the Senate of the United States, provided two thirds of the senators present concur.

THE TEHERAN DECLARATION
Three-Power Agreement

We, the President of the United States of America, the Prime Minister of Great Britain, and the Premier of the Soviet Union, have met in these four days past in this the capital of our ally, Teheran, and have shaped and confirmed our common policy.

We express our determination that our nations shall work together in the war and in the peace that will follow.

As to the war, our military staffs have joined in our round-table discussions and we have concerted our plans for the destruction of the German forces. We have reached complete agreement as to the scope and timing of operations which will be undertaken from the east, west, and south. The common understanding which we have here reached guarantees that victory will be ours.

And as to the peace, we are sure that our concord will make it an enduring peace. We recognize fully the supreme responsibility resting upon us and all the nations to make a peace which will command good will from the overwhelming masses of the peoples of the world and banish the scourge of terror of war for many generations.

With our diplomatic advisers we have surveyed the problems of the future. We shall seek the co-operation and active participation of all nations, large and small, whose peoples in heart and in mind are dedicated, as are our own peoples, to the elimination of tyranny and slavery, oppression and intolerance. We will welcome them as they may choose to come into the world family of democratic nations.

No power on earth can prevent our destroying the German armies by land, their U-boats by sea, and their war plants from the air. Our attacks will be relentless and increasing.

Emerging from these friendly conferences we look with confidence to the day when all the peoples of the world may live free lives untouched by tyranny and according to their varying desires and their own consciences.

We came here with hope and determination. We leave here friends in fact, in spirit, and in purpose.

Signed at Teheran, December 1, 1943.

ROOSEVELT, STALIN, CHURCHILL.

CAIRO CONFERENCE

President Roosevelt, Generalissimo Chiang Kai-shek, and Prime Minister Churchill, together with their respective military and diplomatic advisers, have completed a conference in North Africa.

The following general statement was issued:

"The several military missions have agreed upon future military operations against Japan.

"The three great Allies expressed their resolve to bring unrelenting pressure against their brutal enemies by sea, land, and air. This pressure is already rising.

"The three great Allies are fighting this war to restrain and punish the aggression of Japan.

"They covet no gain for themselves and have no thought of territorial expansion.

"It is their purpose that Japan shall be stripped of all the islands in the Pacific which she has seized or occupied since the beginning of the first World War in 1914, and that all the territories Japan has stolen from the Chinese, such as Manchuria, Formosa, and the Pescadores, shall be restored to the Republic of China.

"Japan will also be expelled from all other territories which she has taken by violence and greed.

"The aforesaid three great powers, mindful of the enslavement of the people of Korea, are determined that in due course Korea shall become free and independent.

"With these objects in view, the three Allies, in harmony with those of the United Nations at war with Japan, will continue to perse-

vere in the serious and prolonged operations necessary to procure the unconditional surrender of Japan."
December 1, 1943.

SECRETARY HULL'S STATEMENT ON FOREIGN POLICY

The text of a State Department statement on U. S. foreign policy:

Secretary of State Cordell Hull on March 21 informed press and radio correspondents that after returning from his recent trip to Florida he had noted a growing interest in the foreign policy of the United States and an increasing number of requests for information about various points in our foreign policy. He said that he was glad of this increased interest. The Secretary said that in addition to many statements and declarations by the President, he had himself made a number of basic statements on foreign policy during the past two years. He thought it would be a convenience and help to the public generally if there could be compiled a brief memorandum of a number of them. Accordingly, the following had been prepared:

In determining our foreign policy we must first see clearly what our true national interests are.

At the present time, the paramount aim of our foreign policy is to defeat our enemies as quickly as possible.

Beyond final victory, our fundamental national interests are the assuring of our national security and the fostering of the economic and social well-being of our people.

Co-operation between nations in the spirit of good neighbors, founded on the principles of liberty, equality, justice, morality, and law, is the most effective method of safeguarding and promoting the political, the economic, the social and the cultural well-being of our nation and of all nations.

Some international agency must be created which can—by force, if necessary—keep the peace among nations in the future.

A system of organized international co-operation for the maintenance of peace must be based upon the willingness of the co-operating nations to use force, if necessary, to keep the peace. There must be certainty that adequate and appropriate means are available and will be used for this purpose.

Political differences which present a threat to the peace of the world should be submitted to agencies which would use the remedies of discussion, negotiation, conciliation, and good offices.

Disputes of a legal character which present a threat to the peace of the world should be adjudicated by an international court of justice whose decisions would be based upon application of principles of law.

International co-operative action must include eventual adjustment of national armaments in such a manner that the rule of law cannot be successfully challenged that the burden of armaments may be reduced to a minimum.

Through this declaration the Soviet Union, Great Britain, the United States, and China have laid the foundation for co-operative effort in the postwar world toward enabling all peace-loving nations, large and small, to live in peace and security, to preserve the liberties and rights of civilized existence, and to enjoy expanded opportunities and facilities for economic, social, and spiritual progress.

As the provisions of the four-nation declaration are carried into effect, there will no longer be need for spheres of influence, for alliances, for balance of power, or any other of the special arrangements through which, in the unhappy past, nations strove to safeguard their security or to promote their interests.

In the process of re-establishing international order, the United Nations must exercise surveillance over aggressor nations until such time as the latter demonstrate their willingness and ability to live at peace with other nations. How long such surveillance will need to continue must depend upon the rapidity with which the peoples of Germany, Japan, Italy, and their satellites give convincing proof that they have repudiated and abandoned the monstrous philosophy of superior race and conquest by force and have embraced loyally the basic principles of peaceful processes.

Excessive trade barriers of the many different kinds must be reduced, and practices which impose injuries on others and divert trade from its natural economic course must be avoided.

Equally plain is the need for making national currencies once more freely exchangeable for each other at stable rates of exchange; for a system of financial relations so devised that materials can be produced and ways may be found of moving them where there are markets created by human need; for machinery through which capital may—for the development of the world's resources and for the stabilization of economic activity—move on equitable terms from financially stronger to financially weaker countries.

The pledge of the Atlantic Charter is of a system which will give every nation, large or small, a greater assurance of stable peace, greater opportunity for the realization of its aspirations to freedom, and greater facilities for material advancement. But that pledge implies an obligation for each nation to demonstrate its capacity for stable and progressive government, to fulfill scrupulously its established duties to other nations, to settle its international differences and disputes by none but peaceful methods, and to make its full contribution to the maintenance of enduring peace.

Each sovereign nation, large or small, is in law and under law the equal of every other nation.

The principle of sovereign equality of all peace-loving states, irrespective of size and strength, as partners in a future system of general security will be the foundation stone upon which the future international organization will be constructed.

Each nation should be free to decide for itself the forms and details of its governmental organization—so long as it conducts its affairs in such a way as not to menace the peace and security of other nations.

All nations, large and small, which respect the right of others, are entitled to freedom from outside interference in their internal affairs.

There is no surer way for men and for nations to show themselves worthy of liberty than to fight for its preservation, in any way that is open to them, against those who would destroy it for all. Never did a plainer duty to fight against its foes devolve upon all peoples who prize liberty and all who aspire to it.

All peoples who, with "a decent respect to the opinions of mankind," have qualified themselves to assume and to discharge the responsibilities of liberty are entitled to its enjoyment.

There rests upon the independent nations a responsibility in relation to dependent peoples who aspire to liberty. It should be the duty of nations having political ties with such peoples to develop materially and educationally, to prepare themselves for the duties and responsibilities of self-government and to attain liberty. An excellent example of what can be achieved is afforded in the record of our relationship with the Philippines.

FLETCHER SCHOOL OF LAW AND DIPLOMACY

Courses of Study

GROUP I

INTERNATIONAL LAW AND ORGANIZATION

Law 1. INTERNATIONAL LAW
A study of the rules and practices accepted by states as international law and applied by them in their international relations. The course embraces both classic and contemporary problems of international law arising in times of peace, war, and neutrality with emphasis upon the interpretations and applications of the law by the United States. Materials drawn upon include the legislation and the practices of states, treaties, and engagements, decisions of national and international tribunals, and diplomatic correspondence.

Law 2. INTERNATIONAL ORGANIZATION AND GOVERNMENT
A review of the historical background (attempts represented by the Treaties of Westphalia, the Congress of Vienna, the Holy Alliance, and the Concert of Europe) serves as an introduction to the subject. Subsequent topics include: the development and essential elements of the state-system, analysis of the traditional organization of the family of nations, and the machinery for transacting business between its members. Concrete study will be made of recent organization based on world-wide (League of Nations) and regional (e.g., inter-American) membership, attention being given to aims and machinery, lessons to be drawn from past experiments, and the outlook for the future.

Law 3a. INTRODUCTION TO THE THEORY OF INTERNATIONAL LAW
An analysis of the principal theories concerning the nature of international law and its fundamental conceptions from the seventeenth to twentieth centuries. Their significance for international law at the present day is considered, particular attention being directed to theories, express or implicit, in the decisions of the Permanent Court of International Justice.

Law 3b. INTRODUCTION TO THE SCIENCE OF LAW
A study of the fundamental conceptions of law and theories of the

end of law, together with a sketch of the history of modern systems of law.

Law 4.   Consular and Diplomatic Law and Practice

This course aims to reveal the functions of the diplomatic and consular services in the pursuit of national interests, and their importance in preserving a system of law and order among nations. It considers the organization and procedure of the Department of State and other foreign offices and foreign services. It takes up the formulation and execution of foreign policy and the impact of contemporary developments upon diplomatic and consular functions and procedures.

Law 6.   International Commercial Law

A study of the interaction of the Roman Law, the common law, and the customs of merchants. The course is concerned with commercial law in its relation to international trade. Built around the transaction of sale, it deals from that point of view with the comparative development under Anglo-American and Continental legal systems of such customary instruments of the international merchant as bills of exchange, letters of credit, bills of lading, trust receipts, and marine insurance policies. Instruction is by the case method with supplementary readings and reports.

Law 7b.   Problems and Conflicts in the Law Merchant

A consideration of specific problems encountered in international trade and arising from differences in the various systems of commercial law. Steps in the direction of unification are noted, and further possibilities in regard to uniformity are discussed.

Law 8.   Maritime Law

Topics dealt with in the course include the history and extent of admiralty jurisdiction, maritime contracts and torts, towage and pilotage, salvage, maritime liens, general average, and the rights and obligations of the parties under the contracts of carriage evidenced in charter parties and bills of lading. Instruction is largely by the case method, but relevant statutes and conventions are studied, and reference is made to comparative materials.

Law 9.   Applied Problems in International Law

A part of the time in this seminar will be devoted to the application of law to current problems of war. The greater portion of the time, however, will be taken up with a consideration of the legal bases of a more stable world order, and the legal situations which may arise in connection with the conclusion of the present war.

Law 10b.   The Law of the Air

A survey of the development of the law in regard to the use of the air for commercial purposes, with reference also to incidental military aspects of the questions considered. Selected problems peculiar to aerial transport and communication are studied, and opportunities for international action are explored.

Law 15. CONTEMPORARY THOUGHT IN INTERNATIONAL POLITICS
Analysis of the principal democratic, authoritarian, and totalitarian political philosophies, chiefly in relation to peace and war. The history of ideas on international organization will be briefly considered. A selected number of suggested plans for postwar collaboration will be examined in detail.

Law 20. RESEARCH IN INTERNATIONAL LAW AND ORGANIZATION
Advanced students may, subject to the approval of their qualifications by the proper authorities, pursue the study of special topics lying within the fields represented in Group I under the personal guidance of the member of the Faculty in whose field the topic lies.

GROUP II

DIPLOMACY AND INTERNATIONAL POLITICS

Diplomacy 1. THE FOREIGN RELATIONS OF THE UNITED STATES
A history of the foreign relations of the United States, including a study of the bases of its foreign policy and a critical evaluation of each of its general and regional policies. Emphasis is placed upon the period since the first World War with especial attention to the present war.

Diplomacy 2. THE HISTORY OF EUROPEAN DIPLOMACY SINCE 1815
This course considers the major problems of European diplomacy in the nineteenth and early twentieth centuries, taking due account of the changing techniques of diplomacy and of the major social and ideological forces bearing upon the conduct of international relations.

Diplomacy 3b. PUBLIC OPINION AND DIPLOMACY
The topics considered during the course include pressure groups and the making of foreign policy; the instrumentalities used in the molding of public opinion, such as the radio, the newspaper, the cinema. Particular attention is given to propaganda at home and abroad during the present war.

Diplomacy 4. LATIN AMERICAN PROBLEMS AND INTER-AMERICAN RELATIONS
After a general historical introduction dealing with physical setting, racial backgrounds, and colonial institutions, a more thorough study is made of modern economic, political, and social problems of the other American republics. Emphasis is placed on international relations with special reference to the United States.

Diplomacy 5a. DIPLOMATIC ISSUES IN THE FAR EAST

A survey of the countries of Eastern Asia followed by a more intensive study of recent and current international issues. Emphasis is placed on the events leading to the Sino-Japanese War and on the Far Eastern problems and policies of the Western powers, especially of the United States.

Diplomacy 6. PROBLEMS OF CENTRAL AND EASTERN EUROPE
A series of timely studies relating to the area from the Baltic to the Balkans. With an historical approach, the course deals with the trends since 1918 and analyzes the reasons for the growing international importance of the states in this area, with emphasis upon recent relations of the German Reich and the Soviet Union.

Diplomacy 7a. DIPLOMATIC RELATIONS OF THE BRITISH COMMONWEALTH OF NATIONS
The topics considered during the course include the organization of the British Commonwealth of Nations; the relations of its members *inter se;* conduct of foreign policy; the organs of consultation; special problems of the United Kingdom; economic imperialism; wartime problems of imperial articulation.

Diplomacy 8. DIPLOMATIC HISTORY OF EUROPE SINCE 1918
A course dealing with the problems inherent in the peace settlement of 1919 and with European diplomacy between the two World Wars. Particular attention is devoted to recent changes and altered diplomatic concepts in the conduct of foreign affairs by European States.

Diplomacy 9a. EVOLUTION OF DIPLOMACY
The course is concerned with the development of diplomatic methods and techniques from their origins to the present time. It traces various conceptions of the diplomatic functions, their practical workings and procedure by the method of selected examples illustrating both general trends and specific diplomatic situations.

Diplomacy 10. CONFLICT OF POLICIES IN THE NEAR EAST
A study of the diplomatic contests resulting from the penetration of Great Britain, France, Russia, Italy, and Germany into the Near and Middle East in the nineteenth and twentieth centuries. Particular attention is given to the problems which have developed since 1919 in the Mediterranean area and along the natural lines of access to the East.

Diplomacy 11b. RESEARCH TOPICS IN THE FOREIGN RELATIONS OF THE UNITED STATES
A seminar course of investigation in the source material within selected fields of American diplomacy. For 1942–43 the topics will deal with the policy of the United States in the Western Pacific and the Far East.

Diplomacy 12. EUROPEAN IMPERIALISM IN AFRICA

An intensive study of the partition of Africa and of the subsequent crises arising from the conflicts of interests of European Powers. The problems inherent in the course of the present war will be given considerations.

Diplomacy 13b. THE NATURE AND PROBLEMS OF WAR

The course opens with a consideration of the evolution of war and of the theories of war. Against this background a study will be made of the chief problems arising in the organization of and in the conduct of war, including the relations between policy, government, and war conduct, and the fundamentals of military, naval, and air strategy.

Diplomacy 20. RESEARCH IN DIPLOMACY AND INTERNATIONAL POLITICS

This course provides an opportunity for qualified students to pursue the study of particular problems lying within the field of diplomatic history and international politics under the personal guidance of a member of the faculty. Work of this nature may be undertaken only with the consent of the proper authorities.

GROUP III

INTERNATIONAL ECONOMIC RELATIONS

Economics 1. INTERNATIONAL ECONOMIC RELATIONS: THEORY AND POLICY

A survey of the ways in which economic life is affected by the existence of political boundaries and of the ways in which political relations between nations are affected by economic factors. The first semester deals with the theory of international economics, including the relation of economic activity to war; the second with governmental policies in such fields as trade, investments, raw materials, population problems.

Economics 2. INTERNATIONAL FINANCE

This course deals with the financial structure and functioning of international society. Topics include: modern monetary theory and policy as a background for the study of international monetary problems; the mechanism of international adjustment; monetary standards and objectives of monetary control; international fluctuations in income and employment.

Economics 3b. INTERNATIONAL ECONOMIC CO-OPERATION

The course is concerned with the institutional side of international co-operation, particularly in the field of economic action by governments and private business. It analyzes the measures taken by national and international agencies with regard to trade, finance, and labor standards. It includes studies of the trends of international organization under the impact of the present political crisis.

Economics 8. METHODS OF ANALYSIS IN INTERNATIONAL ECONOMIC RELATIONS

A methods course, designed to meet the needs of those who wish to prepare themselves for advanced research or for positions involving the handling of economic data. It includes training in the use of certain statistical procedures and economic concepts essential for the analysis of international economic problems.

Economics 9. SEMINAR IN INTERNATIONAL ECONOMIC RELATIONS

The main purpose of the seminar is to provide training in research methods. Student projects and seminar discussions relate mainly to postwar problems of economic adaptation and the economic essentials of a durable peace.

Economics 20. RESEARCH IN INTERNATIONAL ECONOMIC RELATIONS

Individual research work under supervision of faculty members. Open to qualified students who wish to undertake the investigation of particular economic problems lying within the scope of Group III. Consent of the proper authorities is necessary.

GROUP IV

CO-ORDINATIVE COURSES AND SEMINARS

In each of the recent years a special seminar has been given in some field of current interest and concern which the entire student body have been free to attend. Such seminars have been conducted with the co-operation of visiting experts and have been designed to supplement regular curricular offerings. Students who may wish to enroll for credit in these seminars should register for an appropriate "20" course and complete such reading and examination assignments as may be designated by the faculty committee in charge of the seminar.

SPECIAL SEMINAR IN PROBLEMS OF AFRICA AND THE NEAR EAST

Questions of strategy, attitudes of native peoples, and economic potentialities in those parts of Africa, the Near East, the Middle East which are involved largely in World War II. The field will be developed with the collaboration of those who can speak from first hand experience.

SPECIAL SEMINAR IN FAR EASTERN PROBLEMS

A course of lectures by expert authorities bearing on the existing situation in the Far East. The area of concern includes the Dutch East Indies, the Malay States, and the Philippines, as well as China, Soviet Russia, Japan, and Japanese-controlled regions. Particular attention is given to American policy and action, the Sino-Japanese War, and Japan's New Order in Greater East Asia.

SPECIAL SEMINAR ON MILITARY POWER IN INTERNATIONAL RELATIONS
This seminar is designed to explore the relationship between military and naval power, on the one hand, and diplomatic and economic relations, on the other. Among the topics considered are the elements of military power and strategy, the political and physical use of armed force, the development of American naval and military policy, war economics, and the relationship between economic and military policies. Case studies of actual and potential situations are presented by guest experts drawn both from the armed Services and from civilian ranks.

SPECIAL PROBLEMS IN INTER-AMERICAN RELATIONS
A course dealing with the legal, diplomatic, and economic problems and policies arising from our relations with Latin America. The principal feature lies in the participation in class sessions of a considerable number of prominent executive officers of those business organizations and governmental agencies whose activities bring them into constant contact with the countries of Central and South America.

CO-ORDINATIVE SEMINAR ON POSTWAR ORGANIZATION
Members of Law 2, Law 9, Diplomacy 9, Economics 3, and Economics 9 meet together once a month to consider in common, with their respective field backgrounds in mind, some of the problems which must be faced in winning the present war and in establishing the future peace. Taking the Atlantic Charter as the starting point, the seminar took up in 1941–42 the optimum and minimum international organization which should be sought, the problem of raw materials in its bearing on economic and political relations, Anglo-American-Russian collaboration, the place of law in postwar society, and boundaries. Attempts to discover areas of agreement and possible lines of action are kept to the fore.

BIBLIOGRAPHY AND CRITICISM
A course of lectures given by members of the Faculty on the nature and method of research. Following an introductory presentation of general method in bibliography and criticism the lectures treat of the application of these attitudes and processes to the various fields of knowledge and activity represented in the Fletcher School curriculum. The course is not offered for credit and hence is to be taken in addition to a normal program of academic study. Attendance is required of all who expect to become candidates for degrees and who have had no previous instruction in the subject.